Joy to the World!

Mission in the Age of Global Christianity

A Mission Study for 2010 and 2011

by Dana L. Robert
Truman Collins Professor of World Christianity
and History of Mission
Boston University School of Theology

with Study Guide
by Toby Gould

Women's Division • General Board of Global Ministries • The United Methodist Church

Contents

Acknowledgments

I am grateful for the many people who helped me with this book. First thanks go to Cheryl Trent and Glory Dharmaraj, and to the Women's Division, who asked me to write it. Emeritus Dean Ray Hart of the Boston University School of Theology allowed me time off to write the first chapters. His dedication to The United Methodist Church and the support of my School of Theology colleagues for our church connection have made this study possible. Toby Gould has been an invaluable sounding board and experienced expert on study guides, without whose contribution the book would have been less accessible and interesting. I thank him especially for helping with the title of the book, and also for constructing sample questions for preliminary discussions of each chapter. Barbara Dick has gone beyond the call of duty as copy editor, and I have benefited from her encouragement.

At the Boston University School of Theology (BU STH), special thanks go to Doug Tzan, my research assistant. As an elder in The United Methodist Church, he understands the importance of the mission study process and went beyond his normal obligation to research and construct UMC "case studies" on hospitality and healing. Anneke Stasson and Septemmy Lakawa searched for photos and other illustrative material for the volume. Nkemba and Mbwizu Ndjungu allowed me to tell their story in chapter 1. Pamela Couture of St. Paul School of Theology generously provided her interview with Bishop Ntambo for chapter 9, and the bishop approved it. Todd Johnson of Gordon-Conwell's Center for the Study of Global Christianity constructed three maps for my use; they appear both in this study and in my previously-published *Christian Mission: How Christianity Became a World Religion* (Wiley-Blackwell, 2009). Richard Heitzenrater sent me helpful material on the meaning of grace.

One of the most gratifying aspects of writing this mission study has been the opportunity to try out each chapter on the weekly adult forum at the Harvard-Epworth United Methodist Church in Cambridge, Massachusetts. For nine weeks, adults from the congregation read chapters in advance, and came to discuss them and to try out sample questions. Their feedback has made this book and its study guide stronger. I am very grateful for the spiritual support of the congregation. My introductory mission class at the Boston University School of Theology also read draft chapters and provided helpful insights from their perspective as young ministers-in-training.

Finally, I thank my husband Inus and my sons Samuel and John for their ongoing support. I thank my brother and sister-in-law, Kevin and Lisa Robert, and my friends Kip Knight and Peggy Day, for contributions to the Center for Global Christianity and Mission at BU STH. Their financial assistance helped me to produce the book.

I dedicate this book to my parents, Charlie and Mary Ellen Robert, of Broadmoor United Methodist Church in Baton Rouge, Louisiana. Their loving nurture at home and in Louisiana Methodism made me who I am today.

Dana L. Robert
Somerville, Massachusetts

Introduction

Joy to the World, the Lord Is Come!

The Christmas story has been read. The children in the Christmas pageant have assembled in the front of the church, with their shepherds' robes and kings' crowns and angels' wings. Young and old sing the finale with gusto, "Joy to the World!" The baby Jesus has finally arrived. Preparations have ended, and it is time to celebrate!

"Joy to the World" is a shout of celebration, penned by the great hymn writer Isaac Watts in 1819. Although it is a beloved Christmas carol, its message does not stop at Christmas Day. Its deeper message is not about the birth of a baby, but about the fundamental changes brought into the world by the coming of Jesus Christ. Jesus came to bring abundant life in place of human limitations, brokenness, and death (see John 10:10).

Benjamin Franklin once said, "In this world nothing is certain but death and taxes." Governments and economies rise and fall. But at the end of the day, Christians carry a message of hope for the present and for the future. Because God is ultimately in charge, because "the Lord is come," the peoples of the world can partake of God's righteousness, and share in God's bountiful love.[1] Watts writes that even the earth celebrates God's presence, as "fields and floods, rocks, hills, and plains repeat the sounding joy."[2] This glorious affirmation of Christian hope, "the Lord is come," is the beginning of Christian mission.

At its most basic, Christian mission is our response to the Good News that God is present in Jesus Christ, who came into the world with a message of forgiveness, joy, and hope for all of God's creation. We Christians carry this message with us wherever we go. We are living witnesses to the belief in *Emmanuel*—"God with us." Our "proof" of God's presence is the life and ministry, death and resurrection of Jesus Christ, and the coming of the Holy Spirit. In God's name, we go into the world to share the Good News.

The title of this mission study reflects the conviction that for United Methodists, mission and evangelism flow from joyous gratitude for the Good News of Jesus Christ. Its purpose is to explore the theology of mission and evangelism in the twenty-first-century context of Christianity as a worldwide religion. It is divided into three sections of three chapters each. Although the sections reinforce one another, each can also be studied separately.

Part I sets the biblical and historical context for the reality that Christianity is now the largest world religion, comprising roughly one-third of the population. The idea that the Good News is intended for all has helped it spread across many boundaries and barriers. The church today includes persons from all cultures, in all the inhabited regions of the world. Mission and evangelism in the twenty-first century take place within these new global realities. This section discusses changes in the Christian population, mission structures, and women's mission work over the past century.

Part II discusses the theological foundations for Christian mission. It draws primarily upon the New Testament and on Methodist history as sources for United Methodist understandings of mission and evangelism. It discusses the meaning of Jesus Christ as the foundation for Christian mission, and the meaning of the church as a community sent by God into the world as witnesses. Chapter 6 identifies the Wesleyan tradition of free grace as the particular contribution of Methodism to world mission.

Part III examines several contemporary practices of world mission. These models of mission are rooted in both the Scriptures and in history, and are emphasized today by Christians around the world. In the mission of hospitality (see chapter 7), God's love through Christ is revealed as we welcome others to join us in community. In the mission of healing (see chapter 8), we visibly demonstrate God's love for the whole person—body, mind, and spirit. And in the mission of reconciliation (see chapter 9), we seek to mend what is broken—peoples' relationships with God, with one another, and with all of God's creation. As ambassadors for Christ, in the healing power of the Holy Spirit, we share God's love with the whole world. Hospitality, healing, and reconciliation are all ways of witnessing to hope and wholeness for the world through Jesus Christ.

Joy to the world! The Lord is come! We know there is much hard work before us, and yet God is with us. It is time to celebrate!

NOTES

1. See Watt's third and fourth verses: "No more let sins and sorrows grow, nor thorns infest the ground; he comes to make his blessings flow far as the curse is found. . . . He rules the world with truth and grace, and makes the nations prove the glories of his righteousness, and wonders of his love."
2. From verse 2.

Part I

Christianity as Worldwide Fellowship

Chapter One
The Gospel Movement across Cultures

"After this I looked, and there was a great multitude that no one could count, from every nation, from all tribes and peoples and languages, standing before the throne and before the Lamb, robed in white, with palm branches in their hands. They cried out in a loud voice, saying, 'Salvation belongs to our God who is seated on the throne, and to the Lamb!'"
—Revelation 7:9-10

John of Patmos wrote these words at the end of the first century A.D., when the tiny community of Jesus' followers struggled under persecution by Roman authorities. John's vision of the gathered followers of Jesus, who were called out from every nation, tribe, people, and linguistic group, has inspired Christians ever since. Today, in the twenty-first century, John's hopeful dream seems more like a prophecy. For during the lifetimes of the people reading this book, Christianity has undergone one of the biggest changes in its two-thousand-year history. It is now a multi-cultural faith, with believers drawn from every continent, and from multiple nations, tribes, and people groups.

A century ago, one-third of the world was Christian. Today, one-third of the world is Christian. But from the perspective of culture and geography, it is a different one-third. In 1910, at least 70 percent of the world's Christians were of European heritage. By 2010, the European percentage of Christians had shrunk to only about one-fourth of the total. The "average" Christian today is an African or a Latin American woman. Even as Christianity has declined in Europe and stagnated in North America, it has grown by leaps and bounds in Africa, Latin America, and Asia.

Some mission leaders suggest that John's vision means that the fullness of the Gospel will not be revealed until people of all cultures have the chance to worship Jesus Christ. In other words, Christian identity will not be complete until we experience fellowship with believers of other cultures, for different cultural expressions of the Gospel deepen and enrich the message of God's grace. While this interpretation of his vision was probably not exactly what John had in mind, it is certainly the case that he had a revolutionary dream of a faith that spread beyond its origins and that included peoples from around the world. The first step in understanding how and why Christianity has become a multi-cultural, worldwide community is to explore this idea in the Bible. Seen through the eyes of faith, John's dream was a key to God's plan.

The Missionary Vision of the New Testament

A century ago, theologian Martin Kahler remarked that mission is "the mother of theology."[1] Although the New Testament is not a systematic theology textbook, its missionary character reveals that the early followers of Jesus felt a divine call to witness to his ministry, his message, and especially to his stunning defeat of death after the crucifixion. The disciples believed that Jesus was fulfilling the Jewish prophecies that someday a Savior or Messiah would come to save Israel and bring God's reign on earth. They believed that the Good News of Jesus as Lord, or *Kyrios* in Greek, was meant to be shared, even beyond the boundaries of their own ethnic group.

The beginnings of Christianity as a multicultural faith started with the disciples. Although Jesus focused his earthly ministry mostly on his own Jewish people, after his death the Good News spread from the disciples to the "diaspora," the emigrant Jewish community scattered throughout the Roman Empire. The diaspora Jews felt like second class citizens in Israel. Many of them no longer spoke Hebrew but had adopted the languages of the areas in which they lived.

The books of Luke and Acts outline the spread of Jesus' message, starting in Jerusalem and moving outward both geographically and among new groups of people. In Acts 2, after Jesus' death and resurrection, his followers gathered in Jerusalem. They heard the sound of a mighty wind, and they were filled with the Holy Spirit and began to speak in other languages. The gathered crowd of foreign-language Jews and their non-Jewish friends was astonished and asked,

> "How is it that we hear, each of us, in our own native language? Parthians, Medes, Elamites, and residents of Mesopotamia, Judea and Cappadocia, Pontus and Asia, Phrygia and Pamphylia, Egypt and the parts of Libya belonging to Cyrene, and visitors from Rome, both Jews and proselytes, Cretans and Arabs—in our own language we hear them speaking about God's deeds of power." (Acts 2:8-11)

The coming of the Holy Spirit after Jesus' death, at the time of Pentecost, is celebrated as the "birthday" of the Church. Among the earliest believers were Jewish migrants and foreigners friendly to Judaism who traveled from their own countries to Jerusalem and back again. Because they lived in an empire with open internal borders, they could travel throughout the Mediterranean world and carry the message with them to new locations. At the birth of the Church, God brought the fearful, demoralized disciples out of their upper room and into the streets, where they realized that God was doing a new thing. Instead of being limited to

Hebrew, or some other sacred language that people could not understand, the Good News was heard in the spoken languages of ordinary people. The transformation of a defeated handful of Jewish followers into a death-defying, multi-lingual missionary community was an amazing beginning to what is now the largest religion in the world.

Anointed by the Holy Spirit, Jesus' followers moved out from Jerusalem, and they gradually realized that even non-Jews, whom they called *Gentiles*, were part of God's plan of salvation. The book of Acts tells of major encounters between messengers of the Good News and persons from other cultures. By Acts 5, the Good News had reached the Samaritan people, a nontraditional and unpopular community north of Israel. Jesus' own ministry to the Samaritan woman (see John 4) pointed toward the eagerness with which Samaritans heard his message.

In Acts 8, the church leader Philip met an Ethiopian eunuch on the road to Gaza. The Ethiopian was the powerful treasurer for the queen of Meroe in what eventually became the African kingdom of Nubia. Because the African was a eunuch, he was considered an imperfect male and was not allowed to worship in the Jewish temple. As hard as he tried, his physical handicap blocked him from full acceptance by the Jewish community. As the Ethiopian tried to understand the meaning of passages from Isaiah, Philip explained to him that the Scriptures found their fulfillment in Jesus, as the Good News of salvation.

As a follower of Jesus, Philip welcomed the eunuch as an equal child of God. The African was so excited by the Good News of his inclusion among God's special people that he insisted on being baptized at once. Through the act of baptizing the Ethiopian eunuch, Philip became known in Christian tradition as the Apostle of Africa. The eunuch, though physically unable to have children himself, became, like Abraham, the spiritual father of many descendants—millions of African Christians down through the ages.

In Acts 10, the Good News entered the household of Cornelius, a God-fearing and righteous Roman centurion. The conversion of Cornelius was especially important in convincing Peter that it was all right for non-Jews to be accepted as followers of Jesus. Before visiting Cornelius, Peter had three visions in which God told him that he could eat animals and foods that Jewish law considered unclean.(Acts 10:9-16) Three men sent by Cornelius asked for Peter to accompany them to Caesarea to meet him. Cornelius had also had a vision from God, in which an angel told him to find Peter. Even though it was considered taboo for a practicing Jew to meet with non Jews in their homes, Peter followed the vision from God and went to see the Roman centurion.

While in Cornelius' home, Peter testified to the Gospel message about Jesus' life, death, and resurrection, and how Jesus had come to save people from their sins. Upon hearing the message, Cornelius and the others gathered in his home were overtaken by the Holy Spirit. The disciple's response was to order the baptism of Cornelius and his entire household. For Peter realized, "Can anyone forbid water for baptizing these people who have received the Holy Spirit just as we have?" (Acts 10:47).

Non Hebrew-speaking Jewish emigrants, the despised heretical Samaritans, a physically-mutilated African, a Roman oppressor and his family and servants—these were the kinds of marginal people who were attracted to the early Christian message soon after Jesus' death and resurrection. They became followers of the Way of Jesus because they were welcomed as equals by believers in the one God, who had been taught by God's son and messenger, Jesus Christ, and empowered by the Holy Spirit. In God's plan, these marginal people were also bicultural, and thus became the bridges over which the Good News could spread from its Jewish roots into different cultures, within and beyond the Roman Empire.

According to Christian tradition, Jesus' early followers took his message from Jerusalem into new regions where they suffered martyrdom. Mark went to Egypt and became the patron saint of the Christian Coptic Orthodox Church. "Doubting" Thomas, who wished to put his hand into Jesus' wounded side as proof of the resurrection, went to India and was killed there. The Thomas Christians, including the Malankara Syrian Orthodox Church of South India, consider him their founder.

Tradition has it that Philip went to Africa after baptizing the Ethiopian eunuch. Baptizer of the Roman centurion, Peter found his mission in Rome, and was eventually crucified upside down. As the leader of Roman Christianity, Peter became the first bishop—or overseer—of what became the Catholic Church. The popes claim descent from him. Through traditions about the cross-cultural outreach of the disciples, Christians today in Africa, Asia, and Europe can directly ground their own cultural identities in the Scriptures. The Bible thus becomes the sacred founding charter for churches around the world.

Young Christian communities fixed their hopes on the universal vision in which persons from all nations would be drawn to God, through Jesus Christ the Messiah. Despite being a small persecuted minority, poor and needy in the things of the world, early Christians took courage from the words of John in Revelation 7:9, just as do persecuted minority Christians today.

> "After this I looked, and there was a great multitude that no one could count, from every nation, from all tribes and peoples and languages, standing before the throne and before the Lamb, robed in white, with palm branches in their hands. They cried out in a loud voice, saying, 'Salvation belongs to our God who is seated on the throne, and to the Lamb!'"

The Apostle Paul as Bridge to the Gentiles

While the core followers of Jesus when he was alive were known as disciples, Paul is remembered as the *Apostle* to the Gentiles, or in modern terms a "missionary." Scores of books have been written about Paul as the leading cross-cultural missionary of biblical record, on Paul's mission strategy, or "Pauline" methods in missions. Yet Paul was only one of dozens of believers who traveled around the Roman Empire, spreading the Good News about Jesus as Messiah, the chosen one of God. Paul has been remembered as the model missionary by Christians down through the centuries, not just because he traveled an estimated ten thousand miles for his mission but also because the letters to the churches he visited are the oldest documents gathered into the New Testament and are foundational to Christian theology. The narrative of Paul's ministry appears in the second half of the book of Acts.

Paul's personal story makes gripping reading: a follower of a pious Jewish group called the Pharisees, a law-abiding and duly circumcised member of the tribe of Benjamin, and a Greek-speaking Roman citizen, Paul began his relationship with Christians by hating them. The followers of Jesus were standing up in synagogues and proclaiming that Jesus represented the fulfillment of Jewish Scriptures about the coming Messiah. When one of the early church officers named Stephen was stoned to death for blasphemy, Paul held the coats of the mob (see Acts 7).

Yet one day on his way to arrest some Christians in Damascus, a flash of light blinded Paul. He heard the voice of Jesus asking him why he was persecuting Jesus. After three days of blindness, Paul was visited by a church leader who restored his eyesight and told him how Jesus had been resurrected from death. (Acts 9:1-19). This experience was interpreted by Paul as God calling him to preach to Greek-speaking Jews and non-Jews, or Gentiles, about "the way" of Jesus Christ.

Transformed by his encounter with the living God, Paul traveled to provincial cities where he moved into Jewish neighborhoods, supported himself by making tents, and began proclaiming the Good News. The diaspora Jews among whom Paul lived spoke Greek, worked, and traded in the wider Greek-speaking world. They even read the Hebrew Scriptures in a Greek version called the Septuagint.

When Paul interpreted the saving role of Jesus according to the Septuagint, both ethnic Jews and Greeks could understand him. The common Greek language and Paul's theological interpretations were bridges across which the meaning of Jesus' defeat of death traveled from an oral Aramaic-speaking local culture, into the cosmopolitan Greek world. The Greek word for *Messiah* is "Christ." Our term "Jesus Christ," therefore, represents the multicultural nature imbedded in early Christianity, as it combines an Aramaic/Hebrew name with a Greek title.

In Antioch, where Paul spent a year, a decisive breakthrough among Greek-speaking Gentiles occurred. Followers of the way of Jesus began to be called "Christians." Paul's basic message was one of inclusion in God's plan for salvation. Just like a fruitful grapevine grafted on to a sturdy root, through Jesus Christ Gentiles were grafted onto God's promises for Israel: "For there is no distinction between Jew and Greek; the same Lord is Lord of all and is generous to all who call on him. For, 'Everyone who calls on the name of the Lord shall be saved'" (Romans 10:12-13).

The biculturalism of the diaspora Jewish population, as exemplified by Paul himself—a Greek-speaking Jew—was essential for the expanded scope of salvation that included both Jews and Greeks. After Paul had encouraged a community of believers in a particular city, he moved on but sent other workers to help the young churches. A network of Christians—linked together by correspondence and traveling teachers like Paul—grew in the cities across the Roman Empire.

The Jerusalem Council

As more non-Jews became Christians, tensions grew between the Jewish believers who followed Jewish practices and the new believers from other ethnic backgrounds for whom Jewish identity was unimportant. Many of Paul's letters dealt with the struggles of young churches over their internal cultural and economic differences. After fourteen years of successful ministry among the growing Gentile churches, Paul was called to Jerusalem to meet with the Hebrew Christian leadership, directed by Jesus' brother James. The Christians in

Jerusalem were skeptical that the non-Jewish Christians could be fully accepted by God without obeying Jewish law. In a crucial discussion, described in Acts 15, Jesus' chief disciple Peter, Paul, and his friend Barnabas convinced James and the Hebrew church elders that God was clearly speaking to the Gentiles. Evidence of God's love for non-Jews were the miraculous healings and changed lives, the "signs and wonders," being performed among them. The Jerusalem Christians sent off Paul and Barnabas with a few instructions and a generous blessing for their non-Jewish brothers and sisters. This approval by the "Jerusalem Council" of Jewish leaders who had been close to Jesus himself confirmed Christianity's already vigorous expansion into Syria, Cilicia, Antioch, and points eastward.

The response of so many non-Jewish believers to the work of Paul and the other evangelists created a crisis for the original believers in Jerusalem, who sensed that they were losing control over the boundaries of the faith. This same dilemma has been repeated every time the Gospel message makes itself at home among a new group of people. The cross-cultural spread of the message, including translating it into terms that made sense to a Gentile audience, set a pattern that not only separated Christianity from its Jewish background but also created a religion able to transcend cultural differences. The crucial decision to allow Greeks to become Christians and remain within their own cultural framework was the key that opened the future of Christianity to its global potential as a "world" religion, rather than remaining a sect within Judaism.

Christianity Moves Outward

The story of Christianity during its first three centuries was that of a steadily expanding urban network, often along extended family lines, under the leadership of strong local bishops. Christians met in house churches sponsored by wealthy members. Women played prominent roles in the movement that gained a reputation for female leadership and strict personal ethical codes. From the beginning, Christianity was a woman-friendly religion because it considered women equal to men under God. Compared to the general population in the Roman Empire, Christianity had a higher percentage of women. During its first few centuries, Christianity spread through three main linguistic groups. North Africa was the stronghold of Latin-speaking Christians, with their headquarters in Rome. Greek speakers dominated the church in Egypt and the eastern Mediterranean. Syriac, the language most closely related to the Aramaic spoken by Jesus himself, became the sacred language of the Eastern churches that spread beyond the Roman Empire. Each linguistic grouping developed its own traditions of theology and worship.

Many believers identified with Jesus and his sufferings through fasting and other spiritual disciplines. Healings and miracles attracted thousands. Christians were noticed for their care of the sick during epidemics. Critics continued to accuse Christianity of being a superstitious cult that attracted the marginal people—children, the poor, and women. Yet leading philosophers and intellectuals also joined the movement. By the end of the third century, Christianity had spread strongly into areas of Persian control, present day Iran. Christian slaves, captured from Roman territory, began carrying their faith throughout Persia and along the Silk Road across Central Asia.

By the A.D. 400s, Christians could be found from Britannia in the North to North Africa in the South, from Spain in the West to the borders of Persia in the East. The eastward spread of Christianity was so extensive that the fourth-century Persian Empire contained as high a percentage of Christians as the Roman Empire did, with a geographic spread from modern-day Iran to India. By the seventh century, Christians were living as far east as China and as far south as Nubia in Africa.

The rise of Islam in Arabia during the 600s halted Christianity's eastward and southward expansions. Most of the ancient Christian churches, including those in North Africa and Asia Minor, fell under Muslim control and began declining in size and influence. Although Arab armies conquered the country of Jesus' birth, by the end of the first millennium after his death, the Christian religion had pushed northward across

Russia, Scandinavia, and Iceland. The first Christians arrived in North America in A.D. 986 when a short-lived colony settled in Greenland.

From the 600s to the 1200s, Roman Catholicism steadily became the religion of Europe. This process of Christianization was accomplished through a combination of spiritual, cultural, and military force. Less than a century before the birth of Martin Luther, the leader of the Protestant Reformation, in 1483, last European "pagan" tribes became Christian. By the late 1400s, Europeans shared a Catholic identity under a multi-cultural collaboration of church and state known as "Christendom."

In the late 1400s, the most widespread and powerful world civilizations were those of China in East Asia and of Islam from North Africa across Central Asia. But European power rose along with technological advances and royal support for exploration. Spanish and Portuguese explorers sailed around the Muslim blockade and began founding colonies in Asia, Africa, and the Americas.

The policies of Christendom encouraged the forced evangelization of non-Christian peoples. With decrees from the fifteenth-century popes, Spain and Portugal tried to split the world between them. Using horses and guns, young

Percent Christian by current United Nations regional boundaries, AD 400

0 0.4 2 5 10 40 60 75 85 90 95

Source: Center for the Study of Global Christianity, Gordon-Conwell Theological Seminary

conquistadors from Spain and Portugal conquered much of the Americas, coastal Africa, and Southeast Asia. By the late 1500s, due to Catholic missionary efforts, substantial groups of indigenous Christians were thriving in Angola, Japan, the Philippines, Brazil, and Central America. By the 1600s, French missionaries had converted significant numbers in Vietnam and First Nations Canada. After Holland and England became Protestant nations, they began challenging the Spanish, Portuguese, and French for military control of North America and parts of Asia and Africa.

From the 1500s to the mid 1900s, Europeans poured into other parts of the world. As they moved into Asia, Africa, and Latin America, they took many different forms of Christianity with them. Methodism, for example, first came to North America with emigrants from Great Britain in the 1700s, and then in the 1800s spread across the continent. Alongside voluntary European emigration, the cruel and vicious slave trade caused the forced dispersal of millions of Africans. In North America, many slaves became Methodists and Baptists starting in the mid 1700s. Freed slaves took their faith back to West Africa as returning settlers. Methodism was a "diaspora" religion spread by European and African migrants.

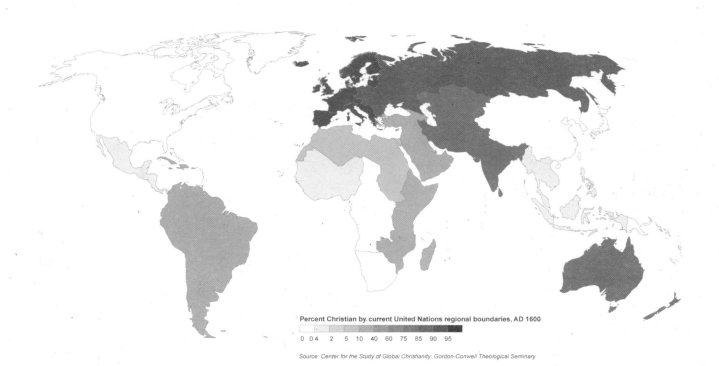

Percent Christian by current United Nations regional boundaries, AD 1600

0 0.4 2 5 10 40 60 75 85 90 95

Source: Center for the Study of Global Christianity, Gordon-Conwell Theological Seminary

Nineteenth-century missionaries took Christianity to Asia, the South Pacific, and Africa. Protestants believed in giving people the Bible in their own languages so that they could found and lead churches for themselves. Bible translations, literacy projects, schools, and medical care spread the Christian message to new groups of people. The most rapid expansion of Christianity took place in the late twentieth century, after the end of European colonialism. Pockets of Christians throughout Africa and Asia grew into widespread movements, and Protestantism began growing rapidly in Latin America.

As the great colonial-era migration of Europeans into Asia, Africa, and Latin America reversed itself after the Second World War, emigrants from Asia, Africa, and Latin American began moving to Europe and North America. Global patterns of migration caused the continued spread of Christianity. Non-Western Christians carried their newfound faith back to Europe and North America and spread it within their home continents. By the beginning of the twenty-first century, Christians from multiple cultures and language groups could be found on all the inhabited continents and in all the countries of the world.

United Methodists and the Changing Face of World Missions

For United Methodists, the Gospel movement across cultures is incomplete unless we recognize that we are part of this complex historical process. As inheritors of the biblical promises, and as the spiritual and physical descendents of generations who paved the way, the unfolding story of world Christianity is our own. Today United Methodists represent the changing face of world missions in the framework of global Christianity. The following tale of two families is but one powerful illustration of the cross-cultural spread of Christianity over the past century.

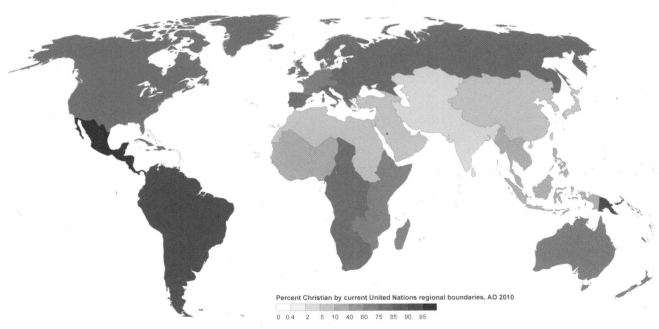

Percent Christian by current United Nations regional boundaries, AD 2010

0 0.4 2 5 10 40 60 75 85 90 95

Source: Center for the Study of Global Christianity, Gordon-Conwell Theological Seminary

Helen and John Springer

In 1901, Helen Chapman Rasmussen sailed to Rhodesia as the first missionary appointed there by the woman's missionary society of the Methodist Episcopal Church, one of the predecessor churches of today's United Methodist Church. This was not Helen's first trip to Africa. Ten years earlier, at age 22 she had answered the call of the famous missionary bishop and revivalist William Taylor for self-supporting missionaries, and volunteered for Angola. On board ship to West Africa, she met and married William Rasmussen, another "Taylor" missionary. The Rasmussens quickly contracted malaria, and Helen's husband died in 1895.

After Helen returned to the United States, her only son died of diphtheria in 1900. So it was as a grieving widow and childless mother that she went to Rhodesia to begin "women's work" among the Karanga (now Shona) people. She moved into a rural village to study the language. She made friends with women and children, including the chief's daughter, and started the first Methodist school for girls in Rhodesia. In 1905 she published the first handbook on the Shona language.

Also in 1901, John Springer arrived at Old Umtali, Rhodesia (now Mutare, Zimbabwe) to supervise the "industrial mission." Industrial mission work included training young men in trades such as carpentry and masonry. In 1905, John and Helen married. Feeling called by the Holy Spirit, they walked across Central Africa scouting possible mission locations—despite the disapproval of the Methodist Board of Missions. The Springers returned to the United States and on faith raised so much money for the Congo that the mission board changed its mind and allowed the Congo Mission to become an official Methodist mission. The Springers spent an arduous two years launching the mission stations, including founding a Bible Training School for teachers and evangelists. Approved in 1915, the Congo Mission was headed by John Springer until 1936 when he was elected bishop for Africa.

When the Springers began their missionary explorations, Africa had the fewest Christians of any continent. Only eight million Christians lived there, mostly in the ancient Christian stronghold of Ethiopia. The Springers were the first Protestant missionaries in a region of Congo as big as Indiana, Michigan, and Illinois combined. Africans in the Springers' day suffered under European colonialism, stemming from a conference in 1885 when European nations cut up the map of Africa and took over different sections for themselves. Congo was put under Belgian control, and its citizens were victimized by cruel forced labor policies and internal slave trading. The Belgian authorities also sponsored Catholicism as a state church, and they persecuted independent ministries, especially those led by Africans. While the Springers did not directly challenge colonial structures, they believed in the power of the Good News to transform human lives. Thus they emphasized conversions to Christ, literacy training, women's ministries, and education for ministers.

From John McKendree Springer, Pioneering in the Congo (New York: The Katanga Press, 1916).

Rev. and Mrs. John M. Springer

Number of Christians in Africa, Europe, and Latin America, 1900-2025				
	1900	1970	mid-2009	2025
Africa	8,756,000	116,451,000	447,277,000	662,881,000
Europe	368,257,000	467,771,000	553,868,000	539,078,000
Latin America	60,027,000	263,719,000	531,393,000	623,207,000

from David B. Barrett, Todd M. Johnson, and Peter F. Crossing, World Christian Database

Mrs. Springer became a famous motivational speaker to students in America, and she wrote mission books on Africa for young people. After a fruitful life of Bible translation and pioneer mission work, she died in 1946. John Springer returned to Mulungwishi Station after his retirement as bishop. After the Second World War, African nations gained independence from European colonialism. Tragically, civil war broke out in some of the newly-independent countries, including Congo. The violence of the early 1960s destroyed most of the mission institutions. The Methodist missionaries of the Congo Mission had to be evacuated from the country. During the violent upheaval, John Springer was forced to leave the Congo at age 90. He died soon afterward. The Bible institute was destroyed in the conflict. [2]

Even though the missionaries left, however, the men educated by Methodist missionaries became leaders of movements for justice and religious freedom. Methodist ministers in Congo led their communities into a post-colonial era. Although anti-colonial upheaval targeted the churches, the memory of the Springers and other missionaries remained strong. In some parts of the Congo, even today Methodists are known as "Springers."

From the vantage point of God's providence, the destruction of Methodist missions in Congo was only a temporary setback in the larger context of building a vibrant, fully indigenous African Christianity. In the mid-twentieth century, Christianity in Africa grew in leaps and bounds. Although foreign missionaries like the Springers could equip only a small number of ministers and lay leaders, African Christians became living testimonies of Christ's love to their people. From the end of colonialism in the 1960s to the present, Africa experienced one of the greatest periods of growth in Christian history. From Africans representing only a small percentage of the world's Christians a hundred years ago, by the early twentieth century there were nearly four hundred million African Christians. It is predicted that by 2025, Africa will be the largest Christian continent.

Nkemba and Mbwizu Ndjungu

In 1998, roughly one hundred years after Emily Rasmussen and John Springer arrived in Rhodesia, another missionary family arrived in Dakar, Senegal. They planned to work in the three-year-old Methodist mission in that largely Muslim country. Their first worship service included fifteen people, eight of whom were their own family members. But these United Methodist missionaries were not from North America. Rather, Nkemba and Mbwizu Ndjungu were from Congo. By the time the Ndjungus became missionaries, eleven annual conferences existed in the United

Mbwizu and Nkemba Ndjungu

Methodist Church in Congo. As theological education was reorganized and expanded, Nkemba Ndjungu was one of the pastors who studied in the Methodist Theological Seminary, the descendent of John Springer's Bible Institute.

As a district superintendent in South Congo, Ndjungu was put in charge of the mission to Senegal. In early 2004, the Senegal Church commissioned the first twenty members of United Methodist Women. Seven hundred people attended services of singing and celebration in March of that year. By June of 2007, eight ministers were ordained as pastors in the United Methodist Church in Senegal, including the first woman ordained in the entire country. Nearly a thousand members worshiped in churches that did not exist ten years before.

One of the main reasons for the growth of the Methodist mission in Senegal was the work of Mbwizu Ndjungu among the women. Just as Helen Springer visited women and children in their homes and organized them for self-support and education, Mbwizu Ndjungu began a nutrition project of feeding needy women and children. Like Helen Springer, Mbwizu suffered hardship and loss. She grew up in an orphanage run by Brethren missionaries. Experiencing the love of Christ through them, she wanted to become a missionary herself. She pursued midwifery training, married Rev. Ndjungu, and had six children—one of whom died. As a missionary to Senegal, Mbwizu was responsible for healing a young girl in a village, after which many people in the area became Christians, including a medical doctor who then joined the work of the mission.

Just as Helen trained women to be partners in ministry with their husbands in Congo, nearly a century later Mbwizu was training women to be partners in ministry with their husbands in Senegal. The holistic work of

Methodist women in Senegal included healing, feeding, and visiting those in prison, in line with Matthew 25:35-36, "For I was hungry and you gave me food, I was thirsty and you gave me drink, I was a stranger and you welcomed me, I was naked and you clothed me, I was sick and you visited me, I was in prison and you came to me."

Christian Missions and Cultures through the Ages

The path from John and Helen Springer to Nkemba and Mbwizu Ndjungu illustrates the meaning of Christian mission as a multi-cultural movement of faith that crosses boundaries of race, geography, time, and nationality. Euro-Americans Emily and John Springer were both inspired in their missionary commitment by Bishop William Taylor, who himself was converted to Christianity upon hearing the testimony of an African American girl in rural Virginia.

As the Springers gave themselves to Africa, they befriended Africans who were seeking missionaries to instruct their people. The Springers went to Congo and began churches and schools that nurtured the teachers and pastors who eventually inspired Nkemba and Mbwizu Ndjungu. Called by God, the Ndjungus received support for their work in Senegal from United Methodists in Illinois, Michigan, and Wisconsin. [3]

As the story of the Springers and the Ndjungus shows, the history of Christian mission is a chain of personal relationships, forged by the Holy Spirit, which stretches across time and place. The great Scottish Methodist mission historian Andrew Walls reminds us that God accepts people into the church on the basis of their own cultural identities. No language group or ethnicity is too weak or insignificant to be loved by God. As the Sunday school song says, "Jesus loves the little children. . . Red and yellow, black and white, they are precious in his sight." The church is a household of faith in which all the peoples of the world are welcome.

The idea that the church is a home is a lot easier to accept in principle than in reality. Did the earliest Jewish Christians in Jerusalem realize that the result of their decision not to require circumcision for membership would eventually cause them to be outnumbered by Gentiles, who would change the character of the church? The changing demographics of world Christianity mean that new groups of Christians have the right to feel at home in their own cultural skins. Each believer must be able to eat of his or her own vine and fig tree (see Isaiah 36:16).

But the idea that God in Christ accepts people as they are must be kept in tension with the idea that God calls people in order to transform them into what God wants them to be. Andrew Walls also reminds us that all Christians are on a journey toward a higher end. Transformed by Christ, persons of faith share in a universal fellowship. Christians live in two worlds—the earthly one to which we belong by nature and the mystical communion of the saints that transcends time and space. As the faith moves from one culture to another, we are linked historically to the whole history of Israel

REV. WILLIAM TAYLOR.

Bishop William Taylor

and down through the stories of Christians of all nationalities. Yet we must constantly remember that because we are called to a higher purpose, we must not make the church so much in our own image that other people cannot find a home with us.

The church's process of cultural change began in Jerusalem on the day of Pentecost, when the gathered people heard the Gospel in their own languages. Today, United Methodists are privileged to see a world in which more kinds of people than ever before are contributing to the fullness of the Good News of Jesus Christ. Although it is neither perfect nor complete, the church is the product of two thousand years of Christian hope. The new reality of global Christianity reminds us that the reign of God is a biblical vision of human unity, with worshipers called from all the nations of the earth.

CHAPTER NOTES

1. Some material for this section is taken from Dana L. Robert, *Christian Mission: How Christianity Became a World Religion* (Chichester, UK: Wiley-Blackwell, 2009). For overviews of the biblical and historical development of mission theologies, see David J. Bosch, *Transforming Mission* (Maryknoll, NY: Orbis, 1991); Stephen Bevans and Roger Schroeder, *Constants in Context: A Theology of Mission for Today* (Maryknoll, NY: Orbis, 2004).
2. For more information on the Springers, including brief bibliographies, see Dana L. Robert, "Springer, Helen Emily (Chapman) Rasmussen," and "Springer, John McKendree," in *Biographical Dictionary of Christian Missions*, ed. Gerald H. Anderson (New York: Macmillan Reference USA, 1998), 635–636.
3. Information on Nkemba and Mbwizu Ndungu is derived primarily from personal conversations with the author.

Chapter Two

From 1910 to the World Church Today

As though in preparation for such a time as this, God has been building up a Christian fellowship which now extends into almost every nation, and binds citizens of them all together in true unity and mutual love . . . Almost incidentally the great world-fellowship has arisen; it is the great new fact of our era."
—Archbishop William Temple, 1944 [1]

In June of 1910, twelve hundred representatives of one hundred sixty Protestant mission societies from around the globe arrived in Edinburgh, Scotland. Over a thousand homes were opened to house the delegates, many of whom had traveled for weeks on trains and steamships to attend the historic event. Never before had so many branches of Protestantism put aside their differences and embraced a common cause—that of world missions. For ten days, Lutherans, Anglicans, Presbyterians, Methodists, Baptists and others gathered in the Assembly Hall of the United Free Church of Scotland. The meeting was chaired by American Methodist layman John R. Mott, who went on to become world president of the

World Mission Conference in Edinburgh (1910)

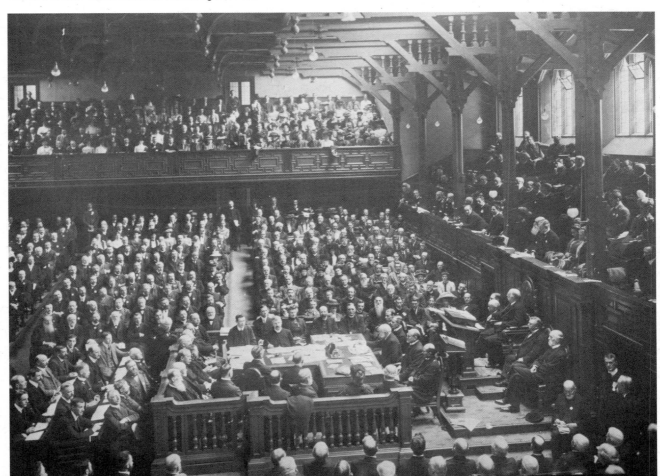

YMCA, and forty years later the recipient of the Nobel Peace Prize.

Four galleries full of observers, including many missionaries, listened intently while church leaders discussed the key issues facing world missions in the twentieth century: What should the Christian message be in relation to non-Christian religions? How should missionaries relate to colonial governments? What is the relationship of mission schools to growing political independence movements? How can churches and missions unite and work together for the improvement of the world? The importance of the World Missionary Conference, or "Edinburgh 1910" as it is called, was such that the Archbishop of Canterbury, the head of the Church of England, judged it to be the most important conference of its kind in the history of Christianity. [2]

John R. Mott

In 2010, Christian groups around the world are celebrating the centennial of Edinburgh 1910 with conferences, study programs, and seminars. Exactly one hundred years after the original conference, representative delegates from all the major church traditions—including this time Catholics, Orthodox, Protestants, and new non-Western denominations—are meeting in the same church hall in Edinburgh, Scotland. But why remember Edinburgh 1910 at all? What was so important about a conference of missionaries and church leaders a century ago? What exactly is being celebrated?

Although most of the delegates were Europeans and North Americans, the World Missionary Conference was the most inclusive meeting of Protestants in modern history to date. It was marked by optimism that the twentieth century would see a great advance in the number of Christians in the world as a result of the missionary movement. It launched the "ecumenical movement" for Christian unity that ultimately led to the founding of the World Council of Churches in 1948 and to other worldwide networks of like-minded Christians. Through its study commissions, for the first time in modern history a global overview of Christianity became available.

From the vantage point of 2010, it is clear that the century after 1910 brought one of the most important changes in the two thousand year history of Christianity. During the twentieth century, Christianity became a worldwide religion. Instead of three out of four Christians being Europeans as was the case in 1910, by 2010 three out of four Christians are Asians, Africans, or Latin Americans. The participants in Edinburgh 1910 would be shocked to know that the twentieth century would be scarred by two world wars, the Cold War, genocides, and the decline of Christianity in Europe. Although the kingdom of God did not emerge as they hoped, they were nevertheless on the verge of a new era in the history of Christianity.

"The evangelization of the world . . . is not chiefly a European and American enterprise, but an Asiatic and African Enterprise." —John R. Mott

Edinburgh 1910 marked the symbolic beginnings of Christianity as a worldwide fellowship. A small but strategic group of non-Western Christian leaders met as equals with their Western counterparts. Although only nineteen non-Western Christians attended the conference as delegates, they delivered six of the 47 major conference addresses. Their presence confirmed the views of conference chairman John R. Mott, "The evangelization of the world . . . is not chiefly a European and American enterprise, but an Asiatic and African enterprise." [3]

A speech by V. S. Azariah (d. 1945) made a deep impression on the delegates. Azariah was a second generation Indian Christian, YMCA leader, founder in 1905 of a groundbreaking Indian Missionary Society, and a future Anglican bishop. While thanking the missionaries who brought the Gospel to India, Azariah asked for true equality and partnership between missionaries and indigenous Christians:

> Through all the ages to come the Indian Church will rise up in gratitude to attest the heroism and self-denying labors of the missionary body. You have given your goods to feed the poor. You have given your bodies to be burned. We also ask for *love*. Give us FRIENDS. [4]

Azariah's cry for friendship captured the spirit of the conference. Delegates pledged themselves to move beyond racism to promote full equality between Western missionaries and Eastern converts, and between older and younger churches. Although the typical missionary in 1910 was a European operating in a colonial context, what thrilled the conference delegates was the prophetic vision they glimpsed of worldwide Christian unity marked by human equality, justice, and shared passion to spread the name of Jesus Christ.

Christianity Spreads in the Twentieth Century

The reasons for the growth of world Christianity during the twentieth century are complex and will not be clear until later generations can look back on where we are today. But a few major factors can be noted. First to mention, of course, is the work of thousands of missionaries like the Springers and the Ndjungus, who were discussed in chapter 1. Missionaries founded schools and mass literacy projects so that people could learn to read. Mission hospitals and clinics led to better health. Dignity for women and children were taught as part of the Gospel message. The most effective missionary message was to offer the whole Gospel for the whole person—mind, spirit, and body. Throughout the twentieth century, cross-cultural missionaries translated the Bible, hymnals, and Christian literature into local languages. Language teams composed of missionaries, linguists, and local people worked together to make the Gospel understandable to ordinary people. By the early twenty-first century, at least part of the Bible had been translated into more than two thousand four hundred of the world's nearly seven thousand languages.

Just as the early followers of the resurrected Jesus heard the word of God in their own languages at the time of Pentecost, so in the twentieth century the ability to hear the Gospel in one's own language was the key to its spread. Once someone has the Bible in her own language, she is empowered to develop her own faith. The history of twentieth-century Christianity is full of stories of local teachers and preachers who took what they learned from missionaries, repackaged the message for their own local cultures, and then founded new churches.

Sometimes these churches remained inside the missionary denominations. But often a prophet figure emerged, broke away from the mission, and then founded a new movement. For each cross-cultural missionary who brought ten people to Christ, a local missionary evangelist influenced hundreds or even thousands because of the ability to express the Gospel to people in terms meaningful to their culture.

People on fire with the Holy Spirit tend to break out of established church structures.

Because Methodism began as a movement characterized by strong belief in the power of the Holy Spirit, it has been an unusually fertile source for the founding of new churches. People on fire with the Holy Spirit tend to break out of established church structures. The powerful combination of Methodist beliefs and church-sponsored education equipped people for independent ministries. For example, although Spanish Catholics controlled the Philippines for centuries, they ordained shockingly few men for the priesthood. But soon after Methodist missionaries arrived there in 1900, they ordained Nicholas Zamora. He pastored the first Filipino Methodist Church and brought many into the faith. Tired of being controlled by foreign missionaries, in 1909 he founded an independent Filipino Church, the *Iglesia Evangelica Methodista en las Islas Filipinas* (Evangelical Methodist Church in the Philippine Islands). Zamora served as its first bishop. In the Philippines, as in many other places, Methodist missions gave rise to multiple denominations.

In 1907, a group of missionaries and native church leaders held a massive revival in Pyongyang, Korea. From that famous revival, Koreans went out to found their own Methodist and Presbyterian churches around the country, including on nearby islands. In 1918, Shona Methodists experienced the "year of the Holy Spirit," and many people were converted and spread across the region as evangelists. Methodism grew among other people as well; in 1932 a Methodist evangelist named Johane Maranke believed that God was

John Bancroft Devins, An Observer in the Philippines (1905), 306.

Nicholas Zamora

calling him to start his own church. He departed in 1932 on missionary tours through six African nations. He founded what became the largest indigenous church in Zimbabwe, the Apostles of Johane Maranke. Similarly, in the late 1920s, Methodist evangelists led revivals in China that resulted in the conversion of Chinese Christian leaders who then founded their own churches.

The successes of the twentieth-century missionary movement cannot be understood in isolation from the stories of the early converts, who despite opposition and persecution became Christian pioneers in Africa, Asia, and Latin America. At the 2008 General Conference, the Methodist Church of Ivory Coast was welcomed into The United Methodist Church. Ivory Coast Methodism is an important example of the partnership between indigenous Christians and missionaries during the twentieth century. In 1910, the same year as the Edinburgh conference of missionary leaders, the largest African-led revival movement broke out in several West African countries. Raised as a Methodist, the Liberian prophet William Wadé Harris was called by God in a vision. Dressed in robes of white and carrying a Bible, he traveled around Ivory Coast with a band of singers. Harris preached repentance from sins, baptized, and instructed people to burn their magical objects.

As people were converted, Harris told them to wait for missionaries who would tell them about the Bible. He told them to reform their morals and to exercise spiritual discipline. Hundreds of thousands of people were spiritually awakened before Harris was arrested by colonial authorities. Although several denominations were founded by his converts, tens of thousands gathered into Methodist Churches under the instruction of English missionaries. Like the work of Paul in the New Testament, who sent teachers to follow up his visits to

William Wadé Harris

new churches, Ivory Coast Methodism resulted from the work of the African evangelist William Wadé Harris with follow up by Western missionaries in partnership with local leaders. Bible translation, church planting and revivals, the founding of schools and colleges, social services, and cross-cultural partnerships are just a few of the reasons for the spread of Christianity worldwide from 1910 to 2010.

Changing Political Contexts Lead to Growth

Until the Second World War, much of Asia and Africa was under the political control of European nations. After war with Spain in 1898, the United States occupied the Philippines and islands in the Caribbean including Cuba and Puerto Rico. Missionaries often operated in colonial situations where they sometimes received privileges from these governments, such as subsidies for mission schools or land on which to build mission stations. Although missionaries provided education, medicine, and social services to the needy, as citizens of the colonial powers, they were unavoidably tainted by the realities of imperialism and occupation by European powers. Sometimes they reacted to colonialism by supporting people's struggles for freedom and human rights or by challenging settler communities that tried to take the land of native peoples. But most of the time they did not see their work as "political" and so avoided confrontations with colonial powers. [5]

The destruction of Europe during the Second World War halted four centuries of European expansion into other continents. Independence movements fought successfully against colonial rule. India in 1947, Burma in 1948, and Ghana in 1957 were a few of the dozens of new nations that had become independent by 1970. The 450-year old flood of European emigration reversed itself as citizens of former colonies—Algerians, Pakistanis, Filipinos, Indonesians, Lebanese, Colombians, Nigerians, and others—began immigrating to the homelands of their former colonizers. In the 1960s, as the tide of Western colonization flowed out, the reverse surge of global migration began.

With the end of European colonialism came a radical rejection of missions as Western assaults on other cultures and religions. New political regimes confiscated mission institutions, including schools and hospitals. Western missionaries were denied visas in India,

In the 1960s, as the tide of Western colonization flowed out, the reverse surge of global migration began.

Indonesia, and other predominantly Islamic and Hindu countries. In China, Communist victory in 1948 meant the expulsion of missionaries and the accusation that even mission hospitals and Christian schools had been tools of "capitalist imperialism." Chinese Christians were treated as traitors to the people. During the 1960s and 1970s, young church leaders from around the world accused missionaries and their supporters of paternalism and of failing to turn over church leadership structures to local control. It appeared to worried observers that Christianity around the world was collapsing rather than growing.

Yet even while church leaders argued over the new form that missions should take in a post-colonial world, behind the scenes Christianity was entering an amazing period of growth in Latin America, Africa, and parts of Asia. The turmoil over the meaning and structures of missions from the 1960s to the 1980s was actually a necessary part of the process of moving to a new phase of Christian history—that of a truly multi-cultural, worldwide church.

The greatest growth in worldwide Christianity began in the mid-twentieth century. Researchers in the 1960s began to notice new churches in the southern hemisphere—churches founded by Africans, Asians, and Latin Americans rather than by Westerners. In his groundbreaking book of 1968, *Schism and Renewal in Africa*, the mission researcher David Barrett counted over six thousand new Christian movements in Africa alone. These "independent churches" typically began when an African prophet broke from a Western mission, but they quickly grew on their own and were not confined by Western structures. Barrett predicted that non-Western Christians would attain a numerical majority of members by the year 2000. In 1977, Catholic scholar Walbert Bühlmann predicted "the coming of the third church" with a growing percentage of future Roman Catholics coming from the Third World. Then in 1979, the Chinese government allowed public worship for the first time since 1966. Far from having been killed off by Communism, Chinese Christianity had increased by millions of members. [6]

Far from having been killed off by Communism, Chinese Christianity had increased by millions of members.

The end of colonialism was important for the health of world Christianity because as long as it was dominated by the West it looked like a European religion. For example, to be a Christian in Kenya in the 1950s was to be accused of being a traitor to Kenyan identity because Kenya was occupied by the British. The "Mau Mau" independence movement specifically rejected Christianity and attacked Kenyan Christians as Europeans in disguise. One of its leaders, the future president of Kenya, Jomo Kenyatta, commented that missionaries had brought the Bible and told people to close their eyes to pray. When people opened their eyes, they had the Bible and the missionaries had the land.

But by the 1970s, after independence from British colonialism, to be a Christian in Kenya was to be someone with desirable international connections and part of a growing world movement. Christians proved themselves to be patriotic citizens whose honesty and hard work was a positive factor in building up independent nations. Once mission work was clearly separated from Western power, Christianity gained credibility among the people.

To be seen as connected with Western imperialism is still the kiss of death for Christians in the Middle East, India, China, Indonesia, and especially in Muslim-dominated parts of the world. An example of this problem can be seen in what happened to Iraqi Christians after the United States invaded Iraq in 2003. Instead of being seen as patriotic citizens, Iraqi Christians were condemned with guilt-by-association with the "Western" religion. Over six hundred thousand Iraqi Christians were forced from their homes. The terrible irony is that Christians in Iraq, Iran, India, Lebanon, Egypt, and Turkey are descended from the ancient churches of biblical times, whose communities pre-date both Europe and Islam.

History shows that when Christianity has been associated with social improvements, material progress, and the patriotic growth of nationhood, people have often supported it. But when Christianity is seen as the religion of foreign invaders, takes the side of dictators, or uses violence, belief falters and the way of Jesus loses credibility. Although Jesus refused to accept political power, and Christianity is not a political program, politics still has a big impact on people's opinions toward Christian mission. Overall, the end of European colonialism by the 1960s led to the growth of Christianity, and in many countries helped remove the stigma of being seen as a foreign religion.

Who Are the Christians Today?

By the 1990s, it had become clear to scholars of Christian mission that even though the percentage of the world that was Christian had not changed much since 1900, Christianity had become a multi-cultural rather than a mostly European or North American religion. The late twentieth century was the greatest period of cross-cultural expansion in the history of Christianity. In the twenty-first century, no one culture will be the dominant force in the church. If present trends continue, by 2025, Africa will have roughly one-fourth of the world's Christians, Latin America one-fourth, and Europe one-fifth, with North America and Asia behind them.

Although population statistics are not perfect, the best scholarly estimates about the number of Christians in Africa illustrate that remarkable growth occurred in the mid- to late-twentieth century. In 1900, the continent of Africa was largely a mission field. As a percentage of the total of Christians in the world, Africans constituted only 1.5 percent, compared to 66 percent in Europe. By the year 2000, of the world's roughly two billion Christians, 350,091,000, or 17 percent were in Africa, compared to 550,729,000 or 27 percent in Europe.[7]

Christianity today is characterized by amazing linguistic diversity. Spanish, not English, is the number one language spoken by Christians around the world.

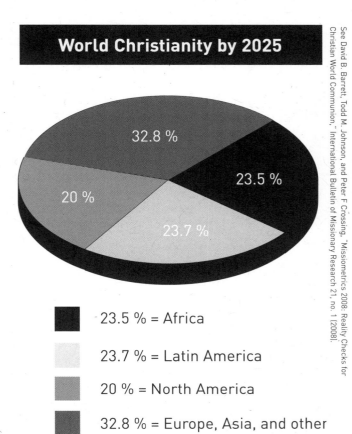

World Christianity by 2025

32.8 %
23.5 %
23.7 %
20 %

- 23.5 % = Africa
- 23.7 % = Latin America
- 20 % = North America
- 32.8 % = Europe, Asia, and other

See David B. Barrett, Todd M. Johnson, and Peter F Crossing, "Missiometrics 2008: Reality Checks for Christian World Communion," International Bulletin of Missionary Research 21, no. 1 (2008).

Christians in the Southern hemisphere constitute six thousand different ethno-linguistic peoples. The fastest growing church today appears to be the church in China. Scholars estimate that already more people attend church every Sunday in China than in all of Europe combined.

Half of the two billion Christians in the world are Roman Catholics (1.142 billion). Although pentecostalism is growing rapidly there, Latin America remains the heartland of Catholicism. Brazil has the largest Catholic Church in the world (144 million) followed by Mexico (93 million) and then the United States (68 million). While the historic Protestant churches such as Methodists, Anglicans, and Baptists still constitute roughly a quarter of the total number of Christians, each of those global communions is becoming less Western. Among Anglicans, Nigeria has 18.5

million members, a figure not too far behind that of the Church of England at 24.3 million, and far exceeding the 2.2 million Episcopalians in the United States.

> The largest concentration of Methodist churches is in North America, including: The United Methodist Church (8 million), the African Methodist Episcopal Church (2.6 million), and the African Methodist Episcopal Zion Church (1.44 million). But the next most populous countries for Methodism are Nigeria (2 million), Korea (1.5 million), South Africa (1.48 million), and India (1.03 million). [8]

One of the most significant changes in the world Christian population from 1910 to 2010 has been the growth of entirely new denominations founded by Africans, Asians, or Latin Americans. While these groups scarcely existed a century ago, today they constitute nearly one—fourth of the world Christian population. Such twentieth-century denominations as the Universal Church of the Kingdom of God in Brazil, the Kimbanguist Church of Congo, and the Redeemed Christian Church of God in Nigeria have multiple millions of members and branches in countries around the world.

Characteristics of Churches Worldwide

Christian churches everywhere trace their shared historic roots to ancient Israel of the Bible. They believe in Jesus Christ as the Son of God, and celebrate common rituals such as baptism and Holy Communion. These common characteristics are honed and affirmed in dialogue and cooperation with other churches around the world. While churches may differ on such practices as whether to baptize children or adults, whether to worship on Saturday or Sunday, and the qualifications for ordained ministry, the basic beliefs and practices they have in common mark them as Christian churches whether they are located in Boston or Baton Rouge or Beijing.

The growing churches of Africa, Asia, and Latin America also share certain similarities with one another. These characteristics are significant not only for the churches themselves but because, through "reverse mission," newer churches are influencing older churches in North America and Europe.

New Churches Are "Four-self" Churches: Self-Governing, Self-Supporting, Self-Missionizing, and Self-Theologizing

In the 1800s and 1900s, Protestants drew the distinction between a dependent "mission" and a "church" based on whether the group of Christians could support themselves, lead themselves, and spread the Gospel beyond their own boundaries. This "three-self" definition of a church was useful as a way to determine when new churches no longer needed outside help from foreign missionaries. By the 1980s, mission theologians began talking about the "fourth self," namely the ability of a church to think about theology from within its own culture and worldview.

New Churches Are "Four-self" Churches: Self-Governing, Self-Supporting, Self-Missionizing, and Self-Theologizing

World Christianity today is characterized by "four-self" churches. Although most churches rely on shared resources for theological education and social services, the growing Christian communities in Asia, Africa, and Latin America typically develop their own leaders from within their local context (self-government), raise their own funds (self-support), spread themselves beyond their own boundaries (self-missionizing), and read the Bible through their own cultural lenses (self-theologizing).

The reality of "four-self" churches requires new discussions on Christian identity. New non-Western churches are not clones of Western churches, even if they belong to the same denominational families. Just as James and Peter argued in the first century over whether followers of Jesus needed to follow Jewish law, the whole church re-examines beliefs and practices every time new groups of people enter our common community. When Christianity grows among new groups of people, arguments over theology and practices are inevitable.

What might be compatible with one group's understanding of God's mercy might be seen as optional to someone from another culture or another generation. For example, many Western churches allow divorce but would never allow polygamy. Some African churches argue that since Jesus forbids divorce, it should not be allowed. But since polygamy is in the Old Testament, it is tolerated. Who is correct? Neither divorce nor polygamy seems consistent with Christian values, yet both exist because of human weaknesses and social realities.

Sometimes new cultural values provide fresh perspectives on old theological concepts. Take, for example, belief in the idea that Jesus died as a sacrifice for the sins of the world. While this idea has been a standard part of Western theology since the early church, many urban Westerners today have trouble identifying with the idea that the blood sacrifice of Jesus is a necessary part of the Christian message. And yet rural Africans and Latin Americans are very comfortable with animal slaughter as a part of life, and are familiar with animal sacrifices by traditional healers and diviners. To them, Jesus died for the sins of the world as a sacrifice to end all sacrifices. Since in traditional worldviews, relationships are made right through appropriate rituals including the offering of sacrifices, the ancient Christian idea of Jesus' sacrifice makes more sense to most non-Western Christians than to secular North Americans in the twenty-first century.

The whole Bible looks different when seen through the eyes of "four-self" churches around the world. For example, in the book of Revelation, the red dragon is a symbol of evil. How do Chinese Christians interpret Chinese tradition, in which the red dragon is a positive symbol of China itself? How do Asian Christians deal with ancient rituals that honor their dead ancestors? Is this idolatry according to the Bible? Many Africans believe that the book of Leviticus is very important

because it deals with purity laws and taboos that are familiar in African traditional religions. But many North Americans would be shocked to think that the book of Leviticus is central to their faith. As new groups and new generations are born into the Christian family, the church struggles with how to remain faithful to the Bible and to tradition, and also to be relevant to the needs of its varied peoples.

New Churches Are Worshiping and Healing Communities

By and large, the churches that are growing worldwide use charismatic or pentecostal worship styles. The singing of praise choruses, speaking in tongues, prophetic utterances, and prayers for healing have become common practices in churches around the world over the past thirty years. Lively worship style and deep emphasis on prayer is something that has already had a positive impact on the churches in the United States. Simple choruses are particularly appropriate worship forms for churches in which people move frequently or migrate from one country to another. Pentecostal type prayer does not disadvantage those who do not speak English. The use of personal "prayer languages" is a unifier that cuts across different linguistic groups.

Every great revival movement in history has been characterized by the development of a new outpouring of music. In the First Great Awakening of the 1730s, the hymns of Dr. Isaac Watts were a major force. Charles Wesley's hymns were vital to the success of early Methodism. Shaped-note singing and the Sacred Harp were keys to the expansion of Christianity on the North American frontier. Gospel hymns and gospel music shaped late nineteenth- and early twentieth-century churches, both black and white. The whole movement toward developing global praise teams in The United Methodist Church has been an exciting response to the growing world church. Today Christian praise music is not just an American practice, but a worldwide phenomenon that draws Christians together across linguistic and ethnic boundaries.

Another feature of pentecostal-style worship is the leadership of women through song and dance. Although men continue to be the preachers in most churches, music provides an important participatory role for women in worship. In fact, in indigenous churches in southern Africa, Methodist churches in Ghana, and others, women break into song to interrupt the male preacher if he goes on too long. Lay-led music provides a check on male pastoral leadership.

One of the major factors that draw people into the growing churches of the southern hemisphere is healing. Healing ministries, through the laying on of hands, the blessing of families, and even the exorcism of demons, is a major reason that people in Latin America, Africa, and China are becoming Christians. Women are the largest group of people being healed and incorporated into churches today. To be healed is not only a physical phenomenon, but a social one. Healing restores not only health but also human relationships. Chinese house churches are places of spiritual power that are growing in response to people being healed. Henri Nouwen's idea of the "wounded healer" makes a lot of sense in non-Western churches; often women with active healing ministries have themselves used sickness, barrenness, or other misfortunes as starting points. [9]

In the United States, old and new churches often find themselves cooperating in community projects or even sharing the same space. An article a few years ago in the

© Paul Jeffrey

Members of the choir of the United Methodist Church in Kamina, Democratic Republic of the Congo, sing and dance during an outdoor worship celebration.

Boston Globe described how a Congregational church with twenty-five elderly members welcomed a youthful, eighty-member Hispanic Pentecostal congregation into their old New England-style white wooden church building with its tall steeple. The two congregations understandably experienced tensions. Elderly Congrega- tionalists disliked the noise, the drums and microphones, and the exuberant worship style. The Hispanics felt hemmed in by the wooden pews, depressed by the stark white walls and wine-colored carpet in the sanctuary, and intimidated by the fluent English of the older parishioners. Some of the members attended each other's services, and the two pastors held joint services with some success. Stated the translator at the joint services, "It is growing pains for both churches. But you cannot afford to stay with one culture anymore. . . . That's not what heaven is going to look like."[10]

The renewed focus on God's power in worship and Christian life can help Western churches to experience anew the work of Jesus and the Apostles as healers. North American Christians can deepen their understanding of the visions of Peter and of Paul and become more open to the power of God in prayer and worship.

The Growing World Church Is a Migrant Church

The twentieth and twenty-first centuries are characterized by the unprecedented movement of millions of people from one place to another: refugees fleeing from wars and bad governments, economic migrants searching for jobs, business people working in global corporations, international students seeking better educations. People on the move take their faiths with them, but they are also open to new forms of belief that fit their new situations.

In 1965, the Immigration Reform Act permanently changed the face of the United States by opening up the country to new immigration from Asia, Africa, and Latin America. At the beginning of the twenty-first century, over 10 percent of Americans are immigrants. By the mid twenty-first century, the United States will be the largest Hispanic country except for Brazil and Mexico. In another twenty-five years, the United States will be like California is now, with no one dominant ethnic group.

Despite all the publicity about Islam in America and the triumph of secularism in the United States, a little-known fact is that the majority of people immigrating to the United States are Christians from the growing parts of the world church. Latin Americans and Africans who have immigrated to the United States in the past few decades tend to be Christians, and the Asians who come here are disproportionately Christian. Just as Swedish Lutherans, Italian Catholics, Greek Orthodox, and others did before, the new immigrants to the United States are bringing their own Christian traditions with them, and in many cases their own pastors. Says sociologist Stephen Warner, "Immigration is creating not so much new diversity in American religion, as new diversity in American Christianity."[11]

Rather than the world becoming a more secular place, faith communities have become even more important political and social movers in the past decade. And as Christian immigrants stream into Europe and the United States, they are challenging what used to be seen as the irreversible march of secularism. Many Chinese and Korean immigrants become Christians after they move to the United States. University Christian fellowships are full of second-generation Asian immigrants who became Christians in college.

Rather than the world becoming a more secular place, faith communities have become even more important political and social movers in the past decade.

African Christian immigrants are changing the profile of Christianity in both Europe and the United States. There are over ten thousand different denominations in Africa alone. A few years ago, African pastors in Europe founded their own support organization because they are now working throughout Germany, Switzerland, and the United Kingdom. The largest congregation in Europe is Ukrainian—and is pastored by a Nigerian. An African congregation is the largest church in London. Although Africans are typically some of the poorest people in the world, many of the Christian immigrants from Africa are highly educated, with masters' degrees. Their high level of education reflects the long history of missionary education in their home countries.

> A large African immigrant church in Dallas illustrates how the growth of Christianity in the non-Western world affects Christians here. The Redeemed Christian Church of God (RCCG) was founded in 1952 in Nigeria and has thousands of branch churches throughout Africa, Europe, and North America. At the beginning of the century it claimed to have 150 churches in North America, and in 2001 "penetrated" the countries of Dubai, Thailand, Norway, and Sweden. It sees the United States as a mission field, just like Africa, and seeks to plant churches within the reach of urban dwellers all over the world. This church descended from the "Aladura" or Prayer churches of Nigeria and so has a charismatic worship style. It has its own school of missions and is sending many missionaries.
>
> The RCCG bought two hundred fifty hectares of land in Farmersville, Texas, to build its U.S. headquarters, including a school, housing for members, and an auditorium for five thousand. This kind of massive headquarters will be similar to what is in Nigeria; it is a particular characteristic of major indigenous churches in Africa to have large physical headquarters that provides space for healing colonies, educational enterprises, and agricultural work. In other words, this church is building a massive mission station outside of Dallas. Mission objectives for 2005 included planting five viable churches in every sub-Saharan country, winning ten million souls, and training twenty thousand new pastors and one thousand cross-cultural missionaries worldwide.

With the rich ethnic mix in American Christianity today, many of the things that older congregations have discarded as irrelevant or old-fashioned are highly relevant and vitally important to the new Christians from the southern hemisphere. As each culture enters the community of Christ, it will ask new questions from within its own cultural milieu. Often the answers are found in literalistic readings of the Bible and new twists on traditional Christian doctrines.

Another important issue for immigrants is the large number who feel called to be ordained pastors. Several church leaders have written a book on the challenges that occur in The United Methodist Church when a pastor of one ethnicity is appointed to be pastor of a church with members of a different ethnicity. Cultural misunderstandings often occur, and the whole appointment must be considered a form of mission for both the minister and the congregation that receives the minister. [12]

The Catholic Church has been dealing with this challenging issue for many years; often the number of people called to become priests is not proportional to the membership. Today, 20 percent of Catholics studying for the priesthood in North America are foreign-born, while the percentage of Irish-American priests is declining. What will it mean in a few decades if, say, half of the Catholic priests in the U.S. are Vietnamese or African in origin, presiding over congregations that are largely Euro-American or Latin American in ethnicity? What will happen in The United Methodist Church if a large number of the appointed pastors are from the growing immigrant churches but do not share the same basic culture as the churches to which they are appointed? These are difficult questions that need sustained reflection by church leaders of all denominations, particularly those in which bishops appoint the clergy to local congregations.

What the immigration of southern hemisphere Christians reminds us is that pastors of every ethnicity need to approach each new church appointment as if they are going into a mission field. What are the questions and assumptions that energize this group of people? How can they be reached for Christ in their own home cultures? What does it mean to be a Christian in this particular place and as part of a multi-cultural, worldwide community? Congregational diversity requires that both immigrant and U.S.-born pastors think of themselves as missionaries, and not force their cultural patterns onto the people they have promised to serve.

From 1910 to 2010

The previous century has seen one of the largest demographic shifts in the history of Christianity, which is no longer a predominantly European or North American religion. Despite their limitations, the missionaries and church leaders who gathered at Edinburgh in 1910 envisioned the possibility of Christianity making itself at home in Asia and Africa. Their shared prophetic imagination encompassed ideals of Christian unity for worldwide witness to Jesus Christ.

Just as the leaders who gathered a century ago were committed to world mission, so the growing non-Western church today is a missionary church. South Korea alone sends over ten thousand cross-cultural missionaries. Brazilian and Nigerian immigrants are busy founding churches in their new neighborhoods. Groups of Chinese Christians are seeking to travel the Silk Road back across Asia toward the Middle East, in a reversal of the process by which Christianity entered China in the first place. Ethnic minority Christians in Indonesia, Sri Lanka, India, and Burma (Myanmar) have bravely shared Christian care and compassion with their non-Christian neighbors in the wake of tsunamis, monsoons, and other natural disasters. An estimated forty thousand to eighty thousand Indians act as missionaries within India itself, mostly without outside support.

As cross-cultural mission is increasingly undertaken by Koreans, Chinese, Brazilians, Nigerians, Filipinos, and others, the connection in people's minds between Western imperialism and missionaries is being broken. Non-Western missionaries can witness for Christ without being seen as the tool of powerful American interests. As the Good News becomes truly international in the twenty-first century, it liberates Westerners from spiritual straitjackets in which they have been bound. Those whose ancestors sent missionaries a century ago may even find their own faith reawakened by the witness of brothers and sisters from the growing world church!

CHAPTER NOTES

1. William Temple, *The Church Looks Forward* (New York: Macmillan, 1944), 2.
2. Charles Clayton Morrison, "The World Missionary Conference, 1910," *The Christian Century*, July 7, 1910. http://www.religion-online.org/showarticle.asp?title=1408 (accessed June 1, 2009). See also *World Missionary Conference 1910*, 9 vols. (Edinburgh: Oliphant, Anderson & Ferrier, 1910). Part of this chapter is taken from chapter 3 of Dana L. Robert, *Christian Mission: How Christianity Became a World Religion* (Chichester, UK: Wiley-Blackwell, 2009). For an overview of the 1910 conference, see Brian Stanley, *The World Missionary Conference, Edinburgh 1910* (Grand Rapids: William B. Eerdmans, 2009).
3. John R. Mott, quoted in *Report of Commission I: Carrying the Gospel to All the Non-Christian World*, World Missionary Conference 1910 (Edinburgh: Oliphant, Anderson & Ferrier, 1910), 404.
4. V. S. Azariah, *Report of Commission IX: Carrying the Gospel to All the Non-Christian World*, World Missionary Conference 1910 (Edinburgh: Oliphant, Anderson & Ferrier, 1910), 315.
5. For an overview of the political and social changes that led to the growth of non-Western Christianity in the twentieth century, see Dana L. Robert, "Shifting Southward: Global Christianity since 1945," *International Bulletin of Missionary Research* 24, no. 2 (2000): 50–58 (reprinted in Robert L. Gallagher and Paul Hertig, eds., *Landmark Essays in Mission and World Christianity*. Maryknoll, NY: Orbis Books, 2009); Philip Jenkins, *The Next Christendom: The Coming of Global Christianity* (Oxford: Oxford University Press, 2002).

6. For references to the work of Barrett, Bühlmann and other sources for this section, see Robert, "Shifting Southward."

7. These figures are extrapolated from David B. Barrett, Todd M. Johnson, and Peter F Crossing, "Missiometrics 2008: Reality Checks for Christian World Communion," *International Bulletin of Missionary Research* 21, no. 1 (2008): 30.

8. For denominational statistics by region, see the World Christian Database at Gordon-Conwell Theological Seminary. http://www.worldchristiandatabase.org/wcd/about/more.asp

9. Henri Nouwen, *The Wounded Healer: Ministry in Contemporary Society* (New York: Image, 1979).

10. Marie Cramer, "Two congregations warily share church," *Boston Globe*, January 16, 2005.

11. Stephen Warner quoted in Joel A. Carpenter, "The Christian Scholar in an Age of Global Christianity," Nagel Institute for the Study of World Christianity, http://www.calvin.edu/nagel/resources/carpenter_bakerpublication.html (accessed June 1, 2009).

12. Ernest S. Lyght, Glory E. Dharmaraj, and Jacob S. Dharmaraj, *Many Faces, One Church: A Manual for Cross-Racial and Cross-Cultural Ministry* (Nashville: Abingdon Press, 2006).

Chapter Three

Women and Changing Structures for Mission

"Yes, Lord, I will do it."
—Belle Harris Bennett's response in 1887 to God's call to found a women's missionary training school.

While the 1910 World Missionary Conference was meeting in Edinburgh, committees of church women were planning inter-denominational gatherings in cities and towns across America. The Woman's Missionary Jubilee of 1910–1911 marked the fiftieth anniversary of the founding of the first major women's missionary society. Jubilee celebrations were held in forty-eight major cities and many smaller locations. Across the country, local women gathered for missionary teas, pageants, and luncheons to hear jubilee speeches by a travelling team of women mission leaders. They celebrated the achievements of what was then the largest women's movement in America—women organized for world mission.

Jubilee participants included three million dues-paying members of over forty denominational women's mission

---

Forerunners of United Methodist Women

1869 The Woman's Foreign Missionary Society (Methodist Episcopal Church)
1875 Woman's Missionary Association (United Brethren)
1877 Woman's General Executive Association (Methodist Episcopal Church, South)
1880 The Woman's Home Missionary Society (Methodist Episcopal Church)
1882 Woman's Board of Missions (Methodist Episcopal Church, South)
1884 Woman's Missionary Society (Evangelical Association)
1886 Women's Department of Church Extension (Methodist Episcopal Church, South)
1890 Woman's Board of Foreign Missions (Methodist Episcopal Church, South)
1891 Woman's Parsonage and Home Mission Society (Methodist Episcopal Church, South)
1898 Woman's Board of Home Missions (Methodist Episcopal Church, South)
1910 Woman's Missionary Council (Methodist Episcopal Church, South)
1921 Wesleyan Service Guild (Methodist Church; for business and professional women)
1939 Woman's Society of Christian Service (The Methodist Episcopal Church, the Methodist Episcopal Church, South, and the Methodist Protestant Church merge to form The Methodist Church. The various women's home and foreign missionary societies and other women's groups of the three uniting churches are joined as one organization.)
1944 Christian Service Guild (Evangelical Church; for business and professional women)
1946 Women's Society of World Service (Evangelical United Brethren)
1972 The Women's organizations in The United Methodist Church merge to form one inclusive organization with the name, "UNITED METHODIST WOMEN."

societies. Women's mission societies held regular circle meetings at local churches. They raised money for missions through church fairs and other activities. Many societies published their own magazines about missionary work among women and children around the world. They recruited and sent female missionaries. As the first women's groups in all the predecessor denominations of The United Methodist Church, they were the forerunners of United Methodist Women.

Starting in 1901, a committee of women from different denominations produced a mission study book that women across the United States read in their mission circles. Each book was written by a prominent author on a missionary theme or area of the world, and contained an outline and study questions. In 1904, the united study committee launched inter-denominational summer schools of mission in which mission circle teachers could study the book they would be teaching throughout the year in their local churches. The summer schools of mission were inspirational gatherings involving thousands of women in Bible studies, pageants, prayer, and fellowship. The summer schools of mission held now in The United Methodist Church are the direct descendants of what women began in 1904.

To celebrate the fiftieth anniversary of the women's mission movement, the textbook for 1910 was *Western Women in Eastern Lands,* by Baptist leader Helen Barrett Montgomery. This textbook gave an historical overview of women's missionary work during the previous fifty years. It showed that by 1910, women's missionary societies were sending thousands of foreign missionaries on their own, in addition to the ones being sent by regular denominational mission boards. All over the world, women missionaries worked to improve the lives of women and children by founding schools, clinics and hospitals, by visiting them in their homes, and by sharing the Good News of Jesus Christ. Montgomery summarized the ideals of the women's missionary movement:

> To seek first to bring Christ's Kingdom on the earth, to respond to the need that is sorest, to go out into the desert for that loved and bewildered sheep that the shepherd has missed from the fold, to share all of privilege with the unprivileged and happiness with the unhappy, to lay down life, if need be, in the way of the Christ, to see the possibility of one redeemed earth, undivided, unvexed, unperplexed, resting in the light of the glorious Gospel of the blessed God, this is the mission of the women's missionary movement. [1]

Helen Barrett Montgomery

The women gathered for Jubilee celebrations in each city and town urged women and children in the years ahead to even greater efforts. Cooperation among mission societies led to a number of important projects. First was the founding in 1912 of the World Day of Prayer. The idea of a united day of intercessory prayer for missions was adopted by women's societies and spread around the world by women missionaries. The World Day of Prayer was also the day when churches took special collections on behalf of women's mission projects, such as the production of Christian reading material for youth in different cultures.

Women's Colleges and Medical Schools in China, India, and Japan Funded by Missionary Women

Year	School
1870	Isabella Thoburn College
1908	North China Union Woman's College at Peking became Women's College of Yenching University
1910	Woman's Union Medical College of Peking
1915	Ginling College in Nanking
1915	Woman's Christian College, Madras
1918	Union Woman's Medical College at Vellore, India
1918	Women's Christian College of Tokyo

from James M. Thoburn, Life of Isabella Thoburn (1903).

Isabella Thoburn

Another concrete outgrowth of the Jubilee was the raising of one million dollars to support ecumenical women's colleges in Asia. Missionary women had founded hundreds of schools around the world, especially since the 1860s. But to raise some of these schools to college level required ecumenical cooperation across multiple denominations. Because missionary women believed that education was the path to social improvement and greater respect for women and girls, together they funded seven women's colleges and medical schools in China, India, and Japan.

Women in Mission and Evangelism from the Bible to the Present

Although largely forgotten today, the Woman's Jubilee of 1910 was a link in the chain of holistic women's witness that stretches from the Bible to the world church of the twenty-first century. The New Testament recounts the stories of many women who followed Jesus during his lifetime and after his death. These women are the mothers of faith who have inspired mission and ministry down through the ages.

As Jesus passed through Samaria on his way from Judea to his home up north in Galilee, he stopped by a well to rest. After talking with him about worship and her own messy personal life, a Samaritan woman ran and called her neighbors to hear him (John 4). Because Jesus looked into her heart and saw her for who she was, she recognized him as the Messiah.

"He told me everything I have ever done." (John 4:39)

The Samaritan woman was the first outsider to mainstream Judaism who understood something of Jesus' identity as the Son of God. As the first "native evangelist," she foreshadowed the day in which people marginal to Judaism—a category that includes most Christians today—would follow Jesus. She also pioneered the important role women have played in sharing the Good News with others.

"Do not be afraid. Go and tell my brothers to go to Galilee; there they will see me." (Matthew 28:10)

After Jesus died on the cross, women who gathered at the tomb were the first to meet the resurrected Christ and to be his witnesses. He told them to "go tell" the disciples that he wished to see them (Matthew 28:9-10). Mary Magdalene, one of Jesus' supporters in life, became the "Apostle to the Apostles," as she spread the news of his victory over death. In the book of Acts, the house church leader Priscilla gave theological instruction to Apollos, who became an important evangelist (Acts 18:24-28). She and her husband Aquila led house churches in several cities and provided hospitality for Paul that gave him a home base for his outreach.

In Acts 9:36-42, Luke tells the amazing story of Peter's encounter with the only woman in the New Testament who is called a "disciple." The leader of the widows, the disciple Tabitha, or *Dorcas* in Greek, had died in Joppa. Peter traveled there and found that Tabitha had been washed for burial and was laid out in an upstairs room. Surrounding her body were weeping women, "all the widows," who showed Peter the clothing that she had made them. Verse 36 says that Tabitha was "devoted to good works and acts of charity." Clearly the widow Tabitha was a major benefactor, if not organizer and leader, of widows in the Joppa church.

Peter sent everyone from the room, and knelt down to pray. He said "Tabitha, get up." At that point she opened her eyes and sat up. The raising of Tabitha, the woman disciple, was the only time Peter brought anyone back to life. As the story of Tabitha spread throughout Joppa, "many believed in the Lord."

Now in Joppa there was a disciple whose name was Tabitha, which in Greek is Dorcas. She was devoted to good works and acts of charity. At that time she became ill and died. When they had washed her, they laid her in a room upstairs. Since Lydda was near Joppa, the disciples, who heard that Peter was there, sent two men to him with the request, "Please come to us without delay." So Peter got up and went with them; and when he arrived, they took him to the room upstairs. All the widows stood beside him, weeping and showing tunics and other clothing that Dorcas had made while she was with them. Peter put all of them outside, and then he knelt down and prayed. He turned to the body and said, "Tabitha, get up." Then she opened her eyes, and seeing Peter, she sat up. He gave her his hand and helped her up. Then calling the saints and widows, he showed her to be alive. This became known throughout Joppa, and many believed in the Lord. (Acts 9:36-42)

Why was the only person Peter raised from the dead a widow? And why was a leader of widows called a disciple? Widows organized the first women's groups in the history of Christianity. Poor women without male providers operated under the leadership of better-off widows for their survival and that of their children. Widowed Christian women refused to be helpless victims of fate. Rather, they worked together for their own self-support by sewing clothing, such as those the mourning widows of Joppa showed to Peter. Not only were the widows and forgotten women the most needy of the church's members, but they were also the most faithful—so faithful that in the New Testament their leader was called a "disciple" of the Lord.

Why was the only person Peter raised from the dead a widow? And why was a leader of widows called a disciple?

Because even poor women found dignity in the early church, Christianity attracted a higher percentage of women than the general population. Consecrated virgins, widows, and female martyrs were some of the most important witnesses to the Gospel during the first few centuries after the resurrection. Christian widows often defied the norms of Roman society by refusing to remarry and pass down their wealth to men. Instead, they used their inheritances to serve the poor and to nurse the sick, and in so doing attracted others to the church.

Christianity attracted a higher percentage of women than the general population.

In some of the earliest churches, the role of the widow grew into that of the "deaconess." According to the early church manual, the *Didascalia Apostolorum*, written in Syria at the beginning of the third century, the deaconess "is required to go into the houses of the heathen where there are believing women, and to visit those who are sick, and to minister to them in that of which they have need, and to bathe those who have begun to recover from sickness." [2] The female deacon was on the cutting edge of an expanding, missionary church. By going into non-Christian homes to nurse the sick, widows and deaconesses set an example of Christian love that attracted non-Christians.

The female deacon was on the cutting edge of an expanding, missionary church. By going into non-Christian homes to nurse the sick, widows and deaconesses set an example of Christian love that attracted non-Christians.

In his book *The Rise of Christianity*, Rodney Stark attributes the expansion of membership in the early church partly to the fact that Christians nursed the sick during the frequent epidemics of the day while most others fled in fear and left the ill to die alone. Not only did Christians recover from sickness at a greater rate than non-Christians, but non-Christians who recovered were welcomed into Christian fellowship. [3] Throughout the history of Christianity, the compassion of women toward the ill and needy has been one of the most important features of mission.

American Women in Mission

When American laywomen organized themselves into mission societies in the 1800s, they were deliberately following in the footsteps of the Samaritan woman, Mary Magdalene, Tabitha, early deaconesses, and other persistent women of faith. As they witnessed to the way of Jesus, they found their own voices. Despite opposition from leading men who predicted they would fail, in 1869, Methodist women in New England formed the Woman's Foreign Missionary Society.

Women were not permitted to raise funds at regular church events, so they depended on five-cent dues and life memberships. Not only did they succeed in sending their own missionaries and supporting indigenous "Bible women" evangelists, but their self-published mission magazine immediately turned a profit. When John R. Mott, who grew up to head the world YMCA and to chair the Edinburgh 1910 conference, was asked how he first got interested in world missions, he recalled reading the Methodist women's missionary magazine his mother left lying around the house.

Methodist women also reached out to immigrants crowded into urban slums.

Methodist women also reached out to immigrants crowded into urban slums. They revived the ancient order of deaconesses as women consecrated to work among the poor. Deaconesses visited the poor in their homes, opened kindergartens and settlement houses, and even founded charity hospitals in cities. Methodist women cared about both the spiritual well-being of individuals, and the goal of making the world a better place. This dual emphasis was expressed by Southern Methodist mission leader Belle Harris Bennett, who founded the Scarritt College for Christian Workers to train women in evangelism and social work. Her biographer summarized her philosophy of missions as "Eternal life for the individual, the kingdom of God for humanity." [4]

Belle Harris Bennett.

At the time of the Jubilee celebrations in 1910, Baptist mission leader Helen Barrett Montgomery considered the Methodist women's mission groups to be the strongest of all the denominations. They had sent more missionaries than any other women's society in America, including thousands of indigenous women workers. Methodist women missionaries pioneered all aspects of mission service. They founded the first women's college in Asia, Isabella Thoburn College in Lucknow, India; and what became the largest women's college in Asia, Ewha Women's University in Korea.

Methodist women were the first female medical missionaries in India and China.

Methodist women were the first female medical missionaries in India and China. They opposed foot binding and female infanticide in China. They introduced government legislation to abolish child marriage in India. They sheltered girls fleeing forced marriages in Africa, and rescued abandoned children. Methodist missionary women exposed sex trafficking by infiltrating brothels established in the late 1800s near lumber camps in Wisconsin and by the British army near troop barracks. Trained as social workers, they founded kindergartens and social service centers in cities around the world, and they ran baby wellness clinics in rural areas. They witnessed to Christ and brought people to the Christian faith in Asia, Africa, and the Americas.

During the early twentieth century, women's mission societies focused on supporting education, health care, social services, and evangelism for women and children. In the American South, Methodist home mission societies opposed lynching and racial segregation by insisting on holding interracial meetings. Although the women's mission societies that celebrated the Jubilee of 1910 do not exist in the same form today, during much of the century they steadily pressured their denominations to make the improvement of life for women and children a core priority for mission work in North America and abroad. Despite the well-known limitations of colonialism and missionary paternalism, women missionaries steadfastly worked to improve women's lives through education and advocacy.

In the American South, Methodist home mission societies opposed lynching and racial segregation by insisting on holding interracial meetings.

Women in the World Church

A century after the Woman's Jubilee, the leadership of women in churches around the world remains a vital part of its legacy. As was the case in early Christianity, the majority of Christians in the world church today are women. Although they are not typically the ordained pastors, women are taking a leading part in what is probably the greatest expansion of Christianity since the conversion of Europe. At least 70 percent of Christians in African indigenous churches are women; 70 percent of house church members in China are probably women; and Latin American Pentecostalism is growing fastest among women, who typically bring their men into the church rather than the other way around. Even as Catholic religious congregations are having trouble attracting Western women, they are being filled with women from Latin America, India, and Africa. The growth of Christianity in the world today is a women's movement.

At least 70 percent of Christians in African indigenous churches are women; 70 percent of house church members in China are probably women; and Latin American Pentecostalism is growing fastest among women.

In every "mission field," missionary women founded women's organizations in the churches. These groups quickly became popular and independent from both missionary and male control. Today women's groups lead local evangelistic and mission outreach. In Southern Africa, for example, married women in the church organize themselves into Mother's Unions. The Anglican Mothers' Union, with its motto "Christian Care for Families Worldwide," had 3.6 million members by 2005, most of them African. Mother's Union members run daycares, soup kitchens, orphan programs, literacy training, pre-marital counseling, and health management for those with HIV-AIDS. They wear special uniforms as a sign of solidarity and spiritual purpose.

In 1907, a South African minister's wife, Mrs. Gqosho, founded the Methodist women's *Manyano* movement. Stemming from women's revival prayer meetings, the movement swept through African Methodist churches. Women in the Methodist Church of Southern Africa hold mid-week preaching and prayer events, as well as send their best preachers on evangelistic crusades from Fridays until Sundays. They run income-generating projects with which to support widows and orphans in the larger community, combating a common and tragic problem in this day of AIDS. They raise money to pay school fees for their children. *Manyanos* and Mothers' Unions each hold meetings for girls, giving them biblically based and culturally appropriate teachings about marriage and child-rearing. In United Methodist churches, the UMW takes the role that Mothers' Unions do in other churches.

Mpho Phiri. Used by permission.

Mosetse (setsese) Staunch Methodist, Member of Manyano Group & Church Choir

One of the most important roles of women's groups in churches around the world is to strengthen families by supporting the dignity of women and the care and education of children. Studies of healthy churches show that women join because they find friendship and support. In societies in which women do not have rights equal to men, church women's groups provide solidarity and strength in numbers.

Studies of healthy churches show that women join because they find friendship and support.

Conversion to Protestantism in Central America has been studied by Elizabeth Brusco as a path to the empowerment of women. When women join Pentecostal churches, it strengthens the household as the women encourage their husbands to give up drinking, smoking, and extramarital affairs that take valuable resources away from the children. If women can reform the behavior of their husbands, family prosperity improves because money is available to feed, clothe, and educate the children. In other words, conversion to evangelical Christianity weakens macho attitudes and empowers women in relation to their husbands. Protestant households eat together around a family table, go to church together, and confer on major decisions. Elizabeth Brusco concludes that evangelicalism is a "strategic women's movement" because it raises the status of women by making the family the center of the man's life. [5]

Conversion to evangelical Christianity weakens macho attitudes and empowers women in relation to their husbands.

Brusco's study of Central America today echoes how Methodism worked in North America in the 1800s. When women had few legal rights, the family could prosper only if male behavior could be controlled. Methodism became the largest church in America in the early 1800s partly because women organized and sought the conversion of their husbands. The traditional Methodist prohibition against drinking alcohol and smoking stems from the fact that such behaviors wasted family income and took the food out of children's mouths. In the late 1800s, Methodist leader Frances Willard led a worldwide "temperance" movement to get men to pledge not to drink liquor. She signed her letters "yours for home protection."

The traditional Methodist prohibition against drinking alcohol and smoking stems from the fact that such behaviors wasted family income and took the food out of children's mouths.

The women's temperance movement was important because bars were the major gathering place for men in the 1800s, and respectable women were not allowed inside them. Hard-drinking men abused their wives, but if a woman left her husband she had no legal rights to custody of her own children. In some states, the legal age of consent at which girls could have sex was eleven. Thus the alcohol culture also encouraged sexual abuse and forced prostitution of girls. The women's temperance movement founded kindergartens, supported the eight-hour working day and workers' rights, petitioned to raise the minimum age of consent, fought for a woman's legal rights to her children in case of divorce, and supported women's voting rights. Women gained the right to vote in 1920, ten years after the Woman's Jubilee of 1910.

Similar to American women in the early twentieth century, the missionary role of women in contemporary African churches grows from their commitments as wives and mothers. They judge the church by the kinds of relationships they see modeled in the homes of church members—where women are respected by their husbands and where children are fed, dressed, and sent to school. Just as American women long used the ideal of improved home life as a starting point for mission, African women use a Christian vision of the home as a source of their evangelistic power, and to justify going into the world to preach, teach, heal, and to support rights for women and children.

> Nineteenth-century Bible women were indigenous evangelists who traveled through villages, visited with women, and taught them to read the Bible.

Another important missionary role for women has been that of the "Bible woman." Nineteenth-century Bible women were indigenous evangelists who traveled through villages, visited with women, and taught them to read the Bible. They were the first non-Western women workers supported by women's missionary societies, and they worked as pioneer evangelists alongside the first women missionaries. Chinese medical doctor and Bible woman Dora Yu, for example, partnered with Mrs. Josephine Campbell as the first female missionaries from the Southern Methodist Church to enter Korea in 1897. For six years, in her official role as "Bible woman," Yu attended female patients, preached and taught the Bible to women, conducted door-to-door visitation, and taught poor children. Today in Southeast Asia, including the Philippines, Malaysia, Cambodia, Oceania, and India, Bible women continue this important tradition by visiting women in villages, teaching them to read, and educating them about HIV-AIDS and other public health issues. [6]

Women's groups in the church can be the key to the survival of Christianity. Before Communism swept over Eastern Europe, a woman missionary named Hazel Anna Craighead founded women's groups in the Baptist churches of Moldova. One of her protégés was Lydia Caldararu, the first woman selected for formal ministry by Baptists in that region. When the Soviets severely persecuted the churches and drove out the missionaries around 1939, Lydia continued to minister underground among women's groups. She was captured, sentenced to death, and sent to Siberia for fifteen years. Many other women leaders died in prison. And yet, the women's groups remained faithful during fifty years of persecution. After the "Iron Curtain" came down in 1989, and the Soviet Union broke apart, "Anna" circles resurfaced in Moldova. Before she died, Lydia passed on the leadership to young women she

had secretly trained. Although the women forgot the name of the missionary who inspired their women's groups, in the past few years they have researched and rediscovered who she was. Now they are collecting the stories of the faithful women who, through their women's groups, kept the Baptist Church alive in Moldova while under Communist rule. [7]

What can we conclude from the history of the 1910 Woman's Jubilee and from recent studies of women in the world church? As we celebrate the growth of Christianity today, we see clearly how supposedly old-fashioned "women's mission work" has remained central to the identity of Christianity, from the Samaritan woman and Tabitha and work for widows, to mothers' movements and deaconesses around the world. Through ministries of compassion and support for economic and social improvement, as well as direct evangelism and mothers' organizations, the outreach of Christian women is a major way in which women and their families are attracted to the church. Statistically speaking, world Christianity is a women's movement. Just as Peter discovered in Joppa, in many parts of the world, the church itself is the community of the faithful poor, most of whom are women. In every culture, Christian women find ways of making the world a better place.

Changing Structures, Renewed Priorities

Thunderous applause greeted Ambassador Gertrude Ibengwe Mongella in November 2004 when she rose to address Boston University faculty on the subject of the African Union Parliament and democratization in Africa. Mrs. Mongella had recently been elected the founding president of the Pan African Parliament of the African Union, thus making her the woman who held the highest political office on the continent of Africa. Among her many distinguished positions, Mongella served in her native Tanzania as Minister of State for Women's Affairs; Minister of Lands, Natural Resources and Tourism; Head of the Social Services Department of the ruling party; and High Commissioner to India. From 1993 to 1995 she was Assistant Secretary General of the United Nations, and more recently a goodwill ambassador of the World Health Organization. A teacher, wife, and mother of four children, in 1995 she acted as Secretary General of the United Nations International Conference on Women held in Beijing.

Mrs. Mongella began her speech by thanking her hosts. Then she paused and said, "I must thank the American missionaries who came and started the girls' school in

achievements of the missionary movement. Scholars have found a direct correlation among missions, the education of women, and improved economic and social indicators such as lower infant mortality rates. Educating a girl means improving the well-being of the next generation. Without the commitment of missionary women to girls' education, Ambassador Mongella would not have achieved what she did.

Ambassador Gertrude Ibengwe Mongella

which I was educated. Without the work of the Maryknoll Sisters, young African girls like me would have had no opportunities to get an education, to become a teacher, or to attend a university. But why are Americans not focusing on founding schools and hospitals like they used to?" she asked. "Where are the missionaries of today?" [8]

The question raised by Ambassador Mongella highlights important issues about both the great achievements and the failures of women's mission work during the past century. First, the work of women missionaries during the early- to mid-twentieth century in educating women and girls is one of the greatest

Ambassador Mongella's comments also raise the issue of the decline of traditional "woman's work" in education, medicine, and social services over the past fifty years. For example, Methodist missionary Clara Swain founded the first women's hospital in India in 1874. For a century, women's circles supported the hospital, and enabled it to care for many poor people unable to afford medical care and to train many doctors and nurses. By the 1990s, the hospital could barely remain open because of its poor financial condition and the lack of long-term personnel. Then in 2009, despite investing millions of dollars to keep it open, the Women's Division was forced to sell it because of its financial collapse. The loss of Clara

Swain hospital illustrates how much the structures of mission have changed since the days of the Woman's Jubilee of 1910, when one out of every ten missionaries sent by women's societies was a medical doctor.

Reasons for the gradual decline in mission-supported women's institutions are many, and are too complicated to mention except in passing. In the early twentieth century, lifetime mission work as a teacher or doctor was one of the most innovative career paths for unmarried women. By the late twentieth century, this was no longer the case. Long-term personnel were replaced by short-term workers who lacked the lifetime commitments of previous generations. Additional problems in continuity were caused by the general rejection of missionaries that took place from the 1960s onward in the older missions of mainline churches—the very missions in which women's institutions were the best developed.

One reason for the decline of women's mission institutions was the "devolution" process itself. When, in the mid-twentieth century, missionary-founded institutions were turned over to national churches, the women's ministries were often allowed to collapse because male leaders did not place a high priority on women's work. Melissa Heim, for example, writes about how the American Madura Mission, one of the oldest missions of the Congregational Church, was turned over to local control in 1934. A combination of loss of financial support from American women's mission societies with neglect by male leaders meant that women's ministries were the first to disappear. Women's education and the sponsorship and training of Bible women were all eliminated by the male-dominated Indian Church. [9]

During the 1950s and 1960s, another wave of devolution occurred in the wake of nationalist independence movements. In many countries newly independent from Western control, mission institutions were nationalized, and the missionaries were thrown out of the country. Sometimes the mission schools thrived under new leadership, but often they were neglected as symbols of colonialism. Under Communist leadership, for example, all mission schools were closed in China during the Cold War, and their work was repudiated as imperialistic. In Muslim countries, mission institutions were often nationalized. Presbyterian Forman Christian College in Pakistan, for example, was seized by the Islamic government, but then reopened many years later by President Musharraf, who appreciated the unique features of the mission school. Similarly in China, renewed appreciation for the pioneering work of mission schools has emerged in the past twenty years.

Another reason women's mission societies lost control over women's ministries was denominational reorganization. In the early twentieth century, women supported their own missionaries. With forced denominational reorganization plans, however, the support of missionaries was stripped away from women's groups. So, for example, Methodist women's mission societies lost the right to send their own missionaries and to promote mission education to children in 1964. As male-controlled denominations took away laywomen's rights in one church after another—often in the name of "efficiency" or of reducing duplication of efforts—women fought to gain voice and vote and then clergy rights within the churches. Thus the end of the woman's missionary society shifted the focus from supporting women's rights in the "mission fields," to struggling for women's rights within the churches themselves. From an historical perspective, there is a straight path from women's mission work to the ordination and mainstreaming of women into the power structures of mainline churches today.

In effect, Methodist laywomen had to pay twice for Scarritt—first to build it, and then later to save it!

Unfortunately historical research reveals a common phenomenon. When women are no longer in charge of ministries they have founded, churches often fail to support them. One notable example of this is what happened to Scarritt College for Christian Workers in Nashville, the mission training institute for women in the Southern Methodist Church. For many decades,

Scarritt was the most important source of female missionaries and deaconesses in the southern branch of Methodism. After the creation of The United Methodist Church in 1968, Scarritt was taken from the control of women in the church and put under a general agency. From there it was allowed to decline. Ultimately the Women's Division had to buy it from The United Methodist Church to keep it from being sold. In effect, Methodist laywomen had to pay twice for Scarritt—first to build it, and then later to save it!

Renewed Priorities

With the realization that Christianity in the twenty-first century is a worldwide religion, it is time to recover and to lift up the central role played by women in mission and outreach in the growing churches around the world. From a global perspective, organizing laywomen into groups, teaching them to read, promoting advances in medical care and human rights, and helping women toward economic self-sufficiency lift entire communities out of poverty. To echo what missionaries of old used to say, the health of societies can be judged by how they treat women and children, and to reach the mother is to improve society. Ambassador Mongella's question "where are the missionaries today?" reminds us that despite understandable changes in structures for mission, the well-being of women and children must remain mission priorities in the twenty-first century. These priorities must not be lost as more women are ordained for ministry.

The renewed relevance of work for women and children is expressed in the Millennium Development Goals (MDG) adopted by the United Nations in 2000. The member states adopted eight goals as focus for the effort to eradicate extreme poverty by 2015. The MDGs express in modern form what missions among women and children have tried to achieve over the past century, including primary education for all, gender equality and empowerment of women, reduction of child mortality, improvement of maternal health, and combating diseases like AIDS and malaria. Worldwide church communions, notably the World Methodist Council, the Lutheran World Federation, and the bishops of the Anglican Church, all adopted the MDGs as missional priorities. The continuity between women's mission work and the MDGs was expressed in July 2008 by Ms. Helen Wangusa, Anglican Observer at the United Nations, when she addressed the assembled Anglican bishops at their once-a-decade Lambeth Conference, "We are there at the grass roots. . . . Before the MDGs, the church was there, working on them as part of our mission."[10]

While churches cannot possibly hope to achieve the Millennium Development Goals without the cooperation of governments and businesses, church people must lead the way in building relationships and showing compassion among the poorest, most needy communities in the world. The raising of the widow Tabitha is just as important a symbol for the church's mission as it was in the time of the Apostles. Women's dignity through education and health care, micro-lending and income-generating projects for the poor, care for families, and women's organizations for fellowship and spiritual sustenance—all these are historic priorities for women's outreach that began in the New Testament and have continued through the history of Christianity into the present.

The Global Church and Changing Mission Structures

Recognition of a global church requires flexibility in the way that United Methodists engage in mission. With Christianity growing in Africa, Asia, and Latin America and the percentage of European Christians steadily dropping, it has become increasingly clear over the last twenty years that mission is no longer a unidirectional movement from the West to the rest of the world. Rather, the vision of 1963 has finally been fulfilled, when delegates to the Mexico City meeting of the World Council of Churches first called for "mission to all six continents."

While United Methodists can be proud of past generations of sacrificial missionary outreach, in the twenty-first century, no one-sized mission structure fits all. As the Millennium Development Goals demonstrate, the need for Christian witness is as great as at any time in human history. Given all the changes in mission structures since the founding of The United Methodist Church over forty years ago, how can women and men best contribute to the mission of the church?

To a certain extent, traditional women's concerns have been institutionalized in greater roles for women within denominational structures. So, for example, women bishops and pastors today make possible continued mission focus on issues like "children at risk." Yet Ambassador Mongella's question in relation to schools for girls, "where are the missionaries today?," reminds us of what can be lost if women do not insist on keeping the well-being of women and children at the center of mission, regardless of changed contexts. The very existence of the United Methodist Women is a visible reminder of the importance of long-term, sustained advocacy and outreach on behalf of issues important to the survival and well-being of ordinary women and children the world over.

Given all the changes in mission structures since the founding of The United Methodist Church over forty years ago, how can women and men best contribute to the mission of the church?

The goals of women's salvation and well-being have remained the same, but ways of being in mission have changed a lot over the past half century. The following discussion highlights only a few trends in organization for mission that impact mission work, including the needs of women and children. The need for traditional, long-term cross-cultural missionaries remains, especially in difficult situations where the Gospel has not been shared before or in places of extreme poverty. But other mission pathways have become increasingly popular for North Americans since the mid-twentieth century. These trends in mission organization reflect Christianity's growing strength as a worldwide rather than predominantly Western religion.

Mission Partnerships

In the late 1960s, as missions moved beyond colonialism and Western control, the idea of "partnership" took hold. In some circles, the word *missionary* was replaced with terms like "partner in mission" to emphasize that mission was a multi-directional, relational form of outreach rather than something that Westerners did to or for others. At first the idea of partnership worked on a formal level between a denominational mission board and a partner "national church," in which a non-Western branch of Methodism would request specific projects and personnel from the General Board of Global Ministries (GBGM).

But early partnership agreements often lacked flexibility and cultural sensitivity. While denominations restricted themselves to "official" partner relationships negotiated through a general church agency, entrepreneurial churches and freelance mission agencies filled people's felt needs and attracted members away. Also, the formal partnerships of the 1960s and 1970s usually focused on the transfer of money from Western churches to non-Western ones. New kinds of dependencies and cultural misunderstandings developed over control of project funds. Church agencies soon learned that for projects to succeed, relationships with ordinary people needed to come first.

As the world church continued to grow in the late twentieth century, the limited formal partnership model broadened into less rigid and more imaginative practices. By the 1990s, the GBGM had moved from being an agency that tried to control mission to a support structure for multiple forms of partnerships among different groups of Methodists. After Methodism re-entered Russia in the 1980s, the Russia Initiative was the first major mission effort in which the GBGM played a coordinating rather than controlling role.

Partnership can mean that one branch of a denomination pays for missionaries from another country to go where its own people cannot. So for example, when North American United Methodists could not serve in Marxist-controlled Angola, the GBGM brokered a partnership with Cuban Methodists to send medical doctors there. Nigerian missionaries witnessed to Christ in the Soviet Union when Americans could not. But all were mission partners within the larger Methodist family.

The recent expansion of Methodism in Cambodia is an example of partnership among historically related churches for spreading the Gospel into new areas. In 2005, the various Methodist missions that had started work in Cambodia—Korean, Malaysian, Singaporean,

Children at play in Cambodia.

Swiss, French, the World Federation of Chinese Methodist Churches and The United Methodist Church—formed the Methodist Mission in Cambodia. According to the mission supervisor, United Methodist missionary Romeo del Rosario from the Philippines, the Methodist Mission in Cambodia runs programs involving women, children, health and agriculture, and

works with 140 churches. As Cambodian leaders are trained, they will take over leadership from their mission partners.

Another partnership model is that of the "companion." The root of the word *companion* is the same as *accompany*—to walk alongside. Over the past few decades, Anglicans (including American Episcopalians) developed a companion diocese program, in which a diocese in one part of the world would be linked with another part of the world. So for example, the Episcopal diocese of Alabama has a companion relationship with the Episcopal diocese of Haiti. The companion dioceses help each other with projects, share a prayer calendar, and send visiting delegations.

In The United Methodist Church, the companion model of mission partnership involves an annual conference committing itself to a long-term relationship with a similar entity abroad. In 1986, the New England Annual Conference entered into a companion relationship with *La Asociacion de Iglesias de Cristo de Nicaragua*, an indigenous Nicaraguan church. Churches in New England have sent numerous mission teams to work there, raised money for needs, developed cross-cultural friendships, and hosted young people from Nicaragua.

The advantage of companion arrangements is that they establish relationships between the privileged and the poor within a denominational framework. The purpose of the New England Conference's companion relationship, for example, is

> to accompany one another in solidarity
> as a self-conscious response to the
> unjust and inequitable dichotomy

between North and South, rich and poor. We do so for the sake of reclaiming human dignity and human rights—education, health care, a decent place to live, potable water, a caring community—for all persons. [11]

The spiritual renewal enabled by such friendships is usually the most meaningful aspect of the partnership for those from more economically privileged churches.

Among Presbyterian and Lutheran congregations, "mission partners" are often specialized agencies to which local churches pledge their support. So for example, a Lutheran congregation in Minnesota will raise money to send to a mission partner for a specific purpose, such as Habitat for Humanity to build houses in India, or Church World Service for relief services in Haiti, or World Vision to set up microloans for local development projects in Tanzania. The "mission partner" provides specialized expertise for development projects that the local church wishes to support.

While traditional missions used to do everything—education, medical work, relief and development, women's work—today specialized Christian agencies handle the complexities of relief and development. Christian NGOs (Non-Governmental Organizations) such as the GBGM (through its subsidiary the United Methodist Committee on Relief) and Catholic Relief Services function within denominational structures; within the National Council of Churches, notably Church World Service; or as independent parachurch agencies like World Vision. As specialized mission partners, Christian NGOs do not do the full work of the church such as evangelism and Christian education. But they provide necessary expertise and support for the social aspects of the churches' mission.

With migration a major social and economic reality in the twenty-first century, creative new possibilities for partnership have emerged. A local church in Texas might partner with Mexican immigrants, for example, to provide resources that will help the immigrants spread the Gospel back in their homeland when they travel to visit their families. Ministry among Chinese international students who return to their home country, for example, is a key way in which the Gospel has entered China over the past few decades. Because nearly 12 percent of Americans today are immigrants, the distinction between local and foreign mission has broken down. Indeed, mission among immigrants in one's own neighborhood may be the most important kind of cross-cultural and cross-racial partnership churches can undertake today—and the most challenging.

Because nearly 12 percent of Americans today are immigrants, the distinction between local and foreign mission has broken down.

Local Churches and Mission Networking

In the twenty-first century, many local churches have become their own mission agencies. Local churches have always been involved in supporting mission and outreach in their own towns and neighborhoods. Soup kitchens, mothers' day out programs, youth-at-risk mentoring, senior centers and activity nights, turkey baskets for the poor at Thanksgiving, vacation Bible schools and music camps, lobbying elected officials for affordable housing and poverty relief—these are but a few of the creative ways in which local churches serve their surrounding communities. Some local churches have conducted inventories of the non-churched in their neighborhoods, or re-evaluated their own priorities as part of a "missional church" network.

By the late twentieth century, advances in communication and air travel made long distance, short-term mission by volunteers a possibility for the first time in human history. Laypeople grew frustrated with being asked to contribute money without being able to see, feel, taste, and experience cross-cultural mission themselves. The short-term-missions movement answered the need for personal involvement with the poor, within a controlled time frame. While "globalization" can be a negative thing when large economic and cultural forces drown out local cultures, it also has positive aspects in making people aware of problems halfway around the world, and enabling them to make direct contact with needy people far away. Instead of cross-cultural outreach being limited to "professional" missionaries who go abroad for lengthy terms, or mission projects negotiated by denominational staff in distant offices, ordinary church members with the time and money can volunteer for a few weeks, using their expertise in construction, finance, medicine, agriculture and earth care, or whatever is requested by churches in other parts of the country or other parts of the world.

Mission teams return home and testify to their life-changing experiences. When effective, the short-term mission experience leads to long-term commitments. United Methodists Charles and Karen Wiggins from Arkansas, for example, were part of short-term mission teams who went to Tanzania. After retiring from their jobs as a minister and a public school teacher in 2005, the Wiggins moved to Bunda, Tanzania, full-time. With the support of some churches in Arkansas, and their own small pensions, they are involved in a comprehensive ministry of church-planting, water projects, education, and of course, hosting short-term mission groups from Arkansas.

Among United Methodists, the growing desire for personal involvement resulted in the formation of United Methodist Volunteers in Mission (UMVIM) by members from the Southeastern Jurisdiction (SEJ) in 1976. Volunteers identified specific needs and matched teams with the necessary interest and expertise. The purpose of UMVIM, SEJ, is "to promote, encourage and enable Christians to exemplify "Christian Love In Action." Our aim is to achieve the Great Commission through providing short-term mission opportunities for everyday Christians." [12]

In 1996, the GBGM made Mission Volunteers one of its six major program areas. The interactive context of globalization that makes possible the short-term volunteer movement is summarized on the GBGM website:

Our neighborhood has expanded. Today we are a global neighborhood and our neighbors are everywhere. There is no place on this planet where we are not called to go if there is a need. There is no place on this planet where we do not have the opportunity to receive those who understand themselves to have been sent. [13]

While globalization has made the volunteer movement possible, the reality of a vigorous world church creates the specific contexts in which mission volunteers can be hosted. Without mission partners abroad, volunteer teams could not operate. Changing opportunities for mission by local churches cannot be separated from either cross-cultural partnership in mission or the twenty-first century reality that Christianity has become a worldwide faith.

Without mission partners abroad, volunteer teams could not operate.

In 2005, an estimated 1.6 million North Americans participated in short-term mission trips of two weeks or less. This represents an explosion of activity, compared to the one hundred twenty-five thousand who went on such trips in 1989. Included in the figures for 2005 were one hundred thirty-five thousand United Methodist Volunteers in Mission, who undertook short-term mission trips to seventy countries and forty-eight states. [14] While the bi-cultural long-term missionary remains the backbone of cross-cultural mission, especially in dangerous places where knowledge of the language and culture are essential, the rise of the volunteer mission movement underscores that mission structures have expanded from "partnership" into "networking."

The networking model for mission is like a spider web of relationships among varied and changing mission partners. Local churches are weaving their own webs, shaped by the interests of their members. Local and global needs and ministries are interconnected by a multitude of non-exclusive partnerships and information networks that stretch from local churches to denominations, parachurch agencies, and international NGOs. Some threads break and the webs collapse, but new ones are spun in their place.

The old bumper sticker "Think globally, act locally" has reversed its meaning in the networked mission context of today. For now, with the age of volunteer missions, congregations are using the global context to meet their own local needs for spiritual formation. Short-term missions provide spiritual inspiration for millions of participants, especially when they are able to establish ongoing relationships with the people they seek to serve. The work teams that went to Louisiana and Mississippi after Hurricane Katrina in 2006 have not only helped people whose homes and churches were destroyed but also revitalized the churches that sent them.[15] An increasing number of young people are deciding to go into the ministry because of their experiences on mission trips.

The old bumper sticker "Think globally, act locally" has reversed its meaning in the networked mission context of today.

But mission trips alone are not an adequate model for mission. There is a danger that such trips can become a "new colonialism" in which the chief benefit of the mission trip is to middle class "mission trippers" who are deepening their spiritual lives on the backs of the poor. A megachurch in California, for example, decided a few years ago to eliminate its support for long-term mission priorities such as Bible translation, and pastoral education for native evangelists, in order to hire a youth pastor who could motivate the church's youth through repeated (and expensive) overseas mission trips. Although the short-term mission trip based in the local church is integral to mission networking, it is not a substitute for sustained commitments to change unjust structures, to empower the world's poor, and to make the Gospel available to those who have never heard it because they do not speak English or Spanish.

The danger of the new popularity of short-term missions was demonstrated in July of 2007, when a group of twenty-three Korean Presbyterians on a short-term missionary trip was kidnapped by the Taliban in Afghanistan. Two were executed and the rest returned home in September after the Korean government paid four million dollars in ransom. While all Christians are called to be in mission, the most difficult mission contexts are not suitable for amateurs who have not fully studied the languages, cultures, and religions of the regions to which they wish to go. Sometimes even the most careful planning cannot prevent tragedies and cultural misunderstandings when short-term mission teams travel to foreign locations. The history of Christian martyrdom shows that mission can be a dangerous business.

Short-term mission trips represent the exciting groundswell of revived mission energy in local churches today, but they are only one aspect of mission networking in the context of world Christianity. The traditional challenges of cross-cultural mission beyond the local area require the infrastructure of mission boards. The sheer complexity of learning about other cultures, getting travel documents, handling currency exchanges, and supporting personnel in dangerous or isolated locations requires greater organizational capacities than those of the typical local church. The expense and expertise required to support institutions, such as schools and hospitals in foreign countries, also need the stability of a denominational or a strong independent parachurch mission agency. In addition, the career missionary is often needed to locate work sites and host short-term teams.

While the denominational mission board, in the case of United Methodists the GBGM, does not dictate how local churches or annual conferences define their own missions, it acts as a clearinghouse for connectional priorities, and as a "server" for the Methodist mission network. Not only does the GBGM continue to undergird and coordinate full-time missionary placement, but through its website it has become "a one-stop" information center to resource the mission priorities of local churches and annual conferences. In the context of the world church today, the denominational mission board no longer controls the shape and direction of cross-cultural mission the way it did forty years ago. It rather seeks to discern where God is calling United Methodists to be in mission, and to support them there.

Conclusion

Given all the changes in mission structures since the founding of The United Methodist Church over forty years ago, what remains of the grand heritage of women's leadership in mission? A hundred years after the Woman's Missionary Jubilee, how can women's groups like the UMW best contribute to the mission of the church?

The missional roles of women in the New Testament remind us that even though church structures change over time, the faithfulness of women in mission never ends. Women's ways of being in mission will continue to evolve in response to human needs and divine possibilities.

In Luke 18:1-8, Jesus told the parable of the persistent widow who kept asking an unjust judge for justice. Finally the judge grew tired of the stubborn widow and granted her justice because she never gave up. Jesus concluded the parable of the persistent widow, "And will not God grant justice to his chosen ones who cry to him day and night?" Like the widow of Jesus' parable, women's organizations in the church must keep reminding the powerful that women are both the poorest of the poor—especially elderly widows and those with young children—*and* the backbone of the church.

Women's ways of being in mission will continue to evolve in response to human needs and divine possibilities.

The persistent widow did not want a short-term charity operation. She demanded justice. The presence of global evils against women, such as displacement by war, sex trafficking, and HIV-AIDS, require diligence, coopera-

tion among different groups, and long-term commitment to systemic change. At the same time, local problems of poverty, racism, and loneliness call women's groups into numerous forms of outreach and advocacy.

The story of the disciple Tabitha reminds us of the continued importance of women's groups who support one another through family problems, economic challenges, illness, and end of life care. As the widows organized themselves for self support, they made friends and helped the needy. They were not in a position to publicly preach the Gospel or to travel to foreign countries in mission teams. But their witness of caring for one another made the church into a family—or what in the New Testament is called *oikos*, the "household of God."

And finally, women in mission are like the Samaritan woman, who, despite her own personal problems, ran and told her neighbors that Jesus knew and recognized her for who she really was. Her relationship with Jesus compelled her to testify to his identity as Lord and Savior. Her role as evangelist, along with Mary Magdalene and other women who witnessed to the resurrection, became the model for women as missionaries through church history.

In world Christianity today, the majority of faithful Christians are women. Women are both the bearers and the receivers of the Good News. Mission structures may change, but human need does not. The Gospel is Good News for women. This is what was celebrated a century ago at the Woman's Missionary Jubilee, and it is still true.

CHAPTER NOTES

1. Helen Barrett Montgomery, *Western Women in Eastern Lands* (New York: The Macmillan Company, 1910), 278; quoted in Dana L. Robert, *American Women in Mission: A Social History of Their Thought and Practice* (Macon: Mercer University Press, 1996), 268.
2. G. Homer, *The Didascalia Apostolorum. The Syriac Version Translated*, Oxford 1929, chapter 16. Women Priests Website. http://www.womenpriests.org/traditio/didasc.asp#instruct. (Accessed June 1, 2009).
3. See Rodney Stark, *The Rise of Christianity* (San Francisco: HarperOne, 1997).
4. Mrs. R.W. MacDonell, *Belle Harris Bennett: Her Life Work* (Nashville: Board of Missions, Methodist Episcopal Church, South, 1928).
5. See Elizabeth Brusco, *The Reformation of Machismo: Evangelical Conversion and Gender in Colombia* (Austin: University of Texas, 1995). For an overview of recent literature on world Christianity and women, see Dana L. Robert, "World Christianity as a Women's Movement," *International Bulletin of Missionary Research* 30, no. 4 (2006): 180–188.
6. For more on the Bible woman movement in United Methodism today, see chapter 8.
7. Catherine Allen, personal communication to the author in 2007. Additional information provided by e-mail July 25, 2008.
8. This anecdote about Ambassador Mongella is taken from Dana L. Robert, *Christian Mission: How Christianity Became a World Religion* (Chichester, UK: Wiley-Blackwell, 2009), chapter 5.
9. Melissa Heim, "'Standing Behind the Looms': American Missionary Women and Indian Church Women in the Devolution Process," in *Gospel Bearers, Gender Barriers: Missionary Women in the Twentieth Century*, ed. Dana L. Robert (Maryknoll, NY: Orbis Books, 2002), 47–61.
10. "Women's needs must be met to meet Millennium Goals," *Lambeth Daily*, July 23, 2008. http://www.lambethconference.org/daily/news.cfm/2008/7/23/ACNS4461 (accessed July 26, 2008).
11. From the New England Conference website, http://www.neumc.org/page.asp?PKValue=177 (accessed September 1, 2009).
12. http://umvim.org/about.htm (accessed October 14, 2008).
13. General Board of Global Ministries, "Mission Volunteers." http://new.gbgm-umc.org/about/us/mv/ (accessed July 28, 2008).
14. For information on North Americans' interest in mission trips, see Robert Wuthnow, *Boundless Faith: The Global Outreach of American Churches*. University of California Press, 2009. For information on United Methodist Volunteers in Mission, see the various websites maintained by jurisdictional and conference programs. A list of such websites is located at http://gbgm-umc.org/VIM/vimpages.html.
15. See chapter 7.

Part 2

Good News for the World

Chapter Four

Jesus Christ: The Messenger and the Message

I have decided to follow Jesus.
I have decided to follow Jesus.
I have decided to follow Jesus.
No turning back, no turning back.

Will you decide now to follow Jesus?
Will you decide now to follow Jesus?
Will you decide now to follow Jesus?
No turning back, no turning back.

—Anonymous

In the twenty-first century, Christians can be found among thousands of ethnic groups, within most countries, and in remote regions of Asia, Africa, Europe, and the Americas. Despite cultural and theological variety, followers of Jesus share an identity based on common commitments. Historian Andrew Walls illustrates the tension between unity and diversity in Christian history by asking his readers to imagine that a Professor of Comparative Inter-Planetary Religions visits the earth from outer space every few centuries to study Christianity. What will he find over the centuries through his investigations? How will he be able to recognize Christians in different times and places?

The space visitor first arrives in Jerusalem around A.D. 37. He observes that all the Christians are Jews. They keep Jewish laws and rituals, worship in the temple, value their close family ties, and read the Hebrew Scriptures. They resemble other Jews except that they believe a recently executed teacher, Jesus of Nazareth, is God's agent on earth—the Messiah— foretold in their Scriptures.

The space visitor visits earth again in A.D. 325 to find that church leaders from around the Mediterranean are gathered in Nicea at a great council. They are no longer Jewish and they worship on the first rather than seventh day of the week. Instead of having children, most are celibate. While they read in translation the same Scriptures as the Christians of A.D. 37, they value another set of writings—a "new" testament or covenant—that talks about Jesus and his followers. They are debating the distinctions among Greek words that refer to his relationship with God the Father. They are passionate about philosophy and theology.

The Council of Nicea, fresco in the Sistine Salon, the Vatican

Christ Enthroned

The third visit of the professor from outer space occurs in Ireland in the 600s. There he observes monks praying on a rocky coast. One is standing in ice water and another is beating himself with a whip as penance for his sins. A few are getting into a small boat with beautifully illustrated manuscripts to share with the inhabitants of other islands. The space visitor is surprised to find that the holy writings and theological language of the Irish monks say the same thing he heard in Greek in 325, but the monks seem far more concerned with being pure and holy rather than with engaging in theological debate.

Many centuries later, the space visitor arrives in London in the 1840s, to find a convention of people listening to speeches about sending missionaries to Africa, "armed with Bibles and cotton seeds." The meeting is opened with readings in English from the same sacred writings of the past, though now in printed book form carried by many of the delegates. While the people talk about holiness, they are not lean and hungry like the Irish monks, but well fed. While they say they accept the theology of Nicea from the church council of 325, they are an activist bunch, sending petitions to the government to suppress the slave trade and raising money for education of the poor.

The Anti-Slavery Society Convention, 1840

Members of the Holy Spirit Church of East Africa gathered by the roadside before marching to their place of worship in Bul Bul.

The final visit of the interplanetary researcher takes place in the 1960s, in Lagos, Nigeria. There he finds a group of Africans wearing white robes, singing and dancing in the streets. They are testifying to the power of God, which is demonstrated through miraculous healings. While they carry the same holy books as the century before, and they say they agree with the Greek theological formulations from 325, they are more interested in preaching and healing and personal visions than either theology or political action. [1]

Andrew Walls asks whether the inter-planetary professor finds anything in common among these representative groups of Christians across nearly two thousand years of history. Are these simply different cultural groups that claim the title *Christian* for themselves? Do they have more things in common with non-Christians of their own location and generation than

with previous generations of believers? Since Christians find themselves at home in many cultures, should we really be talking about multiple "Christianities" rather than one Christianity?

On closer observation, the interplanetary researcher realizes that the groups of Christians are connected in important ways. First of all they are linked by a shared history of mission. Over the centuries, representatives from one group shared the message with others and gave rise in sequence to new communities. Thus each group owes something to those who came before. Another thing they have in common is the consciousness of being rooted in the same sacred history, starting with the people of Israel and expressed in the Bible. Although their worship practices are different, each group hosts special ritual Communion meals and uses water to initiate new followers.

But the central element that binds the groups of Christians together into the same sacred story is the ultimate significance of Jesus as Christ, or Lord. Jesus is the common thread through the many varieties of Christianity in both the past and the present. Despite their different cultures and languages, their different ways of worship, and their different ways of expressing their faith, they all follow Jesus.

Jesus is the common thread through the many varieties of Christianity in both the past and the present.

The Mission of Jesus

As this tale of the space visitor illustrates, down through history the story of Jesus is the basis for the identity of Christians as persons called by God. But what does it mean to follow Jesus Christ, and what was his mission? Understandings of Jesus can be as varied as the peoples who worship him. Visits to different churches in the United States reveal an amazing variety of views about Jesus. Methodist churches from the early 1900s often hung paintings of Jesus in flowing white robes holding a sheep—the Good Shepherd who cares for his flock.

Catholic churches the world over show Jesus hanging on the cross, the ultimate sacrifice for the sins of the world. Orthodox churches often depict Jesus Christ as *Pantocrator*, the ruler of the world in all his glory. At Christmas we celebrate Jesus as a baby, born of a human mother yet recognized as divine by wise men from Persia. Africans and Asians bring their own views of Jesus—Jesus as wandering *guru*, or "teacher," in India, Jesus as the common *ancestor* of humanity in Africa, or Jesus as the *elder brother* in China.

Jesus the Good Shepherd

Pantocrator

Ultimately all our images of Jesus are rooted in the biblical narratives of Jesus' life and ministry and in the testimonies of the early Christians about who he was. Since the stories of Jesus were handed down for many years before they were collected into the Bible, the portrayals of him in the four Gospels each shed light on different aspects of the early communities that followed him. Biblical scholars spend their lives trying to understand Jesus in his own social and cultural context and studying the Bible as a set of literary and historical documents. But through the eyes of faith, ordinary believers can see the different aspects of Jesus' life and ministry in the New Testament as the facets of a priceless diamond—together they make up a beautiful, sparkling jewel that reflects the glory of God.

For Christians in the world church today, the meaning of mission goes back to the ministry of Jesus, as portrayed in its fullness by his early followers and written down in the Bible. To follow Jesus in mission begins with understanding Jesus' mission and that of his followers over time and across cultures. As Andrew Kirk puts it, "Following in the way of Jesus Christ (discipleship) is *the* test of missionary faithfulness." [2]

"Following in the way of Jesus Christ (discipleship) is the test of missionary faithfulness." —Andrew Kirk

---

Jesus as Messenger of God's Kingdom

At the core of Jesus' own mission was his self understanding as a messenger of the good news that God's kingdom was at hand. Jesus as messenger of the kingdom is a theme found in all four Gospels. After the arrest of John the Baptist, the book of Mark tells us that Jesus proclaimed the "good news of God" in Galilee, "The time has come. . . . The kingdom of God is near. Repent and believe the good news!" (Mark 1:14-15 NIV). Jesus then called the first disciples, the fishermen Simon, Andrew, James, and John, to leave their nets and follow him. Accompanied by his disciples, Jesus taught the people, healed, and drove out evil spirits. Through his message of the kingdom, Jesus showed God's compassion toward needy people whom he healed of physical, psychological, and spiritual illnesses.

"The time has come . . . The kingdom of God is near. Repent and believe the good news!" (Mark 1:14-15 NIV)

The Israelites who met Jesus knew what he meant by the kingdom of God. For in the history of Israel, important prophets had pointed toward the day in which evil would be driven out, justice would prevail, equality would occur between rich and poor, and the one true God would restore peace and harmony to all of creation. The kingdom of God would start small, like a tiny mustard seed. But once it was planted, it would grow so large that birds could nest in its branches (see Mark 4:30-32).

Jesus announced the meaning of his mission at the beginning of the book of Luke. After his baptism and time of spiritual strengthening during forty days of temptation in the desert, he returned to Galilee and to his home town of Nazareth. As was his usual practice, he went into the synagogue to read from the Scriptures on the day of worship. The sacred Hebrew Scriptures were written in scrolls. Jesus unrolled the scroll for the prophet Isaiah and read:

> "The Spirit of the Lord is on me,
>   because he has anointed me
>   to preach good news to the poor.
> He has sent me to proclaim freedom
> for the prisoners
>   and recovery of sight for the blind,
> to release the oppressed,
>   to proclaim the year of the Lord's
>   favor."
> [Rolling up the scroll, he sat down and
> said,] "Today this scripture is fulfilled
> in your hearing." (Luke 4:18-21 NIV)

The immediate response of people to Jesus' proclamation of the kingdom was outrage. How could this carpenter's son dare to testify that somehow God's kingdom was being fulfilled in their midst? Hadn't they known him since he was a small boy? The people drove Jesus out of town and threatened to throw him over a cliff.

The Kingdom of God

He also said, "With what can we compare the kingdom of God, or what parable will we use for it? It is like a mustard seed, which, when sown upon the ground, is the smallest of all the seeds on earth; yet when it is sown it grows up and becomes the greatest of all shrubs, and puts forth large branches, so that the birds of the air can make nests in its shade." (Mark 4:30-32)

"The Spirit of the Lord is on me,
  because he has anointed me
  to bring good news to the poor.
He has sent me to proclaim release to the captives and recovery of sight for the blind,
  to let the oppressed go free,
  to proclaim the year of the Lord's favor."
"Today this scripture has been fulfilled in your hearing." (Luke 4:18-19, 21)

But for the next three years, Jesus amazed his critics with the wisdom of his teaching about God, who loved the poor and demanded justice from the rich. Jesus called upon people to repent of their evil ways and turn from their sins. He attracted big crowds by speaking deep spiritual truths in the form of stories or parables. The Sermon on the Mount (Matthew 5–7) contains the teachings of Jesus about the values of the kingdom: God's justice and blessings for "the least, the last and the lost"; compassion toward enemies; and knowledge of God for seekers and searchers. The Gospels of Mark and Luke record that Jesus' first miracle—the first sign of the fulfillment of God's kingdom—was when he drove evil spirits out of people whose lives were being destroyed by uncontrollable forces. The book of Matthew notes that Jesus walked throughout the province of Galilee, teaching and preaching that the kingdom was at hand. As news went out that he was healing the sick, "people brought to him all who were ill with various diseases, those suffering severe pain, the demon-possessed, those having seizures, and the paralyzed, and he healed them" (Matthew 4:23-25 NIV).

Because people experienced healing and liberation from evil when they were near Jesus, they followed him everywhere and tried to keep him from moving on to the next town. But Jesus responded by taking his mission throughout Judea. He said, "I must preach the good news of the kingdom of God to the other towns also, because this is why I was sent." (Luke 4:43 NIV). [3]

Jesus ate with sinners and outcastes, praised poor widows for their faithfulness, and healed the handicapped people who were thought to be cursed by God. He showed that the kingdom of God would upend the normal social order whereby the rich and powerful people had more than they needed, while the poor and weak struggled to survive. In God's kingdom, all are invited to feast at the banquet table (Luke 14:15-24).

Jesus as Lord

An early confession of faith among ancient Christians was *Kyrios Iēsous*, or "Jesus is Lord." The writings of Paul, the oldest part of the New Testament, use the word *kyrios* 275 times, mostly to refer to Jesus. Christopher Wright tells us that by the time Paul wrote his letters, the confession "Jesus is Lord" was accepted as the standard and defining confession among those who accepted faith in Christ.[4] As the faith spread among Greek speakers, believers in Antioch and elsewhere also called him *Christos* (Christ), meaning Messiah, or "anointed one."

Those who answered Jesus' call to live in the light of God's kingdom soon became known as *Christians*. In calling Jesus "Lord," his followers attributed to Jesus qualities associated with the one God (Yahweh), for whom the term *kyrios* was used in the Greek translation of the Hebrew Scriptures. For the Greek-speaking Jews who made up the large group of early followers of Jesus, to say that Jesus was *kyrios* was to stress his identification with God. An early Christian hymn quoted by Paul in the book of Philippians substitutes the name of Jesus in a passage quoted from the prophet Isaiah about Yahweh:

> "that at the name of Jesus
>   every knee should bend,
>   in heaven and on earth and under
> the earth,
> and every should tongue confess
>   that Jesus Christ is Lord,
>   to the glory of God the Father."
> (Philippians 2:10-11)

The confession "Jesus is Lord" means that the living God of Israel chose to be known in the person of Jesus. [5]

For Paul and other early Christians, nothing was more essential to understanding Jesus' divinity than the resurrection. The defeat of death in the resurrection, and Jesus' appearances to his followers afterward, stood as signs that God's kingdom was at hand. As Paul stated, "If Christ has not been raised, then our proclamation has been in vain and your faith has been in vain" (1 Corinthians 15:14).

Followers of Jesus identified him with the one true God—as creator, ruler, judge, and savior. By sharing in God's nature, Jesus fulfilled the divine will to make God's self known among the peoples of the world. To know Jesus was to know God. To early followers of Jesus, to tell the story of Jesus was to make God known to the world's peoples. Through Jesus Christ, the God of Israel became available to the world. And as Wright states, "God's will to be known is the mainspring of our mission to make him known." [6]

Jesus as the Messenger and the Message

Scholarly studies of the Bible often separate Jesus, the messenger of the kingdom, from Christ, the savior of the world. Jesus of Nazareth was a Jewish man. Christ was the idea of divine lordship. Was there a necessary relationship between the two? Some books by scholars of the early church talk about the path "from Jesus to Christ," as if the Jesus who preached the kingdom was unrelated to a Christ of faith who was later invented by his followers. And yet, the earliest affirmation of faith, *Kyrios Iēsous,* existed before the Gospel stories of Jesus' ministry were even written down. From the perspective of the early Christians, the stories they passed down of Jesus the healer and teacher led directly to the bigger story of the crucifixion and the resurrection, and of God's saving purpose for the world.

Victory over death was the culmination of his message of the kingdom.

Jesus' whole ministry was a testimony against the destroyer, against suffering and against evil. Victory over death was the culmination of his message of the kingdom. He suffered torture and death on the cross, but then rose above it with the power of eternal life and hope for the future. For every human being, the worst suffering is that of death itself—the painful passage through illness and depression, the separation from loved ones, the fear of nothingness. Jesus' resurrection was the most important sign that God's love and mercy are stronger than evil and the greatest symbol of hope for the future of humanity. The mission of Jesus began with calling people to repentance and abundant life, and it culminated in his resurrection.

In the person of Jesus Christ, we see the necessary connection between God's kingdom of peace, truth, and justice; and salvation from sin and death. Taken as a whole, the mission of Jesus was to reveal that God loves the world. The relationship between the message and the messenger can be seen in the well-known biblical story of Jesus' encounter with Nicodemus in the third chapter of the Gospel of John. Nicodemus was a holy man, a devout Jew and Pharisee who recognized in Jesus the presence of God. Nicodemus went to see Jesus because he saw the miracles Jesus performed and was convinced that God was with him: "Rabbi, we know you are a teacher who has come from God. For no one could perform the miraculous signs you are doing if God were not with him" (John 3:2 NIV).

Jesus and Nicodemus.

Jesus' response to Nicodemus was to call him into a deeper understanding of what Nicodemus already knew about the nature of God and the nature of God's promised kingdom. Jesus told Nicodemus,

> "For God so loved the world that he gave his only Son, so that everyone who believes in him may not perish but may have eternal life.

> Indeed, God did not send the Son into the world to condemn the world, but in order that the world might be saved through him." (John 3:16-17)

The messenger of the kingdom, Jesus, is not separate from his message—that God loves the whole world.

Word, Sign, and Deed

In his book on transformational development, Bryant Myers points out that the purpose of Christian witness and the purpose of human development are the same—to transform people and their relationships. When we witness to Jesus Christ, we help people recover their true identities as children of God. [7] As people discover that God loves them, they gain confidence to restore their broken relationships with others and with God's creation. Through reaching out to others, people learn about God's love. The love of God and the love of others work together to create psychological, physical, and spiritual wholeness. The connection between love of God and love of others is reflected in Jesus' answer to the question about what must be done to obtain eternal life. He replied that the greatest commandment is to "love the Lord your God with all your heart, and with all your soul, and with all your strength and with all your mind; and your neighbor as yourself'" (Luke 10:27).

Myers argues that understanding the Gospel message in any human community requires communicating it holistically in three ways: as word, sign, and deed. Full communication of the Good News requires all three. First, communicating the Good News requires *words*—telling the stories of Jesus and telling people God loves them. But if our actions do not match our words, then words are hollow and Christians are seen as hypocrites who do not care about real people and their problems. Second, communicating the Good News requires *signs* of God's love—a community of believers whose existence points to God's love for humanity and creation. But if all we seek are miracles and supernatural signs, then our faith becomes sensationalism. And so, third, communicating the Good News requires *deeds*—healing the sick and helping the poor and working to improve society. But if we only do good deeds, then we are not meeting people's deeper spiritual longing to know God. "The gospel is not a disembodied message; it is carried and communicated in the life of Christian people. Therefore, a holistic understanding of the gospel begins with life, a life that is then lived out by deed and word and sign." [8]

* Communicating the Good News requires words.
* Communicating the Good News requires signs.
* Communicating the Good News requires deeds.

Word. The mission of Jesus as messenger of God's kingdom relied on his use of all three modes of communication—word, sign, and deed. To begin his ministry, Jesus stood up in the synagogue and read from the prophet Isaiah, as presented in Luke 4:18:: "The Spirit of the Lord is upon me, / because he has anointed me to bring good news to the poor." Jesus began his ministry by announcing that God's kingdom was coming. He called people to repent of their evil ways and to follow him. He told parables and taught people to care for others. Jesus' mission of the Word was so important that the Gospel of John says that in Jesus the "Word became flesh." (John 1:14) The coming of Jesus was a way for God to communicate with humanity. As Jesus spoke the word of God, he represented God's own speech. As the embodied Word of God (the "incarnate" Word), Jesus bridged the distance between God and humanity.

Sign. Jesus did not just speak words; he immediately backed them up with miraculous signs of the kingdom. The purpose of the miracles he performed was to let people know he was really a messenger of the kingdom. Words without signs would not have persuaded anyone that he was telling the truth. In the book of John, his first miracle was to turn water into wine at a wedding. "Jesus did this, the first of his signs, in Cana of Galilee, and revealed his glory; and his disciples believed in him." (John 2:11) In the books of Mark and Luke, after announcing that the kingdom is near and calling people to repentance, the first sign Jesus offered was cleansing a man of an evil spirit. Through challenging evil spirits and demons, Jesus demonstrated that God's power was greater than the powers of sin and destruction.

Ultimately the most important sign of the kingdom demonstrated by Jesus was his death on the cross, followed by the resurrection. His willingness to die showed the power of God even over death, for he knew that suffering and death were not the final word on the human condition. As Paul exclaimed in the letter he wrote to the believers in Corinth:

"Where, O death, is your victory?

Where, O death, is your sting?"

The sting of death is sin, and the power of sin is the law. But thanks be to God, who gives us the victory through our Lord Jesus Christ." (1 Corinthians 15:55-57)

Deed. Jesus performed the good deeds of the kingdom. He healed many people. He fought moneylenders in the temple who exploited the people for financial gain. He befriended prostitutes and tax collectors and other social outcasts. He treated women and children with respect as full human beings. Taken together, Jesus' ministry of word, sign, and deed communicated the totality of his message of life: "I came that they may have life, and have it abundantly" (John 10:10).

The Good News of the kingdom is that of abundant life for all, given by God who loves the world. This is why mission is an act of celebration, of proclaiming "Joy to the world! The Lord is come!"

Mission in the Way of Jesus

From the days of the disciples until now and into the future, to be in mission means to follow Jesus. The word *disciple* means "follower." To be in mission in the *name* of Jesus, then, is to be in mission in the *way* of Jesus.

After Jesus called the Twelve to follow him, he sent them out to spread his message. The Disciples' kingdom mission consisted of the same holistic message of word, sign, and deed as that of Jesus himself. In Luke 9, Jesus gathered the Disciples "and gave them power and authority over all demons and to cure diseases, and he sent them out to proclaim the kingdom of God and to heal" (Luke 9:1-2). The Disciples were empowered by Jesus to proclaim the Good News (word), to defeat demons (sign), and to heal the sick (deed). They did not force or impose themselves on people who didn't want to hear them. Rather, they visited those who chose to welcome them. They took no extra food or clothing or equipment that would have enabled them to survive without help from others. In their journeys to spread the Good News of God's kingdom, they were dependent on the support of their listeners. If townspeople chose not to welcome them, Jesus told them to "shake the dust off your feet as a testimony against them" (Luke 9:4) and move on.

In chapter 10, Luke tells us that Jesus sent out seventy workers in pairs on a "mission trip." Like the mission of the Twelve, these additional disciples depended on the hospitality of the local people. They were not to lord it over the poor by demanding special food or housing. They lived at the level of the ordinary townsfolk and stayed in homes where they were welcomed. "Whenever you enter a town and its people welcome you, eat what is set before you; cure the sick who are there, and say to them, 'The kingdom of God has come near to you" (Luke 10:8-9).

Luke tells us that Jesus sent out seventy workers in pairs on a "mission trip."

Discipleship as Mission

The close connection between the mission of Jesus and that of his Disciples is expressed in the Gospel of Matthew. Matthew uses the terms *disciple* and "follow after" far more than the other three Gospels. His is the only Gospel that uses the verb "to make disciples" (see 28:19). [9] In Matthew, Jesus urges his disciples to declare the justice and peace that would come in the fullness of God's kingdom. He challenges them to aim for perfection, and he tells them to bear fruit. As in Luke, in Matthew 10 Jesus sent out the twelve to "proclaim the good news, 'The kingdom of heaven has come near.' Cure the sick, raise the dead, cleanse the lepers, cast out demons" (Matthew 10:7-8). The disciples were not to expect payment for their ministry, but they were entitled to be supported by the people they were helping.

During his lifetime, Jesus confined his mission to the people of Israel and forbade his disciples to go beyond the Jewish community. Despite those limits, Matthew frequently refers to the interest of Gentiles in the Good News. It is Matthew who writes of the visit of the three wise men to baby Jesus, the Roman centurion whose faith impressed Jesus, the Canaanite woman who insisted that Jesus heal her daughter, and even the Roman centurion at the cross who declared that Jesus was the son of God. [10] At the beginning of the book, Matthew's genealogy of Jesus names several non-Jewish foreign women among his ancestors. Thus even though the book of Matthew was probably written for a group of Jewish believers, there are hints throughout the Gospel that Jesus' earthly outreach to Israel was only the beginning of a much bigger mission.

In the conclusion to Matthew's Gospel, the reason for the occasional references to Gentile followers during Jesus' lifetime becomes clear. After Jesus died on the cross, he rose and appeared to the women who went to his tomb and found it empty. He told them to have the disciples meet Jesus in his home province of Galilee. Then occurred the single most important statement about "making disciples" that appears in the entire New Testament. The risen Jesus met his disciples on a mountain and said to them,

> "All authority in heaven and on earth has been given to me. Go therefore and make disciples of all nations, baptizing them in the name of the Father and of the Son and of the Holy Spirit, and teaching them to obey everything that I have commanded you. And remember, I am with you always, to the end of the age." (Matthew 28:18-20)

Jesus' post-resurrection command to his closest followers was to "make disciples of all nations." Although Jesus' own mission of the kingdom focused on the nation of Israel while he was alive, after his death he sent his disciples to witness to people of all nationalities and ethnicities. After his resurrection, the disciples embarked on a mission that would take the rest of their lives. The chief task of Jesus' disciples was to make other disciples from among the peoples of the world, including Jews and non-Jews. This mission of the disciples became the link between the life of Jesus and the existence of the church down through the ages.

Jesus' post-resurrection statement to the disciples is known as the "Great Commission," one of the most important mission texts in the history of Christianity. The opening to Jesus' mission to nations other than Israel took the meaning of *discipleship* to a new level. The disciples proclaimed Jesus' message of the kingdom, now including his stunning victory over death. They taught what Jesus taught and baptized followers eager to join the new community. They witnessed to the resurrected Jesus and to his promise to be present with them until the end of time. According to David Bosch, "In Matthew's view, Christians find their true identity when they are involved in mission, in communicating to others a new way of life, a new interpretation of reality and of God, and in committing themselves to the liberation and salvation of others." [11]

Relationship as Mission

As mentioned earlier, each Gospel presents a different facet of Jesus' life and mission. Matthew's concept of "making disciples" involves going into the world in active ministry—teaching, preaching, and baptizing. The focus of John's Gospel, while equally missional, places following Jesus within the framework of shared relationships. Stanley Skreslet notes that John is unique in portraying friendship with other followers as the major way in which people come to know Jesus. Many of Jesus' followers are introduced to him by others. Says Skreslet, "Sharing Christ with friends is what happens when followers of Jesus open up to loved ones or others with whom they are already in relationship and share their experience of faith in personal terms." [12] A prominent example of this is when the Samaritan woman tells her neighbors about her conversations with Jesus, and they give him a hearing because of her testimony (John 4).

Many of Jesus' followers are introduced to him by others.

Throughout the Gospel of John, Jesus uses his oneness with God as the basis for forging relationships with others. He repeatedly tells his followers that his unity with God extends to them through their faithfulness to him. Thus in knowing Jesus, his disciples know God. As the disciples relate to others, they, too, can know God.

The glue that cements the chain of relationships is love. As Jesus waits to be arrested, John develops some of the most profound thoughts in the New Testament on the believers' relationship with God through Christ (chapters 13–17). Jesus tells the disciples,

> "I give you a new commandment, that you love one another. Just as I have loved you, you also should love one another. By this everyone will know that you are my disciples, if you have love for one another." (John 13:34-35)

> "They who have my commandments and keep them are those who love me; and those who love me will be loved by my Father. . . . and we will come to them and make our home with them." (John 14:21-23)

Thus in loving Jesus and keeping his commandments, his followers find that God becomes present in their lives.

In John 15, the relationship of believers with Christ is described as that of branches to the vine. Cut off from the vine, the branches will die. But "abiding" in the vine allows the branches to bear much fruit. The union of the disciples with Jesus connects them to God, the source of life, and allows them to produce fruit that will feed and nourish others.

"I give you a new commandment, that you love one another. Just as I have loved you, you also should love one another. By this everyone will know that you are my disciples, if you have love for one another." (John 13:34-35)

"They who have my commandments and keep them are those who love me; and those who love me will be loved by my Father . . . and we will come to them and make our home with them." (John 14:21-23).

The topic of the mystical relationship between Christ and his followers was explored in detail by the late-nineteenth-century South African spiritual writer, Andrew Murray, in his classic book *Abide in Christ.* Murray notes that the unity with Jesus that results from "abiding in Christ" allows his followers to feel his love and compassion for others. Unity with Christ makes the disciple wish to bless others, and to receive Christ's power of love and service. Murray reflects,

> If we are abiding in Jesus, let us begin to work. Let us first seek to influence those around us in daily life. Let us accept distinctly and joyfully our holy calling, that we are even now to live as the servants of the love of Jesus to our fellow-men. . . . There is work in our own home. There is work among the sick, the poor, and the outcast. There is work in a hundred different paths which the Spirit of Christ opens up through those who allow themselves to be led by Him. There is work perhaps for us in ways that have not yet been opened up by others. Abiding in Christ, let us work. [13]

Furthermore, Murray continues, if we work, then we abide more deeply in Christ. As we serve others, the living Christ lives more deeply within us and we become closer to him.

The relational form of mission described in the book of John culminates in chapter 17, when Jesus prays for his disciples before he is arrested. As he turns toward the cross, he begs God to protect the friends he is leaving behind:

> "I ask not only on behalf of these, but also on behalf of those who will believe in me through their word, that they may all be one. As you, Father, are in me and I am in you, may they also be in us, so that the world may believe that you have sent me. . . . I in them and you in me, that they may become completely one, so that the world may know that you have sent me and have loved them even as you have loved me." (John 17:20-23)

While the Great Commission in Matthew 28 emphasizes the activism of "making disciples," in John 20 Jesus grounds his commission to the disciples in their relationship with him. Through unity with Christ and with one another, the mission of Jesus' followers is to show God's love to the world. After Jesus' death and resurrection, he appeared to the disciples and reinforced that their unity with him is for the purpose of mission to the world. "'Peace be with you. As the Father has sent me, so I send you.' When he had said this, he breathed on them and said to them, 'Receive the Holy Spirit'" (John 20:21-22).

After the resurrection, Jesus grilled fish and broke bread for breakfast with his disciples on the beach. The give and take of human interaction defined his conversation with Peter, as he asked Peter to tell him three times that he loved him. In response each time, Jesus told Peter to "feed my sheep" (John 21:15-17). Ultimately it was the love between Jesus and his disciples that committed them to taking responsibility for his flock of followers, even after his death.

> When they had finished breakfast, Jesus said to Simon Peter, "Simon son of John, do you love me more than these?" He said to him, "Yes, Lord; you know that I love you." Jesus said to him, "Feed my lambs." A second time he said to him, "Simon son of John, do you love me?" He said to him, "Yes, Lord; you know that I love you." Jesus said to him, "Tend my sheep." He said to him the third time, "Simon son of John, do you love me?" Peter felt hurt because he said to him the third time, "Do you love me?" And he said to him, "Lord, you know everything; you know that I love you." Jesus said to him, "Feed my sheep." (John 21:15-17)

Followers of Jesus

Jesus' life, death, and resurrection were all part of his mission to show God's love to the world. Now that we have seen how the New Testament tells the story of that mission, let us return to the question that began this chapter. What do Christians have in common from one era of history to another? In the world church today, what do Christians share across different nationalities, ethnicities, and geographic locations? For example, what do people who take electricity, cars, and the Internet for granted have in common with Irish Catholic monks who hand-copied and illustrated the Bible in Latin during the Middle Ages? What does a church that ordains women have in common with Mediterranean men who argued about theology at the Council of Nicea in 325? What do Nigerian praise singers dancing in white robes through mud streets have in common with North Americans singing from a hymnal accompanied by organ music, in a church with stained glass windows?

The single answer to these questions is that, despite our many differences of culture and geography, we all follow Jesus. To follow Jesus means to share in his mission as outlined in the Gospels:

- As disciples, we witness to the kingdom of God through word, sign, and deed.
- As disciples, we testify that "Jesus is Lord."
- As disciples, we live in the power and hope of the resurrection.
- As disciples, through our unity with Christ, we share the love of God for the world.

In the late 500s, Saint Columba, one of the greatest missionaries in the history of Christianity, founded a monastery on the Scottish island of Iona. From Iona, he and his monks spread the Gospel into pagan Scotland and northern England. Over the centuries, Iona became one of the great spiritual centers of medieval Catholic Europe.

What do Nigerian praise singers dancing in white robes through mud streets have in common with North Americans singing from a hymnal accompanied by organ music, in a church with stained glass windows?

In the 1930s, a group of men led by Presbyterian Church of Scotland minister George McLeod rebuilt the ruined Iona Abbey and founded the Iona Community. Christians of different theological and ethnic traditions gathered in ecumenical unity to find new ways to be faithful in a hostile, violent, and competitive modern world. As a source of experimental worship and renewed Celtic spirituality, Iona has sent hymns and prayers around the world just as the monks medieval did.

The ecumenical community of Iona today is very different from that of St. Columba and his monks fourteen hundred years ago. But the desire to follow Jesus has not changed. In the moving hymn, "The Summons," Iona Community member John Bell expresses the deep longing of Christians through the ages to be united with Jesus Christ in mission. Regardless of our differences, we answer the eternal call to follow Jesus in loving relationship and witness to the world.

The Abbey, Isle of Iona.

Will you come and follow me if I but
   call your name?
Will you go where you don't know
   and never be the same?
Will you let my love be shown, will
   you let my name be known,
    will you let my life be grown in you
    and you in me?

Will you leave yourself behind if I but
   call your name?
Will you care for cruel and kind and
   never be the same?
Will you risk the hostile stare should
   your life attract or scare,
will you let me answer prayer in you
   and you in me?

Will you let the blinded see if I but
   call your name?
Will you set the prisoners free and
   never be the same?
Will you kiss the leper clean, and do
   such as this unseen,
    and admit to what I mean in you
and you in me?

Will you love the "you" you hide if I
   but call your name?
Will you quell the fear inside and
   never be the same?
Will you use the faith you've found to
   reshape the world around,
   through my sight and touch and
   sound in you and you in me?

Lord, your summons echoes true
   when you but call my name.
Let me turn and follow you and never
   be the same.
In your company I'll go where your
   love and footsteps show.
Thus I'll move and live and grow in
   you and you in me.

CHAPTER NOTES

1. Andrew F. Walls, "The Gospel as Prisoner and Liberator of Culture," in *The Missionary Movement in Christian History: Studies in Transmission of Faith* (Maryknoll, NY: Orbis, 1996), 3–7.

2. Andrew Kirk, *What Is Mission?* (Minneapolis: Augsburg Fortress, 2000), 39.

3. On Jesus' ministry of the kingdom see Arthur F. Glasser and others, *Announcing the Kingdom: The Story of God's Mission in the Bible* (Grand Rapids: Baker Academic, 2003).

4. Christopher J. H. Wright, *The Mission of God: Unlocking the Bible's Grand Narrative* (Downers Grove: IVP Academic, 2006), 107–108.

5. Ibid., 108.

6. Ibid., 129.

7. Bryant L. Myers, *Walking with the Poor: Principles and Practices of Transformational Development* (Maryknoll, NY: Orbis, 1999), 211–212.

8. Ibid.

9. David Bosch, *Transforming Mission: Paradigm Shifts in Theology of Mission* (Maryknoll, NY: Orbis, 1991), 73.

10. Ibid., 61.

11. Ibid., 83.

12. Stanley H. Skreslet, *Picturing Christian Witness: New Testament Images of Disciples in Mission* (Grand Rapids: William B. Eerdmans, 2006), 79.

13. Andrew Murray, *Abide in Christ* (Wilder Publications, 2008, 90). Also see http://www.worldinvisible.com/library/murray/5f00.0562/5f00.0562.20.htm, chapter 20 (accessed October 15, 2008).

Chapter Five

Being Sent: The Church in Mission

I am the church!
You are the church!
We are the church together.
All who follow Jesus, all around
  the world!
Yes, we're the church together!

The church is not a building, the
  church is not a steeple,
The church is not a resting place,
  the church is a people.

We're many kinds of people, with
  many kinds of faces,
All colors and all ages, too, from
  all times and places.

At Pentecost some people received
  the Holy Spirit
And told the Good News through
  the world to all who would
  hear it.

I am the church!
You are the church!
We are the church together.
All who follow Jesus, all around
  the world!
Yes, we're the church together!

("We Are the Church." Words and music: Richard K. Avery & Donald Marsh. © 1972 Hope Publishing Company, Carol Stream, IL 60188. All rights reserved. Used by permission.)

The popular chorus from the 1970s, "We Are the Church," is often used in Sunday schools as an activity song. Its cheery lyrics and steady beat make it great for marching children around the room when they tire of sitting still. The song makes appearances in children's sermons, complete with hand motions.

"We are the Church" is available for download as the subject of numerous YouTube audio clips. A few years ago, a graduate student named Joshua Longbrake got dozens of people to make signs saying "I am the church" and snap pictures of themselves for his online blog. This inspirational posting was made into a moving "MySpace" video clip by a man named Russ. Picture after picture moves across the screen, as young people of different races, in settings from subways to restaurants to dorm rooms, hold up signs in different languages that declare "I am the church."[1]

The simple lyrics, "I am the church! You are the church! We are the church together" signifies the deep theological truth that "All who follow Jesus, all around the world" are the church. At its most basic, the definition of the church is the people, from near or far, who together follow Jesus. People of all colors, ages, and "from all times and places" share an identity as followers of Jesus Christ. The idea of the church emerges in the Gospel of Matthew as those gathered in Jesus' name. Jesus told his disciples, "For where two or three are gathered in my name, I am there among them" (Matthew 18:20).

The Greek word usually translated into English as "church" in the Bible is *ekklesia*, from which come the words ecclesiastical (matters concerning the church), ecclesiastic (an ordained church leader), and ecclesiology (the study of the church). In Greek, *ekklesia* is a political term meaning a local assembly of people called out from the surrounding context because of the need for change or reform. Early believers, the *ekklesia*, were called out from the sinful world to live according to the values of the kingdom—love for God and neighbor in the way of Jesus.

New Testament communities described themselves in a hundred different ways, including "the way of the Lord," "saints," the "body of Christ," the "bride of Christ," the "people of God," the "new creation," the "poor," "sojourners and pilgrims," and more. Many of these descriptions of self-identity are images of mission. Just as his disciples followed Jesus in his mission of witnessing to God's kingdom and sharing God's love and salvation, so did the early church. In his book *Images of the Church in Mission*, John Driver explores a dozen biblical images for the community in mission. Empowered by the Holy Spirit, early Christians called out from the world became what Driver calls "God's contrast-society of witness." Only when mission is rooted in the *ekklesia*, "God's contrast-community," can it become an effective witness to "God's saving rule over humankind." [2]

To be called by Jesus Christ is to become part of the *ekklesia*, the community of witnesses. The purpose of being the church is to be in mission. This purpose is shared today by assemblies of Christians throughout the world. As the song "We Are the Church" concludes,

> At Pentecost some people received the
> Holy Spirit
> And told the Good News through the
> world to all who would hear it.
>
> I am the church!
> You are the church!
> We are the church together!
> All who follow Jesus, all around
> the world!
> Yes, we're the church together!

("We are the Church." Words and music: Richard K. Avery & Donald Marsh. © 1972 Hope Publishing Company, Carol Stream, IL 60188. All rights reserved. Used by permission.)

Sent by God in Mission

If you ask the typical church member whether he or she is a missionary or an evangelist, the answer will probably be no. Aren't missionaries professionals who are sent by a mission board or mission society to live in a foreign country? Isn't an evangelist someone who leads big revivals or stands on a street corner preaching? The problem with these definitions of *missionary* and *evangelist* is that they are narrow stereotypes. Their very narrowness makes it easy to distance ourselves from them. If I don't like televangelists, then I can reject evangelism. I can forget about mission except to donate a few dollars a year to the General Board of Global Ministries. Our definition of missionaries and evangelists as paid professionals obscures the simple biblical truth that all followers of Jesus Christ are sent into the world in mission.

If you ask the typical church member whether he or she is a missionary or an evangelist, the answer will probably be no.

As we saw in chapter 4, Jesus' life, death, and resurrection were all part of his mission to communicate the love of God for the world. When Jesus sent the disciples to proclaim the kingdom of God, their unity with him meant that his mission became their mission. After the resurrection, Jesus told them to share the Good News with all the peoples in the world. As people become followers of Jesus, they, too, inherit the mission of discipleship. To be a follower of Jesus Christ, to be a Christian, is to share the mission of Jesus, in the way of Jesus.

> "I am the church" means that
> *I am in mission.*
> "You are the church" means that
> *you are in mission.*
> "We are the church" means that
> *we are in mission together.*

As theologian Emil Brunner wrote in 1931, "The church exists by mission as fire exists by burning."

I am in mission.
You are in mission.
We are in mission together.

The word *mission* is a Latinized form of the Greek verbs for "sending." According to mission theologian David Bosch, the words *send* and *sending* occur 206 times in the New Testament.[3] A person in mission, therefore, is someone who is sent. After he rose from the dead, Jesus appeared to the disciples and showed them his wounded hands and side. He then said, "Peace be with you. As the Father has sent me, so I send you" (John 20:21). Not only is sending a major theme in the New Testament, but the entire New Testament is the story of mission—the story of God sending Jesus to make himself known, and of people sent to spread God's message of love and compassion for the world.

The process of sending and being sent by Jesus is related to the word *apostle*, because *apostellein* is the primary biblical Greek word used for *sending*. An apostle is one who is sent. Thus when we speak of the twelve apostles, we are referring to the fact that they were the ones sent by Jesus. As disciples, they followed Jesus. As apostles, they were sent by him. Paul the apostle was one of the first great missionaries of the church. To speak of "apostolic ministry" is to refer to the missionary nature of ministry. An "apostolic church" is a mission-minded church full of people who understand their Christian calling as being sent into the world to do God's work. In some languages, for example Dutch and German, missionary societies are called "sending" societies.

One of the most significant features of world Christianity today is the widespread conviction that every believer is involved in mission. Many people in Europe and the United States have forgotten that discipleship and mission cannot be separated. They have inherited church membership from their parents and are Christians as a matter of habit. Because they take church membership for granted, they no longer remember that to be the *ekklesia* is to be called out of the world into a community of Jesus' followers. But new Christians who have decided to follow Jesus—sometimes at great sacrifice—are excited about the opportunity of witnessing to their new identities in Christ. They read Jesus' calling and sending of his disciples as meant for them personally, rather than for paid professionals called "evangelists" or "missionaries." To be called by Jesus Christ is to be sent by Jesus Christ. For Christians, being called and being sent are part of the same movement.

Many people in Europe and the United States have forgotten that discipleship and mission cannot be separated.

The dynamism and energy of the world church in the twenty-first century remind us that being the church is like breathing. First of all, the source of life gives us breath. In God, who created the universe, "we live and move and have our being" (Acts 17:28). Being alive through the grace of God, we must breathe. Inhaling and exhaling are matters of life or death. Worshiping God is like inhaling. When the community gathers to worship God, the act of celebration centers us, and builds our strength. As we breathe in, we are filled with the Holy Spirit. Once filled with the power of the Spirit, we exhale. The process of exhaling the Spirit is the act of being in mission. We go out in the power of the Spirit, ready to serve others in the way that Jesus taught us. Worship and mission are thus two parts of the same motion—the motion of breathing, of being alive.

The process of exhaling the Spirit is the act of being in mission.

Orthodox mission theologian Ion Bria characterizes mission as "the liturgy after the liturgy."[4] During worship—and especially in the Communion service—people experience union with God. As people leave the church building, they witness to what they have experienced. Like breathing in and breathing out, the act of worshiping God sends the community in mission to serve others.

UNITED METHODIST VOLUNTEERS IN MISSION
Christian Love in Action!

The United Methodist Volunteers in Mission summarize the idea that being sent is the basis for being a Christian:

> The understanding that we are called and that we are sent is at the foundation of our faith. The scriptures are full of stories of persons who responded to a call and were sent on mission for God. Jesus spent his ministry calling persons and sending them on God's mission. . . .
>
> Putting our faith into action is at the very heart of our Christian calling. The New Testament instructs those who would be followers of Jesus to feed the hungry, clothe the naked, give shelter to the homeless, heal the sick, care for the widows, and nurture the children.
>
> Through volunteers in mission, every person in the church has the opportunity to serve and to live their lives more faithfully. And when we reach out and use what God has given us in the service of others, we have life-transforming experiences. [5]

The *Missio Dei* (Mission of God)

Because the church is full of people, both the strength and the weakness of Christian mission is the church itself. Living in the power of Christ, people of faith have done heroic things. They have risked their lives for others, and cared for the poor, and stood up against war and injustice. The biblical word for "witness" is *martyria*, from which we get the word *martyr*. To witness to Jesus has resulted in martyrdom for millions of Christians down through the ages. The church father Tertullian remarked in the early 200s, "the blood of the martyrs is the seed of the church." One of the side effects of the growth of Christianity in Asia has been a huge increase in the number of martyrs since the mid-twentieth century in largely non-Christian countries like India, Burma (Myanmar), and Indonesia.

Witness to Christ despite the lack of earthly power provides some of the most heroic and inspiring moments in the history of mission: the hiding of the first Chinese missionary by Korean women in the early 1800s, the protest of the theologian Alcuin against Charlemagne's slaughter of the Saxons in the 800s, the resistance of missionaries Jeremiah Evarts and Samuel Worcester against the forced removal of the Cherokees from their land in the 1830s, the steadfast faith of Huron Indian Kateri Tekakwitha despite persecution in the 1670s, the forgiveness of Australian missionary Gladys Staines toward the Hindu militants who burned alive her husband and two sons in 1999. Mission history is full of the stories of saints who were faithful against all odds.

But some of the worst moments in the history of Christianity have occurred when the idea of mission has been co-opted by the powerful or by the state: the conquest of the Americas and enslavement of the native people in the name of evangelization, the Crusades to take the Holy Land from the Muslims in the 1100s, the forced "unequal treaties" that allowed opium and missionaries into China's port cities in the name of "free trade" during the mid-1800s, and the many times war has been declared in the name of God. The most heroic actions by missionaries have occurred in protest against violations of human rights by citizens of their own countries.

Mission history is full of the stories of saints who were faithful against all odds.

One of the most important Gospel values is the self-criticism that comes from awareness of human sinfulness and the ongoing need of every person for the grace and forgiveness of God. Because the church in each time and place reflects the culture and conduct of its people, it often has trouble recognizing its own involvement in sinful behavior or unjust systems. As Jesus commented, it is easier to see the sawdust speck of sin or weakness in a brother's eye than to see the plank in one's own eye (see Matthew 7:3-5). From a human perspective, being "in the world but not of it" is a very difficult position to sustain. At the same time, Scripture promises that through abundant life in Christ we can do all things (see Philippians 4:13). As the early pioneer missionary William Carey said, "Expect great things from God. Attempt great things for God!" [6]

William Carey

The period between the two world wars of the twentieth century was a particularly challenging time in history for the church. Despite increasing criticism of European rule over vast swaths of Asia and Africa, missions around the world were still operating within colonial contexts and keeping church leadership in Western hands according to Western priorities. Another problem of the era was the rise of Nazism. The main churches in Germany caved in to Nazi propaganda in the guise of being true to the spirit of the German people. In Russia, an anti-religious communist dictatorship liquidated hundreds of thousands of church leaders and ultimately killed millions. In the United States, the Great Depression had thrown millions of people out of work and led to serious doubts about unrestrained capitalism as an economic system. Mission leaders meeting in conferences during the 1930s had to grapple with these massive problems.

One major response by theologians was to argue that no human cultural or social system could be mistaken for the kingdom of God. According to the Bible, the full reign of God would occur only at the end of time. There was a gap between God the Creator and the human creature that could be filled only by Jesus Christ, not by human effort. No human political systems—neither Nazism nor communism nor colonialism nor capitalism—could be confused with the will of God.

It was in this context of "crisis" that the German Karl Hartenstein, head of the Basel Mission, in 1934 began speaking of the *missio Dei* or the "mission of God" as a foundational idea for Christian mission. Christian mission should be rooted in God's loving initiative toward the world in sending Jesus Christ. The basis of mission was participation in God's work, not in building human systems such as colonialism or national socialism or communism. The biblical idea of mission could not be co-opted or captured by human cultures. The true goal of mission was to announce the reign of God, which had broken into the world with the work of Jesus but would not be fulfilled until the end of time. God's plan of salvation could not be co-opted by the church or state or nation. Following Jesus, the church on earth lived "between the times" as exile and stranger.

By the 1960s, the idea of the *missio Dei* gained popularity with the understanding that the focus of God's love and grace was the world, not the church. Jesus did not say that God loved the church, but that "God so loved the *world* that he gave his only Son" (John 3:16, emphasis added). The role of the church in mission was not to build its own empire, but to serve God in the world. Mission belonged to God, not the church. The *missio Dei* thus created a foundation for critiquing the mistakes of missions. It became an ideal to measure up to. Since mission is not owned by the church, it could not be reduced to self-serving ways of seeking power or oppressing persons from other cultures. The *missio Dei* also was a way to defend the concept of mission from those who rejected it because they cynically believed that mission was only a cover for colonialism.

By the 1970s, the idea that mission belongs to God had become widely accepted by Protestant, Catholic, and Orthodox Christians. The *missio Dei* reinforced the idea of mission as "sending," as being sent by God. The idea of being sent into the world in mission emanates from the Trinity—God as Creator, Son, and Holy Spirit. God the Father sent Jesus Christ. Jesus called upon the Holy Spirit, which rested upon his followers at the time of Pentecost. Together the Trinity sends the church into the world in mission. Mission flows from the nature of God, who loves the world and sends the church to witness to that love.

For United Methodists, the most expressive statement of the *missio Dei* as the theological basis for mission appears in the official mission statement *Grace Upon Grace* adopted by the General Conference of 1988. The mission statement opens by rooting mission firmly in the idea that mission flows from the nature of God:

> Mission is the action of the God of grace who creates out of love, who calls a covenant community, who graciously redeems and reconciles a broken and sinful people in Jesus Christ, and who through the Holy Spirit calls the church into being as the instrument of the good news of grace to all people.[7]

Mission begins in the action of God, unfolding through the Trinity, which calls the church to spread the Good News. "The triune God is grace who in Christ and through the Holy Spirit prepares, saves, and makes a new people."[8]

To United Methodists, a mission theology of the *missio Dei* starts with God, who created all things. The church's reaction to God's goodness and love is to go out in mission. "Mission is also the church's grateful response to what God has done, is doing, and will do."[9] *Grace Upon Grace* makes it clear, therefore, that mission is part of the church's identity, as sent by the triune God—Creator, Son, and Holy Spirit.

Although in church circles we talk about *our* mission programs, *our* mission priorities, *our* mission trips, and *our* missionaries, God's mission is not a program owned by the church. Mission is what it means to *be* the church. Because God loves the world, grace comes again and again, in wave after wave.[10] As a community called by God's self-giving grace, the church can't help but share that grace with the world. Sent by God, United Methodists engage in mission as a joyful celebration of God's love.

Text and Context

A great theologian told young ministers-in-training that they should prepare their sermons with the Bible in one hand and the newspaper in the other. As Christians, we see the world through the eyes of faith, handed down through many generations of believers who were grounded in the sacred story of Jesus as found in the New Testament. At the same time, we live in a world in which wars displace and kill thousands, people starve to death, children are ill with preventable diseases, old people are lonely, and violence tears families apart. God's mission of love is directed toward a hurting world, a creation "groaning as in the pains of childbirth" (Romans 8:22 NIV).

One of the most difficult issues in Christian mission is how to relate the Gospel message—the "text"—to its many different contexts. This is not a simple matter of applying selected verses of the Bible directly to life today. For example, verses in the New Testament tell slaves to obey their masters and women to cover their heads and ask their husbands if they do not understand what is going on in church. A lot has changed since those verses were written. Today in North America these ideas make little sense because slavery is seen as a relic of barbarism. Women are now educated, hold jobs, and ask their own questions. Most people would argue that abolishing slavery and liberating women are two of the distinctive accomplishments of Christian witness throughout the world. As Paul states in Galatians 3:28, "There is no longer Jew or Greek, there is no longer slave or free, there is no longer male and female; for all of you are one in Christ Jesus."

Abolishing slavery and liberating women are two of the distinctive accomplishments of Christian witness throughout the world.

In the light of God's love, of "grace upon grace," God is always doing something new. The Gospel of John tells us that even as Jesus prepared for his death upon the cross, he told the disciples that "the Advocate, the Holy Spirit, whom the Father will send in my name, will teach you everything, and remind you of all that I have said to you" (John 14:26). Luke describes in the book of Acts how after Jesus' resurrection, the Holy Spirit fell upon the disciples as tongues of fire. "All of them were filled with the Holy Spirit and began to speak in other languages, as the Spirit gave them ability" (Acts 2:4).

The birthday of the church was marked by the promised coming of the Holy Spirit. In the centuries since the death of Jesus, the Spirit of Christ has animated the church and given it the wisdom to witness in new contexts and challenging situations. The link between text and context becomes possible in the power of the Holy Spirit. While the Bible is the foundation of our faith, it is not a blueprint or users' manual for exactly how to be in mission in different times and places. Sent in mission by the Holy Spirit, Christians combine text and context in creative synthesis and bring forth new insights relevant to the situation at hand. To speak in terms missionaries often use, the Gospel must find "points of contact" with the cultures and events important to the people it encounters.

For mission to be effective, the Good News must meet the real world. For mission to be faithful, it must be grounded in the Scriptures, guided by the Holy Spirit, and pointed toward the kingdom of God. To be part of the *ekklesia*, the called-out community, means to live according to the kingdom vision of salvation and liberation for all of God's creation. Because the task of the church is to communicate God's love to a complicated and diverse world, there are many different ways to be in mission.

Biblical Models of the Church in Mission

Led by the Holy Spirit, early Christians witnessed to the Gospel message in many ways. Their mission practices grew naturally from the situations in which they found themselves. Both the book of Acts and Paul's letters describe young churches that tried to remain faithful to the way of Christ while they lived in the cities and towns of the Roman empire. Just as today, early Christians faced competing religions and worldviews, war, poverty, and unstable family lives. Unlike most Americans today,

Pentecost

they also lived in a society marked by slavery, a complete lack of social safety nets, no legal rights for women and children, rampant violence, epidemic-level disease and filth, and widespread fear of evil spirits.

Living a Christian life meant upholding a visible alternative community of love and concern for others. To live as a Christian was to reject the law of the streets and to care for the poor and the vulnerable. It meant rejecting idolatry, decadent lifestyles, and practices associated with worshiping other gods. It meant suffering persecution. It meant repenting from sin and worshiping God in the joy of salvation. A description of early Christian witness appeared in a second-century letter to the enquirer Diognetus:

> Christians love all men, but all men persecute them. Condemned because they are not understood, they are put to death, but raised to life again. They live in poverty, but enrich many; they are totally destitute, but possess an abundance of everything. They suffer dishonor, but that is their glory. They are defamed, but vindicated. A blessing is their answer to abuse, deference their response to insult. For the good they do they receive the punishment of malefactors, but even then they, rejoice, as though receiving the gift of life. . . . As the soul is present in every part of the body, while remaining distinct from it, so Christians are found in all the cities of the world, but cannot be identified with the world. . . . Christians love those who hate them just as the soul loves the body and all its members despite the body's hatred. It is by the soul, enclosed within the body, that the body is held together, and similarly, it is by the Christians, detained in the world as in a prison, that the world is held together. [11]

In this description of the witnessing community, mission unfolds in multiple ways—as loving the people who hate you, as peacefully accepting persecution, and as serving the world without being defined by it.

In the Bible, it is impossible to talk about mission without talking about the church, and it is impossible to talk about the church without talking about mission.

Biblical scholar Donald Senior shows that the nature of the church and the meaning of mission as practiced by early Christians could not be separated. When the church reached out, it defined itself in new ways. The multiple images of mission in the New Testament give us confidence that Christians in the twenty-first century can engage in many forms of mission while remaining faithful to the Spirit of Christ.

Of the many images of mission in the New Testament, there are three major patterns. [12] Exploring these will give us a deeper understanding of the possibilities for the church in mission today. And because being in mission means being the church, these images of mission deepen our understanding of the nature of the church itself. In the Bible, it is impossible to talk about mission without talking about the church, and it is impossible to talk about the church without talking about mission. Mission and church cannot be separated in the three major categories of mission in the New Testament:

1. Proclaiming the Gospel to the world
2. Witnessing through love and holiness
3. Inclusion through healing and receiving.

Proclaiming the Gospel to the World

How shall the gospel be proclaimed that
sinners may repent?
How shall the world find peace at last if
heralds are not sent?
So send us, Lord, for we rejoice to speak
of Christ with life and voice.

["How Shall They Hear the Word of God." Words: Michael Perry. © 1982 Mrs. Beatrice Perry/Admin by The Jubilate Group/Hope Publishing Company, Carol Stream, IL 60188. All rights reserved. Used by permission.]

The first biblical image for mission is *proclaiming the Gospel to the world.* As we saw in the last chapter, during his lifetime Jesus sent the disciples to proclaim the kingdom of God to the people of Israel. After his resurrection, he sent them out again. With the coming of the Holy Spirit, the disciples gained the courage to move beyond their own national borders. In the power of the Spirit, the followers of Jesus went into Africa, Asia, and Europe proclaiming the Gospel. As Peter quoted from the Old Testament to the crowd at Pentecost, "everyone who calls on the name of the Lord shall be saved" (Acts 2:21).

The apostle Paul saw proclamation of the Gospel as his calling from God. After he met the risen Jesus Christ on the road to Damascus, he knew that his mission in life was to preach that Jesus was the son of God (see Acts 9:20-22). As time went on, he saw more and more clearly that his own special calling was to preach the Gospel to the Gentiles and to found churches among them. As a Greek speaking Jew, he was a bridge over which the Good News passed from Jewish to Gentile communities.

The church in Antioch set apart Paul and Barnabas, blessed them, and sent them out as missionaries to Cyprus and Pamphylia. Paul was thrown out of many synagogues when he tried to preach that Jesus was the Messiah. But Gentiles responded to his message, and Paul decided to preach to them. Using words, signs,

St. Paul on the road to Damascus.

and deeds, Paul and Barnabas reached Gentiles with the message of salvation.

Later Paul worked in partnership with Silas, Timothy, and other evangelists throughout the Roman Empire. Paul's own description of his ministry is found in his letter to the church in Rome,

> "For I will not venture to speak of anything except what Christ has accomplished through me to win obedience from the Gentiles, by word and deed, by the power of signs and wonders, by the power of the Spirit of God, so that from Jerusalem and as far around as Illyricum I have fully proclaimed the good news of Christ. Thus I make it my ambition to proclaim the good news." (Romans 15:18-20)

Paul's desire in proclaiming the Gospel to both Jews and Gentiles was that people might believe in Jesus Christ, repent, and be saved. Without preachers, ordinary people would not have access to the message of Jesus Christ, the word of God. As Paul wrote to the Roman church,

> "'Everyone who calls on the names of the Lord shall be saved.'
>
> But how are they to call on one in whom they have not believed? And how are they to believe in one of whom they have never heard? And how are they to hear without someone to proclaim him? And how are they to proclaim him unless they are sent? . . . So faith comes from what is heard, and what is heard comes through the word of Christ." (Romans 10:13-17)

Following the example of the disciples, the apostle Paul, and others like Apollos, Barnabas, and Silas; one of the major images of mission in the New Testament is that of a community sent into the world to proclaim the Good News by word, sign, and deed.

Witnessing through Love and Holiness

We will walk with each other, we will
walk hand in hand.
And together we'll spread the news that
God is in our land.
And they'll know we are Christians by
our love, by our love,
Yes, they'll know we are Christians by
our love.

("They'll Know We Are Christians" ("We are One in the Spirit") by Peter Scholtes. © 1966 F.E.L. Assigned 1991 to The Lorenz Corporation. All rights reserved. International copyright secured.)

A second biblical image of mission is *witnessing to the love of God.* As Jesus prepared to be arrested, he gave the disciples a "new commandment" to prepare them for the days when he would no longer be with them.

> "I give you a new commandment, that you love one another. Just as I have loved you, you also should love one another. By this everyone will know that you are my disciples, if you have love for one another." (John 13:34-35)

The book of 1 Peter contains the most detailed description of the church as a community living according to its vision of God's kingdom rather than the competitive and violent ways of the world. Just as Jesus was holy, the church is called to be holy. Writing to believers scattered in exile, Peter reminds them that they are a "sanctified" or purified people chosen by God to live in a different way than the norm. The purpose of being a holy people is to reveal God's ways to the world.

> But you are a chosen race, a royal priesthood, a holy nation, God's own people, in order that you may proclaim the mighty acts of him who

called you out of darkness into his marvelous light. (1 Peter 2:9)

Peter exhorts the Christians to live disciplined lives of purity that will win over even non-Christian spouses and masters. Believers are to deal honestly and honorably with non-believers, so that they might glorify God. Relationships of respect give a public witness to the truths by which the church lives.

One of the realities of the life of love and holiness is that of suffering. The exiled believers to whom Peter is writing expect to suffer. Indeed, they have already suffered for their beliefs and their commitment to Jesus. The suffering of those who witness to Jesus—of "martyrs"—is part of the oneness of believers with him. Jesus' own suffering is replicated in the community of witnesses. Peter warns the community to be prepared for the end of human existence: "Therefore be serious and discipline yourselves for the sake of your prayers. Above all, maintain constant love for one another, for love covers a multitude of sins" (1 Peter 4:7-8). Just as Jesus suffered to show God's care for humanity, so the refusal of the persecuted church to engage in violence is a witness to God's love. Love for one another demonstrates God's love for the world.

Inclusion through Receiving and Healing

Help us accept each other as Christ
accepted us,
Teach us as sister, brother, each person
to embrace.
Be present, Lord, among us, and bring
us to believe
We are ourselves accepted and meant to
love and live.

("Help Us Accept Each Other." Words: Fred Kaan; Music: Doreen Potter. ©1975 Hope Publishing Company, Carol Stream, IL 60188. All rights reserved. Used by permission.)

The third major theme is the mission of *inclusion through receiving and healing.* Like the mission of proclamation, the mission of inclusion crosses boundaries to share the Gospel. In order to be complete, the action of being sent as apostles and of calling people into a community (*ekklesia*) requires the complementary action of receiving. When Jesus sent out his disciples, he instructed them to stay with people who welcomed them, and to eat the ordinary food they were given. Only as the people received the disciples could the Gospel be heard. Those sent in mission likewise needed to accept the hospitality of those they wished to reach. Receiving is an integral part of sending. Together, sending and receiving create mutual relationships through which the love of God is revealed.[13]

Jesus himself practiced radical forms of inclusion by eating with known sinners and outcasts, by calling a tax collector to be one of his disciples, and by welcoming as followers women of uncertain virtue (see Mark 2:13-17). As the disciples spread out in mission, many of the notable early converts were the unwanted people of the world—eunuchs, widows, foreigners, and soldiers from the hated imperial army. Early Christianity was pegged by outsiders as the religion for "losers"— for women, children, and slaves. But the model of inclusion became a powerful, counter-cultural witness to the power and love of God for all persons.

Early Christianity was pegged by outsiders as the religion for "losers"—for women, children, and slaves.

To be sent is to receive and to be received. And to be received into the Christian community is to find a safe, healing place in which to know the Lord. To be received into the Christian community allows hurting people to find a home and to feel love and connection with others. Much of the dynamic in the idea of inclusion is that of healing. Jesus and his disciples were healers. The healing ministry not only showed the power of God but also brought people into the community. "Healing or exorcism takes the form of liberation from evil and inclusion in a life-giving community."[14]

In the many stories of healing in the New Testament, a common theme is that of being an outcast. To be ill, whether physically or mentally, isolates people. Just as

HIV-AIDS and mental illness drive people apart today, lepers and people possessed by evil spirits were some of the loneliest and most isolated persons in Jesus' day. The Gerasene demoniac in Mark 5, for example, lived among the tombs, howled, and bruised himself with stones. After Jesus healed him, he was able to go home to his friends. Through his ministry of healing, Jesus

Jesus healing the sick.

was not indicating that all persons can automatically find physical healing by knowing him. But he was sending a strong message that the Good News includes everyone, even those commonly rejected as less than full persons.

The mission of inclusion challenges the church. The book of Acts and the Epistles are filled with examples of the church struggling with its mission of inclusion. In Acts 6, the issue of how to treat poor widows with equity required the election of deacons whose special job was to manage food distribution and charity. The problem was that Jewish widows were receiving more food than Greek widows. Even though the fellowship of Greeks and Jews within the church was a sign of the kingdom, to live with ethnic differences on a daily basis was not easy. In addition to ethnic tensions, another issue of inclusion was class differences. In 1 Corinthians 11–12, Paul's discussion of the church as the body of Christ focused on the need to care for and to respect the least members of the body. Because of economic and status issues in the Corinthian church, the Communion meal had left some people hungry, while others got drunk and had plenty of food. Such disparities in the treatment of people inside the church show that the mission of inclusion was a challenge to the early church, and it remains so today.

As with the images of mission as proclamation and as witness, the ultimate purpose of the mission of inclusion was to reveal God's own mission. In the book of Ephesians, Paul discusses the challenges of including both Greeks and Jews into one fellowship. Through Jesus Christ, the distinctions between them are broken down: "For he is our peace; in his flesh he has made both groups into one and has broken down the dividing wall, that is, the hostility between us" (Ephesians 2:14). Through his sacrifice, Christ created a "new humanity" in which Greek and Jew could reconcile in him. Jesus' death on the cross symbolized the "death of hostility" between different ethnicities. Now members of the same household of God, both Greeks and Jews have the same access to God through the Holy Spirit. No one ethnicity or class is better than another or more special to God. A core message of Jesus' mission was that of welcoming all to the house of the Lord.

The Church for the World

The study of the Scriptures shows us that the New Testament contains multiple images of the church in mission. Just as we do today, early Christians struggled to be faithful followers of Jesus Christ in their own context. They commissioned and sent out missionaries like Paul to proclaim the Gospel. Even though they faced persecution, they tried to live in holiness as witnesses to God's love. They welcomed Jews and Greeks, rich and poor, males and females, young and old, oppressors and victims into the household of faith, and included them in the body of Christ. Together these ways of being in mission reveal the fundamental purpose of the church: to be a sign of God's compassionate love for the whole world.

What can we learn from the early church in mission that applies to the multi-cultural world church today?

- To be the church is to be in mission; and to be in mission is to be the church.
- The church is sent into the world by God, grounded in the missionary nature of the Trinity, the *missio Dei*.
- The church lives to share Jesus' message of the kingdom of God, of salvation and liberation, in multiple contexts and situations.
- The church in mission proclaims the Gospel, witnesses to God's love, and welcomes all who wish to follow Jesus.

As Christians around the world seek to be faithful to God's mission, they find themselves in spiritual unity with one another. Jesus prayed that his followers would be one, so that the world would believe (see John 17:23). Visions of worldwide unity both point to the church's common mission and grow from it.

In 1908, an English Congregational church deacon and writer named William Arthur Dunkerley wrote some verses for a missionary exhibit by the London Missionary Society. In his poem "No East or West," the biblical missions of proclamation, of loving witness, and of inclusion come together in celebration of the worldwide church. First put to music in the mid 1920s, Dunkerley's poem became one of the great hymns of the ecumenical mission movement of the twentieth century, and is a fitting conclusion to this chapter on the church in mission.

> In Christ there is no east or west, in
> him no south or north;
> But one great fellowship of love
> throughout the whole wide earth.
>
> In Christ shall true hearts everywhere
> their high communion find;
> His service is the golden cord close
> binding humankind.
>
> In Christ is neither Jew nor Greek,
> and neither slave nor free;
> Both male and female heirs are made,
> and all are kin to me.
>
> In Christ now meet both east and
> west, in him meet south and north;
> All Christly souls are one in him
> throughout the whole wide earth

CHAPTER NOTES

1. "I am the church!" http://vids.myspace.com/index.cfm?fuseaction=vids.individual&VideoID=14099118 (accessed June 5, 2009).
2. John Driver, *Images of the Church in Mission* (Scottdale, PA: Herald Press, 1997), 44.
3. For the classic overview of Protestant mission theology, see David Bosch, *Transforming Mission* (Maryknoll, NY: Orbis, 1991).
4. Ion Bria, *The Liturgy after the Liturgy: Mission and Witness from an Orthodox Perspective* (Geneva: WCC Publications, 1996).
5. General Board of Global Ministries, "Why We are Volunteers." http://new.gbgm-umc.org/about/us/mv/ (accessed November 2, 2008).
6. Theme of William Carey's address to the annual Baptist association meeting in England, May 30, 1792, on the eve of the founding of what became the Baptist Missionary Society. For additional information on William Carey and other Protestant pioneer mission thinkers, see the History of Missiology website at http://digilib.bu.edu/mission.
7. The United Methodist Church, *Grace Upon Grace: The Mission Statement of the United Methodist Church* (Nashville: Graded Press, 1990), 4.
8. Ibid., 5.
9. Ibid., 4.
10. Ibid., 7.
11. Spiritual Theology Department of the Pontifical University of the Holy Cross, "From a letter to Diognetus: the Christian in the World." http://www.vatican.va/spirit/documents/spirit_20010522_diogneto_en.html (accessed June 2, 2009).
12. See Donald Senior, "Correlating Images of Church and Images of Mission in the New Testament," *Missiology* 23, no. 1 (1995): 3–16.
13. On the spirituality of sending and receiving in mission, see Anthony Gittins, *Ministry at the Margins: Strategy and Spirituality for Mission* (Maryknoll, NY: Orbis, 2002).
14. Senior, 12.
15. For the original version, see John Oxenham [pseud], "No East or West," *Bees in Amber: A Little Book of Thoughtful Verse* (1913). http://www.gutenberg.org/dirs/etext06/8bees10.txt (accessed June 2, 2009).

Chapter Six

United Methodist Mission Traditions

O for a thousand tongues to sing my
   great Redeemer's praise,
The glories of my God and King,
   the triumphs of his grace!

My gracious Master and my God, assist
   me to proclaim,
To spread through all the earth abroad
   the honors of thy name.

Jesus! the name that charms our fears,
   that bids our sorrows cease;
'tis music in the sinner's ears, 'tis life,
   and health, and peace.

He breaks the power of canceled sin, he
   sets the prisoner free;
His blood can make the foulest clean; his
   blood availed for me.

He speaks, and listening to his voice,
   new life the dead receive;
The mournful, broken hearts rejoice, the
   humble poor believe.

Hear him, ye deaf; his praise, ye dumb,
   your loosened tongues employ;
Ye blind, behold your Savior come, and
   leap, ye lame, for joy.

In Christ, your head, you then shall
   know, shall feel your sins forgiven;
Anticipate your heaven below, and own
   that love is heaven.

—Charles Wesley

This passionate poem, written by Charles Wesley, has been hymn number one in nearly every Methodist hymnal since John Wesley published *A Collection of Hymns for the People called Methodists* in 1780. Charles wrote the poem to commemorate the first anniversary of his conversion in 1738. At the time of his conversion, he was ill and being cared for by devout Christian friends. His despair turned into joy when he read the Bible and realized that the peace and protection of the loving Christ applied to him personally. The next day his strength began to return, and he wrote the first of more than six thousand hymns. After writing this poem in 1739, he asked that it be sung by Christians on the anniversary of their conversions.

The Methodism of the Wesley brothers became one of the greatest migratory and cross-cultural mission movements in the history of Christianity. It spread throughout the British Isles and Ireland and traveled to North America with emigrants in the 1700s. Approximately one-third of the early American Methodists were African Americans. Despite hostility and severe persecution by slave owners, Methodism spread among African slaves in the Caribbean. Former slaves took Methodism with them when they founded Liberia and Sierra Leone in West Africa. Methodist ideas and practices also spread in the 1700s among German immigrants in the United States, under leaders like Philip Otterbein and Jacob Albright, the forerunners of the Evangelical United Brethren Church.

Under Bishop Francis Asbury, Methodism moved across the United States so that by 1850 it comprised 34 percent of the churchgoing population. A brilliant mission strategist, Asbury perfected a system in which young, itinerant ministers worked the margins of the American population, seeking out poor immigrants, former slaves, and frontier folk, and founding class meetings among them. Two Congregationalists reporting on Methodism noted in 1814,

> "This denomination has greatly increased within a few years, and this must chiefly be attributed to their complete system of missions, which is by far the best for domestic missions ever yet adopted. They send their laborers into every corner of the country; if they hear of any particular attention to religion in a place, they double the number of laborers in those circuits, and place their best men there, and endeavor generally, to adapt the character of their preachers, to the character of the people among whom they are to labor." [1]

In the early days of American Methodism, there was no distinction made between missionary and preacher, and early historians used the words interchangeably.

Methodism moved into South Africa and Australia along with settlers from Great Britain in the early 1800s. Missionaries spread the faith to Latin America, Southeast Asia, India, China, Germany, Italy, and Bulgaria in the mid to late 1800s. By the mid-1800s, strong indigenous Methodist leaders in Africa and the South Pacific had emerged. From the 1880s, Methodist revivalists began founding their own churches in Africa and Asia, in many cases breaking off from white missionary control. American missionaries in the 1880s and 1890s spread Methodism to Korea and the Philippines, both of which became denominational strongholds. In South Africa during the twentieth century, Methodism remained the largest interracial church. It continued to expand, as Methodists moved into Congo, Russia, Nepal, and other countries.

By the end of the twentieth century, there were seventy-five million Methodists worldwide. Numerous "daughter" churches, such as the Nazarenes, Church of God, Salvation Army, and Church of God in Christ left behind the Methodist name but kept many of its core beliefs and early practices. Other Methodist denominations merged into national churches like the United Church of Canada, the Church of South India, and the Uniting Church of Australia.

Charles Wesley's vision of "a thousand tongues to sing" heralded the founding of a worldwide family of churches. In light of the global nature of Christianity today, the question is how and why does Methodism appeal to so many? What is distinctive about its mission and message? What is the special contribution of the Methodist family to the Gospel? And more specifically, what is the mission of United Methodism in the world today?

The Mission Message of Methodism

While the reasons for the expansion of Methodism are complex and have attracted the attention of many historians,[2] its basic message can be seen in Charles Wesley's hymn: the grace and power of the Good News of Jesus Christ. In response to his healing experience of God's love, Charles Wesley wanted to celebrate! His desire to praise God with a thousand tongues came in response to the victory of grace in his life: "The glories of my God and King, the triumphs of his grace." Through Jesus, Wesley experienced new hope. He was liberated from the paralyzing fear caused by his own sense of sin, inadequacy, and ill health: "Jesus! the name that charms our fears, that bids our sorrows cease; 'tis music in the sinner's ears, 'tis life and health and peace." His response to renewed life, health, and peace was the desire to be in mission for Jesus Christ "—'to spread through all the earth abroad the honor of thy name."

Although his language may seem old-fashioned and even condescending to people today, Wesley's vivid picture of the inbreaking kingdom of God included the liberation of people from disease and physical handicaps: "Hear him ye deaf, his praise ye dumb, your loosened tongues employ; ye blind behold your savior come, and leap ye lame for joy." Jesus' ultimate victory over suffering was not limited to abstract notions of sin, but included the physical realm of life, as shown in the Gospels when he healed the blind, the deaf, and the paralyzed (see e.g., John 9; Mark 10:46-52; Mark 7:32-37; Matthew 9:2-7).

The morning breaks, the shadows flee,
pure Universal Love thou art:
To me, to all, thy mercies move—
thy nature, and thy name is Love.[3]

The Kingdom of God

The kingdom of God was the main topic of Jesus' preaching. Judaism had long taught that God's reign would bring justice to earth, and some expected this to happen through a messianic figure. Thus, Christian belief in Jesus as the Messiah is rooted in Jesus' teaching about the kingdom of God. Jesus taught that the kingdom of God was concerned with all aspects of life, personal and social. He taught that while the inbreaking of the kingdom was a work of God it also required human participation. Jesus' exorcisms and healings demonstrated that the kingdom brought both spiritual and physical transformation. Jesus also taught that full realization of the kingdom lay in the future. Thus, Christians today speak of the kingdom of God as being "both now and not yet." It was initiated in Jesus' life, death, and resurrection, but it will not be complete until Christ's second coming.

Grace

Wesley scholar Richard P. Heitzenrater defines grace as "God's transforming presence/power within us." Original sin isolates us from God's presence, but God's unmerited grace convicts us of our sin and allows us to repent and turn to God in faith (prevenient grace). Out of grace, God forgives us our sin (justifying grace) and enables us to do good works and grow in holiness (sanctifying grace).[4]

To Americans in the twenty-first century, the message that God is love, that God's grace is universal, and that Jesus died for all, may not seem revolutionary. After all, Americans pride themselves on believing in human equality and opportunity for everyone. But such was not the case in the 1700s, nor is it the case in much of the world today. People at the time of the Wesleys were locked into a vicious class system with little social mobility between rich and poor. Without widely shared ideas of human equality, slavery flourished. Factory workers and other laborers endured long hours with no days off, minimal pay, and sub-human working conditions. And even wealthier people had no decent medical or dental care, no antibiotics or pain killers, no electricity or sanitation systems, and no social security to fall back on if the bread winner got sick. Common ideas of "double predestination" assumed that people had little control over whether God would choose to save them for eternal life, or damn them to hell.

The core reason for the spread of Methodism was its message of free grace available to all, without exception. In Wesley's original poem—in a verse typically not sung in churches—Wesley wrote, "Harlots and publicans and thieves, in holy triumph join! Saved is the sinner that believes from crimes as great as mine." To Charles Wesley, God's saving grace through Jesus broke the grip of sin over the human personality. "He breaks the power of canceled sin, he sets the prisoner free." The grace of God flowed from God's nature, as pure love poured out on humanity. As Wesley wrote about God in his poem "Wrestling Jacob," one of his finest verses,

'Tis Love! 'tis Love! Thou diedst for me,
I hear thy whisper in my heart.

The message of God's love for every sinner and every sufferer and of Jesus' death for all rather than for just a few lucky ones remains a revolutionary message of hope, optimism, and empowerment for ordinary people. The Wesleys took their new message to the coal miners and other workers of the British Isles who were being ignored by the official Church of England. On one occasion in which John Wesley was forbidden to preach to the poor from the pulpit, he wrote a letter declaring that "the world is my parish." If he were not allowed to preach inside the church, he would go outside and preach in the fields to people neglected by the system. The idea of free grace for all carries with it the assumption that all people are equal, and all—including slaves, women, and day laborers—can find dignity in this life and eternal salvation in the next. Methodism's idea of universal human potential and persons transformed by the power of God's grace is a missionary theology. As old-time ministers might say, this message "preaches"!

On one occasion in which John Wesley was forbidden to preach to the poor from the pulpit, he wrote a letter declaring that "the world is my parish."

Methodism's great contribution to world Christianity is its heritage as a missionary movement of free grace. As stated in *Grace Upon Grace*, the official mission statement of the United Methodist Church (emphasis added), "We are a people called by God to be a people for God in the world. Recipients of grace, we become witnesses to grace. As United Methodists, we envision *lives changed by grace, a church formed by grace, and a world transformed by grace.*"[5]

Methodism's great contribution to world Christianity is its heritage as a missionary movement of free grace.

Free Grace in Methodist Mission History

The history of Methodism is partly the story of human failures, fights, and divisions. But the deeper message of Methodist history is the outpouring of God's grace through the mission and ministry of people formed by grace.

The message of free grace has given rise to distinctive traditions of mission practice. These traditions build upon the three major missional emphases of the New Testament—proclaiming the Gospel to the world, witnessing through love and holiness, and inclusion through receiving and healing—as discussed in the last chapter. But they also follow the Holy Spirit into new modes of discipleship. In his hymn "A Charge to Keep I Have," Charles Wesley's words apply to the believers' call to mission—"to serve the present age."

Transformed Lives

A central result of the reality of free grace throughout Methodist mission history is that of transformed lives through encounter with the Good News of Jesus Christ. Methodist history is full of personal testimonies, starting with those of its founders. The belief that Jesus died for one's own sins and the personal conviction of God's love and acceptance are historic hallmarks of Methodist identity. Experiences of God's acceptance come when people discover the church as a witnessing community and fellowship of love.

Early conversion stories reveal the revolutionary power of the Methodist message. Olaudah Equiano was a former slave from Nigeria, a seaman and explorer who became the most prominent African abolitionist of the 1700s. His autobiography published in 1789 was one of the first books written by an African, the first important first-person slave narrative. Equiano's life was lonely and difficult, as he had to worry constantly about being kidnapped back into slavery. A series of friendships with individual Christians enabled him to buy his freedom and learn to read. His life of struggle caused him to turn to the Bible for help in overcoming his problems and sense of worthlessness.

In chapter 10 of his autobiography, Equiano recounts how he met an old Christian sailor who shared with him about "the love of Christ to believers" and invited him to a "love feast," as early Methodist services were called. To Equiano's surprise, the chapel was full of people singing, praying, and speaking of their experiences of God's mercy. He was amazed that they "seemed to be altogether certain of their calling and election of God; and that no one could ever separate them from the love of Christ, or pluck them out of his hands." The group shared buns and water in mugs with everyone. Equiano wrote

> This kind of Christian fellowship I had never seen, nor ever thought of seeing on earth; it fully reminded me of what I had read in the holy scriptures, of the primitive Christians, who loved each other and broke bread. [6]

After the four-hour love feast, Equiano was overcome with a sense of the goodness of God, showed to even the worst sinner, and he prayed to God for salvation. Continued visits with the old Methodist seaman and his wife gave Equiano the assurance he needed that no matter what happened, God was with him in this life and the next.

Olaudah Equiano.

In early Methodism, as in the early church, lives were transformed by the free grace experienced in encounter with the worshiping community. Methodists welcomed Equiano as an equal in the love feast, and that experience changed his life.

Another person whose acceptance by the Methodist community transformed his life was William Apess, a Pequot Indian in New England. His mother was part African American of slave background. An indentured servant, Apess was abused and beaten by his alcoholic parents and by hard masters. Despite severe public opposition to the "noisy" and low class Methodists in 1810s Connecticut, Apess began attending their meetings.

Apess was especially affected by hearing a sermon on John 1:29 (KJV), "Behold the Lamb of God, which taketh away the sin of the world," preached by "Brother Hill" about Jesus taking on the sins of the world. Apess wrote in his autobiography of his conversion March 15, 1813,

> I felt convinced that Christ died for all mankind—that age, sect, color, country, or situation made no difference. I felt an assurance that I was included in the plan of redemption with all my brethren. No one can conceive with what joy I hailed this *new* doctrine, as it was called. It removed every excuse, and I freely believed that all I had to do was to look in faith upon the Lamb of God that made himself a free-will offering for my unregenerate and wicked soul upon the cross.[7]

Apess learned to read and write, and in 1829 he was ordained a minister in the Methodist Protestant Church. He served as minister among the Mashpee Indians on Cape Cod and agitated to have the unjust white overseer system removed. He was arrested, but his appeals led to the incorporation of the Mashpee Indian village as a town equal to others in Massachusetts.

The lives of Equiano and Apess demonstrate the amazing personal transformations that came through Methodist conversion. The experience of acceptance, of equality, and of free grace and forgiveness through the death of Jesus Christ, gave even former slaves and indentured servants new lives of hope. The Methodist message emphasized that even the most downtrodden people were equal to all under God. It also assumed that the poorest could improve themselves through self-discipline. The dignity expressed through hard work and personal self-control were important values to the ordinary people empowered by the Methodist movement.

Personal transformation created the self-discipline that made it possible to get an education. Both Equiano and Apess were remarkable for their literacy and writings. Apess's writings were the largest body of publications by a Native American before the 1840s. The radical Methodist message of personal empowerment led to the founding of thousands of schools in North America during the 1800s, including the education of girls and African Americans. Methodism founded the largest number of colleges and universities in America during the late 1800s and early 1900s. The vast network of Methodist schools is a direct result of the unique contribution of Methodist theology—belief in a God of love and free grace to all through the sacrifice of Jesus Christ for the transformation of persons and the improvement of society.

Organization for Cross-cultural Mission

For early Methodists, many of whom were migrants on the move, the message of free grace was too important to keep to themselves. The radical equality of free grace required carrying the message to persons of other cultures, races, and classes. Thomas Coke, one of Wesley's superintendents for America, was the greatest supporter of missions in early Methodism and almost single-handedly organized the spread of Methodism to the West Indies, Nova Scotia, and Sierra Leone. In 1786 he wrote the first Methodist missionary tract, and he was appointed head of the first missionary committee in 1790. He died in 1814 on shipboard while leading a group of preachers to India as missionaries.

In the United States formal organization for cross-cultural missions began in response to the appeal of John Stewart, a Virginian of mixed African and European descent. Suffering agony of soul, he joined a Methodist camp meeting near Marietta, Ohio, and obtained spiritual relief. Stewart became ill from resisting a call to preach and only recovered after agreeing to obey God. In a vision he heard God calling in the voice of a man and a woman telling him to preach to the Indians. Setting off in a northwesterly direction, Stewart sang and preached to the Delawares.

When he reached the Wyandott Indians in 1816, Stewart began singing and preaching to them, warning them to "flee the wrath to come." His ministry resulted in the conversion of a small band of followers. As was often the case on the frontier, rival missionaries quickly appeared on the scene to steal Stewart's converts and accused him of having no credentials from any organized group of Christians. Stung by the accusation but supported by his native converts, Stewart approached the Ohio Annual Conference and requested ordination. [8]

In 1819, the Ohio Conference recognized Stewart's call from God as part of the divine plan for the expansion of Methodism, and it immediately licensed him. The conference collected money for his work and appointed a regular missionary to follow with a circuit. Back in New York City, Methodists heard of Stewart's success and promptly organized the Methodist Missionary Society to raise money for missions and book publishing. Of the nine ministers who founded the society, six had been circuit rider/missionaries in Canada.

Leading women founded the New York Female Missionary Society, which assisted the missionary outreach through fund-raising, an idea that quickly spread to Methodist women in Albany, Boston, and other Methodist centers. Conversion, literacy, and the path toward education were interconnected in the Methodist mission ethic. Therefore in 1825, the women's society sent a circulating library to the Wyandott Indians. The women's society's greatest success came a few years later as a chief support for the new Liberia mission. These two societies, one general and one female auxiliary, were the first significant voluntary organizations American Methodists founded specifically for the mission of the church.

The example of John Stewart demonstrates the Methodist pattern during the early nineteenth century—expansion in obedience to the Holy Spirit, followed by sound organization. Despite requests in 1824 by African American settlers in Liberia for a missionary to organize churches, no experienced pastors would volunteer because of Liberia's reputation as the "white man's grave." Finally in 1832, the widower Rev. Melville Cox of Hallowell, Maine, already dying of tuberculosis, volunteered and was accepted. When told by a heckler at Wesleyan University that he would die in Liberia, Cox replied; then come write my epitaph, "Let a thousand fall before Africa be given up."[9]

Cox survived only three months, but he organized the Liberian church according to the Discipline, planned a school, bought a building, and held a camp meeting. The first reinforcements after his death lived about a month, with only one unmarried woman missionary who remained. Over the decades, most missionaries to Liberia died or were sent home as invalids.

Despite a permanent haze of malaria and the deaths of nearly all her colleagues, the Liberia missionary who provided continuity for nineteen years was the teacher Ann Wilkins—sustained by her holiness piety and by prayers, supplies, and correspondence from the New York Female Missionary Society. Wilkins founded the first Methodist girls' school abroad. Her correspondence with her mother also reveals that she was separated or divorced from her husband.

Wilkins and her female supporters' investment in education still matters nearly two hundred years later. Ellen Johnson-Sirleaf, the first female African head of state, elected president of Liberia in 2005, is a product of the Methodist girls' high school there. Gracia Machel, former first lady of Mozambique, also attended Methodist schools founded by missionaries, as did her husband Nelson Mandela, the former president of South Africa. As the pioneer cross-cultural educational missionary of United Methodism, Ann Wilkins deserves to be honored today.

Thomas Coke, who worked alone and died at sea; Stewart, an unlicensed mixed-race visionary; Cox, a widower on his deathbed; and Wilkins, a laywoman of uncertain marital status—these were a few of the pioneers

Ann Wilkins.

Ellen Johnson-Sirleaf.

of Methodist cross-cultural missions. They were "jars of clay" (2 Corinthians 4:7), empowered by the message of free grace to risk their lives for God in seemingly impossible circumstances. By the late twentieth century, the missionary movement they founded had spread around the world.

Social Holiness

Another central aspect of free grace through Methodist mission history is the commitment to social transformation. When preachers gathered to found the church in America in 1784, they declared as its purpose "To reform the continent, and to spread scriptural Holiness over these lands." One of the unique contributions of Methodism to the world church is the conviction that personal salvation is inseparable from working toward the "kingdom of God." The commitment to social transformation is often termed "social holiness," a phrase coined by John Wesley to mean that Gospel values must be practiced in community and not limited to individual persons.

The idea of social holiness was the starting point for a Methodist social ethic. John Wesley urged believers to practice "works of mercy," which he described as

> the feeding the hungry, the clothing the naked, the entertaining or assisting the stranger, the visiting those that are sick or in prison, the comforting the afflicted, the instructing the ignorant, the reproving the wicked, the exhorting and encouraging the well-doer; and if there be any other work of mercy, it is equally included in this direction. [10]

"Works of mercy" comprise one key component of "social holiness" in Methodist mission tradition. The founding of small fellowship groups and churches were accompanied by outreach to the needy. One strong example of this was the work of Phoebe Palmer and other women in New York City. Palmer and her sister held regular meetings on Tuesdays for the promotion of holiness. Out of their commitment to the discipline of holiness, women divided the city into zones for systematic evangelization. They founded schools for poor children and undertook prison ministry.

Phoebe Palmer.

In 1850, Palmer founded the Five Points Mission in the worst slum in New York City. Gangs of thieves, sex trafficked young girls, prostitutes, and other hustlers crowded into filthy tenement houses. She persuaded Methodist men to buy a brewery at Five Points and then converted it into a settlement house with a chapel, classrooms, baths, and twenty units of low-income housing. By 1854, the Five Points House of Industry was providing five hundred jobs for abused women and girls. In 1858, Palmer and her home mission group had opened a home for young women who were pouring into the city in search of work, but who lacked safe housing.

In an age before government support of any kind for the poor, the comprehensive approach of the Five Points Mission became the model for similar church-based outreach over the next century. Missions and "institutional churches" came to characterize the

Methodist approach to social holiness. Ranging from holiness "rescue" missions in Chicago and San Francisco, to the Deaconess Hospital and Goodwill Industries in Boston, to social service centers in Cuba and Johannesburg, to industrial missions among factory workers in Japan and Korea, Methodists founded a vast network of "works of mercy."

By the late 1800s and early 1900s, the "kingdom of God" took hold in Methodist circles as a shorthand phrase for the missional task of social transformation. With the rise of the "social gospel" as a way to tackle the massive social problems of urbanization and industrialization, mission was increasingly framed as working for the "kingdom of God." Social transformation attempted to attack the causes of poverty and injustice rather than stopping at works of mercy, as important as those continued to be.

The roots of mission as social transformation lay in the anti-slavery activity of early Methodism. Not only did John Wesley oppose slavery, but his superintendents for America, Thomas Coke and Francis Asbury, threatened to excommunicate slaveholders. In 1785, they took an antislavery petition to George Washington. Early Methodist missionaries in the Caribbean suffered imprisonment and severe persecution for teaching slaves to read and opposing slavery. The logical extension of the idea of free grace even for slaves and outcasts spread to the institution of slavery itself. Coke's opposition to slavery and his support for missions were two sides of the same coin.

While later Methodism failed to uphold the anti-slavery ideal with consistency, the "DNA" of Methodist ideals of social transformation began with the issue of slavery and extended over time to include women's rights, anti-racism work, civil rights, and human rights for all of God's children. For missionaries in the 1970s alone, Methodist work for the "kingdom of God" included such issues as supporting land rights for the poor in the Philippines, standing in solidarity with the victims of dictatorship in Korea, supporting equality for outcastes and minorities in India, organizing boycotts to support farm workers in the Americas, opposing apartheid in South Africa and Rhodesia, and protesting U.S. military aid to Latin American military governments. While opposition to "principalities and powers" (Romans 8:38) has often resulted in severe penalties for and even persecution of the missionaries involved, visions of the reign of God give hope to seemingly hopeless causes.

The missionary whose ministry most embodied the ideals of the kingdom of God was E. Stanley Jones, called the "world's greatest Christian missionary" by *Time* magazine in 1938. Throughout his career as evangelist to hundreds of thousands in India, Jones opposed the imposition of stagnant, Western forms of the church. He worked to contextualize the Gospel in Indian form, as reflected in the title of his most famous book, *The Christ of the Indian Road*. An early supporter of Indian nationalism, Jones opposed the continued British control of India and befriended Gandhi, the great leader of the independence movement. The British responded to Jones' influence by closing down his *ashrams* (religious communities) and banning him from India in the 1940s.

Throughout his ministry, Jones' inspiration came from deep prayer and the idea of the kingdom of God. Through it he came to embrace the restructuring of society toward peace and justice. In his 1972 book *The Unshakable Kingdom and the Unchanging Person*, he called for a rediscovery of the kingdom as a "total life plan to be practiced now, both in individual and collective life."[11] As did Wesley, Jones used the Sermon on the Mount (Matthew 5–7) as the foundation for the kingdom on earth, along with Jesus' own announcement of the inbreaking reign of God. While the entrance to the kingdom lay in individual commitment through Jesus Christ, the kingdom itself covered all of life.

As a cross-cultural missionary, E. Stanley Jones could see the dangers of a triumphalist North American church that too easily equated itself with God's reign.

Of all mission thinkers in the twentieth century, E. Stanley Jones most clearly articulated the "classic" Methodist mission theory of personal faith in Christ combined with social holiness. Jones also warned against reducing the idea of the kingdom to the culture and ways of the North American church. From his vantage point as a cross-cultural missionary, he could see the dangers of a triumphalist North American church that too easily equated itself with God's reign. Jones' dual emphasis on personal transformation and God's kingdom, and his warnings against the cultural captivity of the church, have been extended in the writings of José Miguez-Bonino, Mortimer Arias, and other noted Latin American Methodist mission theologians of the late twentieth century.

Creative Tensions in Mission Practice

While a full treatment of Methodist missions is too large a subject to consider here, it is important to mention some of the creative tensions that routinely cut across mission practice. The strength of Methodist mission tradition flows from the dedication of its people. But it also results from a holistic and practical approach that maintains creative tensions between the movement of the Holy Spirit and human organization, evangelism and mission, and individual vocation and general discipleship. These tensions occur in different forms throughout the history of Methodism, and they continue today.

Spirit and Organization

As shown in the stories above, the origins of Methodist mission lie in the message of free grace. The early converts and pioneer missionaries of the Methodist movement were called and energized by the Holy Spirit. At the same time, sound human organization was necessary to conserve the Spirit's work. As we have seen, John Stewart was called into mission by the voice of the Holy Spirit. But without the organizing of the mission society to support and follow up his ministry, mission work like his would not have delivered lasting results.

The call of the Holy Spirit and the founding of stable structures go together. Maintaining their balance was never easy and is not easy today. New pathways emerge when administrative structures become too ponderous or inflexible to accommodate the movement of the Spirit. Sometimes tensions arise between laypeople and structures under clergy control. For example, the Volunteers in Mission Program was founded partly out of frustration with the expansion of church bureaucracy in the 1970s that multiplied staff positions while failing to encourage personal participation by laypeople. UMVIM has been successful because it fuses people's need to serve with sound organization. Ultimately the persistence of UMVIM assisted denominational structures to become more responsive to the needs of the laity for hands-on mission service.

Another example was the work of Bishop William Taylor in the late 1800s. Taylor was a freelance evangelist, and he preached around the world. His high view of the Holy Spirit meant that he worked in partnership with local people. In South Africa, for example, he preached to Zulus in 1866. His translator, Charles Pamla, also became an effective evangelist who brought twenty-five thousand converts into Methodism. British missionaries and local preachers organized the church, and Pamla was appointed evangelist at the church's first conference in 1883. Today the Methodist Church of Southern Africa remains the largest interracial church in the country.

Charles Pamla.

William Taylor, Story of my life: an account of what I have thought and said and done in my ministry of more than fifty-three years in Christian lands and among the heathen (Toronto: W. Briggs, 1895), 372.

Taylor took groups of faith missionaries to open missions in India, Angola, and South America. Because "Taylor" missionaries had very little financial or structural support, many died or left the work. Some founded other denominations. One moving record of Taylor missions lies in the scrapbook of the Withey family, who went to Angola in the late 1800s from a working-class church in Lynn, Massachusetts. The scrapbook shows the church sending the Witheys on a tiny ship to a malaria-filled outpost in Angola in response to an appeal by Bishop Taylor. While the Withey family persevered as missionaries for several generations, the scrapbook ends with pictures of some of their premature graves.

After the death of Bishop Taylor himself, many of the "Taylor" missionaries were taken under the wing of the Methodist Mission Board. Otherwise they would not have survived. And yet the founding of Methodism in Angola and several countries in Latin America can be traced to the risky pioneer Taylor faith missions. Expansion in Methodist mission occurs when both elements are present—the call of the Holy Spirit upon the hearts of people and the founding of flexible yet supportive structures to back them up. When the Spirit outruns the organization, little progress is made. When organization stifles the Spirit, the church turns inward and dies.

Evangelism, Social Justice, and Mission

The hallmark of Methodist mission has been its creative combination of personal evangelism—telling the story of Jesus and calling people to follow him; and of social holiness—working in disciplined community to make the world a better place. As we saw in the life of the Native American Methodist preacher William Apess, his decision to follow Jesus ultimately led him to advocate for the civil rights of the Mashpee Indians. In Methodist tradition, evangelism and social justice are inseparable.

And yet in practice it can be very difficult to keep the two interconnected. On the one hand, the human tendency is to privatize the call to follow Jesus so that it has few social responsibilities. On the other hand, it is often easier for Americans to stay busy working for social justice than to share their faith in Christ. Many United Methodists find it difficult to state the theological or spiritual reasons behind such good works as founding soup kitchens and working for low-income housing. Fights about the proper balance between evangelism and social justice become politicized whenever evangelism is targeted as "conservative," and social justice is termed "liberal." Because of human weakness, it is hard to do both equally well.

In Methodist tradition, evangelism and social justice are inseparable.

Sometimes evangelism is limited to personal testimony while social transformation is seen as a synonym for "mission," and they are put in competition with each other. In some discussions, mission and evangelism are connected to separate biblical mandates. The so-called "cultural" mandate of "love your neighbor as yourself" (Matthew 22:39) is pitted against the "evangelical" mandate of "therefore go and make disciples of all nations" (Matthew 28:19). Should eternal salvation take priority over caring for God's creation? Should concern for liberation override human need for a relationship with God?

In Methodist tradition, evangelism and mission cannot be quantified and then debated as a 50/50, 60/40, or 40/60 proposition. John Wesley's concern for the souls of coal miners was inseparable from his efforts to feed the hungry, clothe the poor, and visit the prisoners. Together, personal and social transformation constitute the mission of the church.

A helpful metaphor about the relationship of evangelism to mission is that of the heart to the body. Mission is the body. It walks and moves in different contexts and reacts to changing circumstances and conditions. The tasks of mission differ depending on the needs of the day. Sometimes the hands are busy and sometimes the feet. Sometimes the eyes are ineffective because the night is so dark that they are useless and the hands are needed to feel the way. At other times the hands are full and the way must be made by sight alone.

But always the heart beats, sending the blood through the body, nourishing the other organs and keeping the body alive. Evangelism is the heart. It is both the pump that circulates the life force and the seat of the emotions. Without the emotional fervor of the heart, the love of Christ and desire to make him known, mission dies. To separate the heart from the body is to kill the body. To take evangelism out of mission is to cut the life out of it. At the same time, a heart pumping for itself, unconnected to a body at work in the world, is not very useful. For United Methodists, evangelism is the heart of mission. [12]

General Calls to Discipleship and the Missionary Call

Another of the creative tensions that runs through mission history and practice is that between the general call to discipleship and the specific call to the missionary vocation. As we have seen in chapters 4 and 5, to be a follower of Jesus Christ is to be in mission. All Christians are sent by God into the world as witnesses.

Yet while all Christians are called to discipleship, the church has always set aside persons with a special call to full-time mission and ministry. On the road to Damascus, Paul was called by Jesus to be an apostle. Although Paul's calling came directly from the Lord, he also carried the stamp of approval from the Christians of Jerusalem (see Acts 15) and carried offerings from one group of Christians to another. The difficult nature of Paul's evangelistic work among the Gentiles required a lifetime commitment. It required changing his name from Saul to Paul as a visible symbol of his task. It required that he become a "missionary."

John and Charles Wesley were profoundly affected by the Moravians, one of the earliest groups of Protestants. Moravians emphasized prayer, Bible reading, and strong community life. On their way to Georgia as missionaries in 1735, the Wesley brothers were impressed by the calm bravery and hymn singing of Moravian women and children during a violent storm at sea. Throughout history, the Moravians have sent more missionaries, for their size, than any other church.

Traditionally they divided themselves into two groups—those who went as missionaries and those who supported them. Each group was equally important. The Moravians graphically demonstrate that the ordinary mission of discipleship should not be separated from the special apostolic call.

For United Methodists, evangelism is the heart of mission.

The twenty-first century provides an unprecedented opportunity for ordinary Christians to become actively involved in God's mission. The new context of the global church makes much of this flexibility possible, along with ease of communication and transportation. The middle class can also afford mission trips and projects in a way that was impossible for previous generations.

But progress in mission outreach requires long-term and sustained commitments. It is also the privilege of the church to support those whom God calls into full-time mission and ministry. Mission workers make visible the connectedness and unity of the Christians who send them. Without Paul, Thomas Coke, John Stewart, Melville Cox, Ann Wilkins, Phoebe Palmer, E. Stanley Jones, and those who supported them, the Good News would have remained boxed up and domesticated. In reality, increased commitment to the ordinary mission of discipleship and sacrificial support of representative full-time mission workers go hand in hand.

The Paradox of Free Grace

As the historical record shows, the greatest contribution of the Methodist movement has been the message of free grace, of God's love, forgiveness, and acceptance poured out upon all of creation. The United Methodist statement on missions, *Grace Upon Grace,* points out clearly that mission is grounded in the nature of God as love. As Charles Wesley wrote of God, "pure Universal Love thou art."

Mission is the natural response to God's gracious love. This view of mission is based on the first chapter of John's Gospel. Jesus is the Word of God from whom the fullness of grace, "grace upon grace," spills over into blessings for all. Safely grounded in God's love made visible in Jesus Christ, the believer loves God back through fellowship, evangelism, and service.

The paradox of free grace is that those who are conscious of receiving it work so hard! Because God's grace unleashes human potential, it creates the confidence to strive for personal and social holiness. Thus United Methodists are also heirs to a tradition of institution building, multiple programs and projects, all manner of good works, and extreme busyness. The blessings of grace create not only a desire to serve others but also a positive view of human nature that creates a frenzy of activity. Sometimes it seems that United Methodist identity is more attached to endless committee meetings than to the theology of grace.

In the fall of 2004, the bishops of The United Methodist Church united around a shared denominational vision of mission, expressed as "Making disciples of Jesus Christ for the transformation of the world." This phrase distilled two years of discussion by the bishops and their identification of seven "vision pathways" in which they committed themselves to provide leadership throughout the denomination, including across the general agencies of the church. The vision pathways led to concrete goals, or Four Areas of Focus: 1) combating the diseases of poverty by improving health globally; 2) engaging in ministry with the poor; 3) creating new places for new people and revitalizing existing congregations; 4) developing principled Christian leaders for the church and the world. In the report of the planning team, the bishops noted:

> John Wesley affirmed personal holiness and social holiness as the twin spires of the Christian faith. We join in affirming that there is no personal holiness apart from social holiness. Invitation into the Body of Christ and formation through the Body of Christ cannot be separated from bearing witness to and advocating for the Reign

of God in all of creation. Disciples of Jesus do not just believe in Christ, they follow Christ into the world. And, the Church will not be in the world without effective systems of reaching, forming, equipping and sending disciples. [13]

"Making disciples of Jesus Christ for the transformation of the world" attempts to recapture the historic Methodism mission vision. It echoes the Great Commission and concentrates on discipleship as found in the book of Matthew. [14] Its dual structure of "making disciples" and "transforming the world" links the awakening of the individual with a higher purpose and links evangelism with social justice. This "new" mission vision is consistent with those that have gone before, such as E. Stanley Jones' dual emphasis on the person of Christ and the kingdom of God; or Belle Bennett's commitment to salvation for the individual, and the kingdom of God for humanity. [15]

While the new motto has brought excitement and a renewed focus on discipleship, it carries with it the danger of forgetting that mission flows from the nature of God, the *missio Dei*. Our commitment to mission is our joyous response to God's gift of love: "Joy to the World!" Mission is not a set of programs put into place for the sake of strengthening local congregations. God gave his only Son for the sake of the world, not for the sake of the church (John 3:16). It is God working through us who makes disciples. We do not have the power to transform the world apart from God's "grace upon grace," poured out through God the Creator, Son, and Holy Spirit. Without the power of God's love, we will neither make disciples nor transform the world.

While the role of the bishops is to guide the church as an institution, laypeople are called to dance and sing the song of grace. As we see from Methodist history, the message of grace is all about taking risks, of moving toward the margins and into the world according to the call of the Holy Spirit. At the period of Methodism's greatest expansion in the mid 1800s, the *Book of Discipline* was only five inches tall and half an inch thick.

In the context of Christianity as a worldwide religion today, our call to mission as United Methodists is to celebrate God's love. The paradox of grace is that because we are "safe in the arms of Jesus," to quote blind hymn writer Fanny Crosby, we are free to take risks and to cross boundaries of unbelief, sin, injustice, and suffering. Because God loves us, we are free to make disciples and to transform the world. Let us sing with Charles Wesley,

> O for a thousand tongues to sing my
>   great Redeemer's praise,
> The glories of my God and King, the
>   triumphs of his grace!
>
> My gracious Master and my God,
>   assist me to proclaim,
> To spread through all the earth abroad
>   the honors of thy name.
>
> Jesus! the name that charms our fears,
>   that bids our sorrows cease;
> 'tis music in the sinner's ears, 'tis life,
>   and health, and peace.
>
> He breaks the power of canceled sin,
>   he sets the prisoner free;
> His blood can make the foulest clean;
>   his blood availed for me.
>
> He speaks, and listening to his voice,
>   new life the dead receive;
> The mournful, broken hearts rejoice,
>   the humble poor believe.
>
> Hear him, ye deaf; his praise, ye dumb,
>   your loosened tongues employ;
> Ye blind, behold your Savior come,
>   and leap, ye lame, for joy.
>
> In Christ, your head, you then shall
>   know, shall feel your sins forgiven;
> Anticipate your heaven below, and
>   own that love is heaven.

CHAPTER NOTES

1. Quoted in Nathan Hatch, *The Democratization of American Christianity* (New·Haven: Yale University Press, 1989), 89.
2. See, for example, David Hempton *Methodism: Empire of Spirit* (New Haven: Yale University Press, 2006); Charles Yrigoyen, Jr., ed., *The Global Impact of the Wesleyan Traditions and their Related Movements* (Lanham, MD: Scarecrow Press, 2002).
3. Charles Wesley, "Come, O Thou Traveler Unknown," *The United Methodist Hymnal* (Nashville, The United Methodist Publishing House, 1989), 387.
4. Richard Heitzenrater, communication to author, May 31, 2009. See also his sermon "The best of all is, God is with us," in Elisabeth Stagg, ed., *With God in Mind: Sermons on the Art and Architecture of Duke Divinity School* (Durham: Duke University Divinity School, 2008).
5. The United Methodist Church, *Grace Upon Grace: The Mission Statement of the United Methodist Church* (Nashville: Graded Press, 1990), 4.
6. Olaudah Equiano, *The Interesting Narrative of the Life of Olaudah Equiano*, ed. Robert J. Allison, 2nd ed. (Boston: Bedford/ St. Martins, 2006), 171.
7. William Apess, *On Our Own Ground: The Complete Writings of William Apess, a Pequot*, ed. Barry O'Connell, Native Americans of the Northeast: Culture, History, and the Contemporary (Amherst, MA: University of Massachusetts Press, 1992), 19.
8. See *The Missionary Pioneer; or a brief memoir of the life, labours, and death of John Stewart, (man of colour,) founder under God, of the mission among the Wyandotts, at Upper Sandusky, Ohio* (New York: Joseph Mitchell printed by J.C. Totten, 1827); N.B.C. Love, *John Stewart, Missionary to the Wyandotts* (New York: Missionary Society of the Methodist Episcopal Church, n.d.).
9. See *Remains of Melville B. Cox, late missionary to Liberia, with a memoir* (Boston: Light and Horton, 1835).
10. John Wesley "Upon the Lord's Sermon on the Mount, VI," quoted in Joyce D. Sohl, *God's Mission. God's Song* (New York: Women's Division, GBGM, UMC, 2006).
11. E. Stanley Jones, *The Unshakable Kingdom and the Unchanging Person* (Nashville: Abingdon Press, 1972), 69.
12. See Dana L. Robert, "Evangelism as the Heart of Mission." Mission Evangelism Series # 1. (New York: General Board of Global Ministries, The United Methodist Church, 1998).
13. For more information on the Four Areas of Focus, see http://www.umc.org/site/c.lwL4KnN1LtH/b.4443111/k.D720/ Four_Areas_of_Ministry_Focus.htm(accessed September 15, 2009).
14. See chapter 4.
15. The motto "Making disciples for the transformation of the world" seems similar to the Discipline of the Methodist Church, which stated in 1939 that the purpose of missions was "to make the Lord Jesus Christ known to all peoples in all lands as their Divine Savior, to persuade them to become his disciples, and to gather these disciples into Christian Churches; to enlist them in the building of the Kingdom of God; to co-operate with these Churches; to promote world Christian Fellowship, and to bring to bear on all human life the spirit and principles of Christ." *Doctrines and Discipline of the Methodist Church, 1939,* (New York: Methodist Publishing House, 1939), 275.

⋛ Part 3 ⋚

Hope and Wholeness:
Practicing Mission Today

Chapter Seven

Hospitality as Mission

Do not neglect to show hospitality to strangers, for by doing that some have entertained angels without knowing it.
—Hebrews 13:2

On September 20, 2007, between fifteen and twenty thousand protestors marched on the small town of Jena, Louisiana. Six African American youth had been convicted of assault against a white student. The trial occurred against a backdrop of growing racial tension, and the young men faced the prospect of long prison sentences. Some months earlier, several nooses were hung from the limbs of a large tree where teenagers often gathered to hang out. White youngsters did not know that lynching was a brutal crime against African Americans earlier in American history. But to older Americans, the noose remained a symbol of racism every bit as powerful as a swastika or a burning cross. Dubbed the "Jena 6," the situation of the young men awaiting their sentences attracted attention from around the world. Their trial seemed yet another example of the United States' sad history of unequal justice for African Americans.

The largely white town of Jena, with a population of only three thousand, reacted with fear to the arrival of the mostly African American marchers. On September 20, stores and the town hall remained closed. People hesitated to leave their houses . . . except for the members of Nolley United Methodist Church. They erected a sign at the edge of town that proclaimed "Open Hearts. Open Minds. Open Doors." Members of the largely white congregation arrived in their church parking lot at 7 a.m. to greet the marchers. Led by the pastor, the Rev. Lyndle Bullard, Nolley UMC was the only place in town where marchers could use the toilet or rest. Said Bullard, "We just started greeting people and finding out where they were from. We thanked them for coming and welcomed them to Jena. We talked about hospitality." [1]

Marchers gather Sept. 20 in Washington for one of the regional rallies protesting the treatment of six African-American high school students following a series of racially charged incidents at their school in Jena, La.

A year after the peaceful demonstration in Jena, Reverend Bullard reflected, "I think the events of Sept. 20 changed my church. . . . I think it scared them at first that we were opening up the church, but when nothing happened to the church and they came up and spoke to the people who came, it opened up their hearts. Wonderful is the only way I can describe it." [2]

In the months following the protest march, the ministers in Jena led efforts to help the townspeople search their hearts and make sure that race and racism would not divide them in the future. The local paper commented, "Nearly everyone you talk to in Jena credits faith and religion for the community's evolution and ability to weather the storm that came with such events like the rally and the national media converging on Jena." [3] Early in 2008, what began as a one-week revival in a local church stretched into a nine-week event that drew hundreds of people nightly from the surrounding area and involved all the churches in town. The revival became the source of healing and reconciliation for the townspeople. Night after night, black and white people came together to worship and to share with one another. Reverend Bullard noted how the black and white ministers presented a united front and also held services of thanksgiving and interracial prayer meetings throughout the year.

In other concrete actions, one woman opened an Internet coffee shop so youth would have a place to socialize after school. The tree from which nooses had been hung was cut down for the rebuilding of the high school, which had burned down earlier. Blacks and whites visited one another's porches and hugged when they saw each other at the Wal-Mart. The Department of Justice opened a special program for high school students to help them deal with racial issues. United Methodists throughout the Louisiana Conference prayed for "justice and healing" in Jena. In September of 2008, the black Baptist pastor, Reverend Jimmy Young, summarized the spirit in Jena in the months after the revival:

> "In every city and state in this union, we have the problems we have here. . . . No legislation can be passed, no law made, to make people love one another. The only way is to change their heart

through God. And that has happened here. I think we've done well. I think we took the right steps for the positive changes to take place." [4]

Hospitality in Today's World

As the events in Jena show, transformational mission in today's divided world often begins with simple but courageous acts of hospitality. The biblical tradition of welcoming strangers is the beginning of Christian outreach. Hospitality to strangers breaks down the boundaries that separate people. When people reach beyond their own comfort zones and insecurities to welcome or to visit others, they demonstrate God's love for the whole world—including for outcasts, the poor, the needy, and those of different nationalities and races. The new relationships that occur are the pathway by which the assurance of God's love can pass from one person to the next. The mission of hospitality not only bridges human differences, but as the example of Nolley United Methodist Church in Jena shows, it also deepens the faith of those who practice it. Hospitality is a two-way street. The "give and take" of reaching out to strangers changes everyone—the giver, the receiver, and the communities in which they live.

The "give and take" of reaching out to strangers changes everyone—the giver, the receiver, and the communities in which they live.

The mission of hospitality is especially important in the twenty-first century. The world is full of people on the move. On average, 13 percent of Americans move every year. As neighborhoods change, Christians are called to welcome strangers into their communities. Emigrants leave rural villages to seek new homes in foreign cities where they can find work. Millions of people are separated from their families while they earn money to send back home—Filipina domestic servants in Saudi Arabia, Mexican farm workers in California, factory workers in China, day laborers in South Africa, and call-center staffers in India. Refugees flee wars in Sudan, Iraq, Afghanistan, Congo, Sri Lanka, and situations of violence. Young women from Moldova, Ukraine, Thailand, Cambodia, and other countries are transported across national lines for sex trafficking. All over the world, soldiers serve in outposts far from home.

With so many of the world's people in transition, there is no need to become a full-time missionary to a foreign country in order to begin the mission of hospitality. In the twenty-first century, even the smallest communities have opportunities to reach out to the poor or homeless or newly unemployed, to high school students, or to persons of other ethnicities, races, and religions. Catholic spiritual writer Henri Nouwen describes the movement from "hostility to hospitality" as creating "a free space where the stranger can enter and become a friend instead of an enemy."[5] Hospitality is the launching pad for mission anywhere and everywhere, and at any time.

Hospitality is the launching pad for mission.

Biblical and Historical Roots of Hospitality as Mission

The roots of the Christian vision of hospitality lie in Jesus' own life and ministry.[6] In Luke 14, Jesus dines at the house of an important leader. In the context of receiving hospitality, Jesus tells his hosts a parable: It seems that a man gave a great banquet and sent his servant to invite the guests. But one after another the invited guests made excuses. One had just bought a field and needed to inspect it; a second bought some oxen for his farm; and a third had recently married. They all declined the invitation. When he learned that potential guests were too busy to attend, the host of the banquet sent out his servants to invite "the poor and maimed and blind and lame." When even that action failed to fill the banquet hall, the master sent the servant to "the highways and hedges," with orders to fill the house with guests. But he declared that none of the original invitees would get to taste the delicious food of the banquet. (Luke 14:15-24)

One of the dinner guests, on hearing this, said to him, "Blessed is anyone who will eat bread in the kingdom of God!" Then Jesus said to him, "Someone gave a great dinner and invited many. At the time for the dinner he sent his slave to say to those who had been invited, 'Come; for everything is ready now.' But they all alike began to make excuses. The first said to him, 'I have bought a piece of land, and I must go out and see it; please accept my regrets.' Another said, 'I have bought five yoke of oxen, and I am going to try them out; please accept my regrets.' Another said, 'I have just been married, and therefore I cannot come.' So the slave returned and reported this to his master. Then the owner of the house became angry and said to his slave, 'Go out at once into the streets and lanes of the town and bring in the poor, the crippled, the blind, and the lame.' And the slave said, 'Sir, what you ordered has been done, and there is still room.' Then the master said to the slave, 'Go out into the roads and lanes, and compel people to come in, so that my house may be filled. For I tell you, none of those who were invited will taste my dinner.'" (Luke 14:15-24)

While this parable has been variously interpreted by scholars, it shows that the kingdom values Jesus came to announce were based on hospitality to strangers. It turns upside down the ways of the world, in which people only befriend others like themselves, or share with those who might help them get ahead in their jobs or personal lives. But in God's house, persons of all socioeconomic groups, nationalities, ages, and races eat together at the same table. Shared fellowship is a sign of God's reign. Welcoming the poor and eating with them are acts of faith that, despite how things may appear, God is really in charge.

While church people take for granted the ordinary "pot luck supper" to which all are invited to share food and fellowship, its deeper meaning lies in its connection to Jesus' practices. The books of Luke and Acts emphasize the fellowship of the table as a sign of human unity under God. The relationship between guest and host was frequently experienced by Jesus, who often dined at the homes of others and used discussions over meals to spread his teachings.[7] The sacred value of shared meal time was best expressed at the last supper, when Jesus gathered his disciples into an upper room and ate with them (Luke 22:7-23). The shared meal was a foretaste of the heavenly banquet, when the followers of Jesus will rejoice in the eternal presence of God.

The book of Matthew also emphasizes the importance of hospitality from the perspective of both host and guest. Shortly after Jesus' birth, his family became refugees in Egypt to escape King Herod's attempts to murder him. This meant that the child Jesus experienced what it was like to be a refugee in a foreign country, in need of charity and hospitality from Egyptians. Today the Coptic Christians of Egypt still use icons or paintings of the holy family as refugees to symbolize their spirituality and their important place in Christian history. Egyptians showed hospitality to a Jewish refugee family. In sheltering the baby Jesus, they welcomed God into their midst.

The child Jesus experienced what it was like to be a refugee in a foreign country, in need of charity and hospitality from Egyptians.

Matthew records the most profound words of Jesus about hospitality in chapter 25. As in the book of Luke, outreach to the stranger is lifted up as a sign of God's kingdom of justice and mercy. Jesus talks of the end times and God's final judgment.

> "Then the king will say to those at his right hand, 'Come, you that are blessed by my Father, inherit the kingdom prepared for you from the foundation of the world; for I was hungry and you gave me food, I was thirsty and you gave me something to drink, I was a stranger and you welcomed me, I was naked and you gave me clothing, I was sick and you took care of me, I was in prison and you visited me.' Then the righteous will answer him, 'Lord, when was it that we saw you hungry and gave you food, or thirsty and gave you something to drink? And when was it that we saw you a stranger and welcomed you, or naked and gave you clothing? And when was it that we saw you sick or in prison and visited you?' And the king will answer them, 'Truly, I tell you, just as you did it to one of the least of these who are members of my family, you did it to me.'" (Matthew 25:34-40)

Christine Pohl, in her important book on the practice of Christian hospitality, writes, "God's invitation into the Kingdom is tied to Christian hospitality in this life."[8]

In this famous passage from Matthew, it becomes clear that in caring for the unknown and needy "other," the followers of Jesus are caring for God. In God's kingdom, every person is valued and loved and carries the image of God inside himself or herself. Thus hospitality to strangers is a way to proclaim the Good News of God's love for all persons. Hospitality as a form of mission enacts what the great missionary Saint Francis meant when he allegedly said, "Preach the Gospel always, and when necessary use words."

The idea that Jesus Christ can be found in the stranger has energized ministries of hospitality throughout the history of Christianity. Monasteries sheltered and fed strangers in early Christian Europe. The root word of *hospitality* is the same as that for *hospital* and *hostel* and *hospice*. The founding of hospitals to care for the sick poor was an important pioneer ministry of churches over the centuries. Hostels sheltered pilgrims and strangers. The hospice movement is a modern-day effort to provide dignified care for the dying. John

Wesley, the founder of Methodism, insisted that his followers obey Jesus' words in Matthew 25 to feed the poor, clothe the naked, welcome strangers, and visit prisoners. Early Methodists founded societies to support the urban poor, who were needy strangers in the cruel cities of the industrial revolution.

"Preach the Gospel always, and when necessary use words." —*Saint Francis of Assisi*

One of the best known ministries of hospitality in the twentieth century was that of Dorothy Day in New York City. A newspaper journalist, Dorothy was profoundly moved by the plight of unemployed men in the 1920s. She was also inspired by the Catholic Church's historic stance on behalf of the poor. She partnered with a Catholic priest, Peter Maurin, to found a paper, *The Catholic Worker*. In the paper, they applied Catholic principles to support issues of economic justice. Day also founded Houses of Hospitality where the

homeless could live and where the unemployed could eat and keep warm. By 1938, in the midst of the Great Depression, her soup line at Mott St. in lower Manhattan was feeding twelve hundred people a day. A devout Christian who took Communion every day, Dorothy devoted her life to following Jesus' direct command to "feed the hungry." [9]

Dorothy Day continued her ministry to the hungry and homeless until her death in 1980. When asked why she did not focus only on changing social structures instead of providing hospitality to the poor, she replied that it was actually harder work and took more discipline to serve poor people day after day. The Catholic Worker movement supported social change, but its daily actions celebrated the divine worth of individual persons. This "personalist" philosophy was illustrated in the beautiful woodcuts of the movement made by Fritz Eichenberg. In one of the most famous, the "Christ of the Breadlines," Eichenberg etched a line of unemployed men waiting for food. In the middle was Jesus,

Christ of the Breadlines.

an anonymous worker, waiting his turn patiently with the others. This is stated in the book of Hebrews 13:2 as, "Do not neglect to show hospitality to strangers, for by doing that some have entertained angels without knowing it."

The offering of food, drink, and shelter is a core practice of hospitality. The centrality of food and shelter means that hospitality has always been one of the most important forms of mission undertaken by women. Throughout history, women have prepared food and bedding, clothed the poor, and listened to people's problems. Without women's hospitality, the early Methodist circuit riders would not have succeeded in setting up churches all over the country. In many neighborhoods, the grandmother with a pot of soup or coffee on the stove has provided a listening ear and life-saving hospitality to troubled youth.

In foreign missions, countless missionary women have routinely opened their homes to visitors, friends and strangers alike. Missionary women have adopted orphans and educated children, many of whom grew up to become the first strong Christians in their home countries. From the mid-nineteenth century to today, deaconesses, Bible women, and evangelists have visited the homes of non-Christian women to establish relationships across cultural and racial divisions. This unsung ministry is often unpaid and unrewarded. Yet without it, relationships of trust do not grow. And without the building of relationships, the meaning of the Gospel message is lost. The amount of time Jesus spent in people's homes, eating and talking with people—including the sisters Mary and Martha—affirms the necessity of hospitality as foundational to mission.

And without the building of relationships, the meaning of the Gospel message is lost.

Today in The United Methodist Church, "radical hospitality" is being promoted as one of the five "practices of fruitful congregations." As explained by Bishop Robert Schnase,

> Christian hospitality refers to the active desire to invite, welcome, receive, and care for those who are strangers so that they find a spiritual home and discover for themselves the unending richness of life in Christ. . . . It describes a genuine love for others who are not yet a part of the faith community; an outward focus, a reaching out to those not yet known, a love that motivates church members to openness and adaptability, willingness to change behaviors in order to accommodate the needs and receive the talents of newcomers. Beyond intention, hospitality practices the gracious love of Christ, respects the dignity of others, and expresses God's invitation to others, not our own." [10]

As a movement for congregational effectiveness, the "radical hospitality" movement links to the ancient Christian tradition of hospitality as a central practice of Christian mission, whether near or far, local or global, past, present, or future.

United Methodist Practices of Missional Hospitality: Hurricane Katrina Relief

[This case study was written by the Rev. Douglas D. Tzan.]

"We have gathered together to seek God's blessings upon this home, which by the favor of God and human labor has been made ready. This home is not only a dwelling but a symbol to us of God's loving care and of our life together as the family of Christ. Let us therefore bring praise and thanksgiving for goodness and mercy, offering ourselves as God's servants and as loving sisters and brothers to one another. . . . Eternal God, bless this home. Let your love rest upon it and your promised presence be manifested in it." [11]

Those words and ones like them repeated countless times at home dedications or blessings in the Gulf Coast, marked yet another link in a widening cycle of missionary hospitality that began in late August 2005 when Hurricane Katrina slammed into the Gulf Coast. Coming ashore southeast of New Orleans and affecting communities from Alabama to Texas, the storm felled trees and damaged roofs, while surging tides flooded homes that would mold and become unlivable. Unfortunately, the wind and waves of Katrina represented only the first stage of the disaster. The breach of the levees in New Orleans flooded most of that city, endangering those who had been unable to flee in advance of the storm. Tens of thousands sought shelter in the city's domed sports stadium—the Superdome—only to find it lacked enough fresh water, food, generator fuel, or security to service the crowds. Across the region, the failure of governments to care for their citizens made bad problems worse. In the most destructive storm to hit the U.S., hundreds of thousands of lives were dislocated and over eighteen hundred mostly poor and elderly people died in the catastrophe. The size and duration of the Katrina disaster is of a scale that exact numbers never will be known. [12]

While a major American city and the surrounding region drowned, and first responders bravely struggled to rescue survivors, United Methodists

http://www.katrina.noaa.gov/helicopter/helicopter-2.html

New Orleans, 2005.

around the United States were already in mission offering hospitality to those fleeing the storm. The Lessie Bates Davis Neighborhood House has been a Methodist mission in East St. Louis, Illinois for almost a century. Its history begins in the early 1900s when Eastern European immigrants were settling in the community. Methodist deaconesses and women working through the Woman's Home Missionary Society supported missionary work in East St. Louis by providing for the needs of the immigrant community. Today, the Neighborhood

House continues to welcome the community by providing social and economic development services for children, families, and senior citizens in East St. Louis.

When Katrina made landfall, the Neighborhood House began to collect donations to send to the suffering people, but within days the staff discovered that residents of the Gulf Coast were arriving in their community to stay with friends or family. As many of the host families were already living below the poverty line, this influx strained already limited resources. Redirecting its effort, the Neighborhood House cooperated with churches and other agencies to assist people with finding emergency food, clothing, and shelter. Over time, with money given by United Methodists to UMCOR (The United Methodist Committee on Relief) for Katrina relief, these survivors were helped on an individual basis to rebuild their lives through job training and education. [13]

United Methodists were also involved in an even more massive welcome staged in Houston, Texas. Three days after landfall in Louisiana, the first of over twenty thousand evacuees began to arrive at the Astrodome and surrounding buildings. Bussed from the horrific scenes at the Superdome, they came with only what they could carry, such as photographs or a treasured possession. United Methodists, working together with others from the Houston area and beyond, came to help set up cots, unload, sort, and distribute donations of clothes, toiletries, and food. Kathleen Buttolph of Wesley United Methodist Church in Johnson City, Tennessee, was visiting Houston for a friend's wedding, but went to help sort donations, saying, "I couldn't help but come here. It seems like you shouldn't be doing anything else."

At times, hospitality took the form of a hug or a listening ear as survivors began the process of recovery by recounting their stories of survival.

Patricia Groves, a member of St. Luke's United Methodist Church in Houston, spoke for many who turned out to help when she said,

> "I cannot sit on my you-know-what and not do anything when these people have absolutely nothing but the clothes on their backs. The first night I was here, I saw this 4-and-a-half-year-old running down the ramp at the Astrodome. She opened her arms, and I picked her up. She was wet, her diaper needed changing, she was dirty, but she had a smile on her face because she finally got in some place that was air-conditioned. Everybody was just so glad to be someplace where they could lay down because they were so exhausted." [14]

Similar stories of missionary hospitality were repeated around the country.

Those who had survived Katrina were thankful for the welcome they received and often expressed a desire to repay their hosts. And as the cycle of hospitality turned, those who survived the storm themselves offered a mission of hospitality! In welcoming the visiting volunteers, Katrina survivors provide the basis for the recovery and rebuilding of the affected region.

Just two years after Katrina, UMCOR estimated that over one hundred thirty-six thousand UMC volunteers had visited the Gulf Coast to assist with recovery efforts. [15] It is often said that an army marches on its stomach; and every person in that army of volunteers represented an opportunity for United Methodists in the disaster zone to continue the cycle of missionary hospitality as they housed or fed visiting workers.

For generations, Gulfside Assembly had provided hospitality to Methodists in the years before the Civil Rights movement, when segregation closed large meeting and retreat facilities to African

Gulfside Assembly.

several multi-purpose recovery centers around the state. The ten-thousand-five-hundred-square-foot building provides warehouse space for construction supplies purchased at lower cost in bulk and dormitory space for eighty-six volunteers. [17] Today the sanctuary of Vancleave UMC is the home for banners from states around the country, giving witness to the different groups who have come to assist in the rebuilding. [18]

Very often, work teams and homeowners develop special bonds with each other so that a sense of mutuality in mission develops. Keith Wells, the coordinator of construction projects in the area noted that "A lot of the families being helped want to cook for the volunteers. Sometimes that's all they can do. Some do it every day. If they have a team at their home, they scrounge up money and feed them. They help us while we're helping them." [19]

Jeri McBroom, the coordinator of Katrina's Kitchen, a ministry at Vancleave that feeds visiting volunteers, said, "This is something we feel called to do. There's no other recourse but to do it. I could not go to my home at night with a roof knowing there are people who didn't have one." [20]

Built on this foundation of missionary hospitality, the United Methodist Katrina Recovery effort in Mississippi grew to become one of the state's largest home builders. Robert Sharp, the director of that conference's recovery work said, "At one point we had thirty-two homes going at once." Using a mix of skilled builders and unskilled volunteers, people on day trips from elsewhere in the state and people from much further afield have come to put up sheetrock, hammer nails, and install plumbing and electricity. [21]

Near Mississippi's Camp Gulfside, when a new home is complete, a dedication is held, or a blessing is offered if the house has been renovated. All workers quit construction to go to the site for these

Americans. Katrina destroyed all the facilities at this camping and retreat facility located on the Mississippi Gulf Coast, including a brand new lodging and meeting building. [16] In the recovery and rebuilding from Katrina, however, Gulfside would become one of several United Methodist sites in the region to offer missionary hospitality to visiting volunteers there to help rebuild.

Another such location in Mississippi is Vancleave United Methodist Church. While survivors were still arriving in East St. Louis, Houston, and elsewhere around the country, the people of Vancleave UMC began to house volunteers arriving to help with the cleanup. In time, Sunday school classrooms were converted into dormitories with bunk beds. Twenty months after Katrina, with about one hundred thousand Gulf Coast residents still residing in temporary housing, the church grounds began to take on the appearance of a large hardware store as it became host to Camp Hope, one of special worship services. Naturally, the services vary according to the pastor who leads them, the homeowners, and the workers present; but in one variation, Psalm 93:3-4 (NKJV™) is read testifying,

The floods have lifted up their voice;
The floods lift up their waves.
The Lord on high is mightier
Than the noise of many waters,
Than the mighty waves of the sea.

Workers are then asked to lay their hands on the house and pray, "Eternal God, bless this home. Let your love rest upon it and your promised presence be manifested in it." At the close of the service, the homeowner is presented with a Bible signed by the various volunteers who have helped in the work, and at times with a quilt or prayer shawl work teams have brought with them from their home church. Finally, the homeowner is given their certificate of occupancy. [22]

And in one final turn of the cycle of hospitality, the homeowners invite those present inside their new home, often providing refreshments. Recalled Jennie Lowrey, the Host Site Facilitator at Camp Gulfside, "The homeowners will say, 'I remember which group worked on this part and which group worked on that part,' so they really feel their home has been rebuilt with love instead of nails." [23]

Conclusion: Hospitality as Transformational Mission

As the above examples show, hospitality transforms people. The amazing thing about the practice of hospitality is that it transforms the host as well as the guest. The people of Nolley and Vancleave United Methodist Churches were changed by their decision to risk moving "from hostility to hospitality." Hospitality is a gracious gift both to the giver and the receiver. The mutual transformation of hospitality can be seen in the story of the disciples on the road to Emmaus, recounted in Luke 24:13-35. After Jesus' resurrection, two of his followers walked to the village of Emmaus, a distance of about seven miles. Along the way, a stranger approached and they began talking together about the events of the past few days—the death of Jesus by crucifixion, and the claim by women at the tomb that they had seen him alive. Together they vigorously discussed the meaning of Scripture. The stranger interpreted the texts in ways that pointed to the death and resurrection of Christ.

Now on that same day two of them were going to a village called Emmaus, about seven miles from Jerusalem, and talking with each other about all these things that had happened. While they were talking and discussing, Jesus himself came near and went with them, but their eyes were kept from recognizing him. And he said to them, "What are you discussing with each other while you walk along?" They stood still, looking sad. Then one of them, whose name was Cleopas, answered him, "Are you the only stranger in Jerusalem who does not know the things that have taken place there in these days?" He asked them, "What things?" They replied, "The things about Jesus of Nazareth, who was a prophet mighty in deed and word before God and all the people, and how our chief priests and leaders handed him over to be condemned to death and crucified him. But we had hoped that he was the one to redeem Israel. Yes, and besides all this, it is now the third day since these things took place. Moreover, some women of our group astounded us. They were at the tomb early this morning, and when they did not find his body there, they came back and told us that they had indeed seen a vision of angels who said that he was alive. Some of those who were with us went to the tomb and found it just as the women had said; but they did not see him." Then he said to them, "Oh, how foolish you are, and how slow of heart to believe all that the prophets have declared! Was it not necessary that the Messiah should suffer these things and then enter into his glory?" Then beginning with Moses and all the prophets, he interpreted to them the things about himself in all the scriptures. As they came near the village to which they were going, he walked ahead as if he were going on. But they urged him strongly, saying, "Stay with us, because it is almost evening and the day is now nearly over." So he went in to stay with them. When he was at the table with them, he took bread, blessed and broke it, and gave it to them. Then their eyes were opened, and they recognized him; and he vanished from their sight. They said to each other, "Were not our hearts burning within us while he was talking to us on the road, while he was opening the scriptures to us?" That same hour they got up and returned to Jerusalem; and they found the eleven and their companions gathered together. They were saying, "The Lord has risen indeed, and he has appeared to Simon!" Then they told what had happened on the road, and how he had been made known to them in the breaking of the bread. (Luke 24:13-35)

Upon arriving at Emmaus, the disciples asked the stranger to join them in a meal and to stay overnight.

At the dinner table, the stranger blessed and broke the bread and handed it to them. In that act of shared blessing, the disciples realized that the stranger was actually the resurrected Christ! Jesus disappeared, and the disciples raced back to Jerusalem to tell the others that "the Lord has risen indeed." Through their act of hospitality, through sharing with a stranger, the disciples discovered Jesus Christ in their midst. They thought they were being the generous hosts. But when Jesus Christ broke the bread, they realized that they were the guests—the beneficiaries of the Lord's hospitality. In the mutuality of this shared relationship, their hearts "burned" within them, and Christ was revealed. Hospitality transformed their lives!

Today courageous acts of hospitality continue to bring Jesus Christ into our midst. Miriam Adeney, professor of world mission at Seattle Pacific University, tells the story of a group of illegal Chinese immigrants who were captured by the Department of Homeland Security and put into a detention center in the Pacific Northwest. [24] They had been smuggled into the United States in ship containers. Their sufferings were immense. As they awaited deportation, they were visited in prison by local Christians who brought them food and personal items, and helped them to navigate the American legal system. Although they were deported in the end, they had become Christians in response to the hospitality shown to them in their time of need. These "container Christians" witnessed to the Good News while in prison. Many came to Christ because of their testimony, and they carried their witness to other Chinese immigrants to the United States.

Hospitality is a form of mission in the way of Jesus. It transforms both the host and the guest. The practice of hospitality witnesses to the life, death, and resurrection of Jesus Christ. It changes people, and it can change the world.

Hospitality changes people, and it can change the world.

CHAPTER NOTES

1. Lyndle Bullard, quoted in Joel Wendland, "Jena Six Case Exposes Right-wing Media Double Standard," politicalaffairs.net, September 24–30, 2007, http://www.politicalaffairs.net/article/view/5893/1/285/ (accessed January 11, 2009).

2. Lyndle Bullard, quoted in Abbey Brown, "September 20, 2008: 'Jena Six' rally, spotlight left impact on community," thetowntalk.com, http://www.thetowntalk.com/article/99999999/NEWS/399990261 (accessed January 11, 2009).

3. Ibid.

4. Jimmy Young, quoted in ibid.

5. Henri Nouwen, *Reaching Out* (New York: Bantam Dell, 1986), 71.

6. Jesus' teachings on hospitality were grounded in the Jewish biblical tradition of welcoming strangers, and particularly the actions of Abraham (see Genesis 18).

7. See John Koenig, *New Testament Hospitality: Partnership with Strangers as Promise and Mission* (Eugene, OR: Wipf & Stock, 2001), chapter 4. On "table fellowship" as hospitality and as a metaphor for the church itself, see Letty Russell, *Church in the Round* (Louisville: Westminster John Knox Press, 1993).

8. Christine Pohl, *Making Room: Recovering Hospitality as a Christian Tradition* (Grand Rapids: William B. Eerdmans, 1995), 22.

9. For information and bibliography on Dorothy Day, see the website of the Catholic Worker Movement, http://www.catholicworker.org/dorothyday/ (accessed June 5, 2009).

10. Robert Schnase, *Five Practices of Fruitful Congregations* (Nashville: Abingdon Press, 2007), 11–12. For discussions of the five practices, go to http://www.fivepractices.org/

11. Stan Lowrey, "A Service for the Blessing of a Home: Mississippi United Methodist Disaster Response."

12. The Earth Institute at Columbia University, "Hurricane Katrina Deceased Victims List—the Earth Institute at Columbia University," http://www.katrinalist.columbia.edu/index.php (accessed March 6, 2009).

13. Susan J. Meister, "Neighborhood House Assists Katrina Survivors," *United Methodist News Service*, March 7, 2008, http://archives.gcah.org/UMNews/2008/March/5090939.htm (accessed March 12, 2009).

14. Steve Smith, "United Methodists Mobilize to Help Evacuees at Astrodome," *United Methodist News Service*, September 5, 2005, http://archives.gcah.org/UMNews/2005/September/9756.htm (accessed March 18, 2009).

15. UMCOR, "Serving Survivors: The United Methodist Response to the Hurricanes of 2005," http://new.gbgm-umc.org/umcor/media/donors%20report/hurricanes_2005.pdf (accessed March 6, 2009).

16. Ciona Rouse, "'We Have to Rebuild Gulfside,' United Methodists Say "*Global Ministries News Archives*, September 19, 2005, http://gbgm-umc.org/global_news/full_article.cfm?articleid=3511 (accessed March 12, 2009).

17. Woody Woodrick, "Facility Dedicated to Hope," *Mississippi Annual Conference of The United Methodist Church*, April 17, 2007, http://www.mississippi-umc.org/news_detail.asp?pkvalue=982 (accessed March 18, 2009).

18. Mississippi Annual Conference of the United Methodist Church, "Mississippi United Methodist Church Katrina Recovery Camps," http://www.mississippi-umc.org/page.asp?PKValue=763 (accessed March 18).

19. Woody Woodrick, "United Methodist Church among Top Home Builders," April 1, 2008, http://www.mississippi-umc.org/news_detail.asp?pkvalue=1696 (accessed March 18, 2009).

20. Woodrick, "Facility Dedicated to Hope."

21. Woodrick, "United Methodist Church among Top Home Builders."

22. Personal communication, Douglas D. Tzan with Jennie Lowrey; Stan Lowrey, "A Service for the Blessing of a Home: Mississippi United Methodist Disaster Response."

23. Personal communication, Douglas D. Tzan with Jennie Lowrey.

24. Personal communication Dana Robert with Miriam Adeney. See Miriam Adeney, *Kingdom Without Borders: The Untold Story Of Global Christianity* (Downers Grove, Ill.: InterVarsity Press, 2009).

Chapter Eight

Healing as Mission

When the woman saw that she could not remain hidden, she came trembling; and falling down before him, she declared in the presence of all the people why she had touched him, and how she had been immediately healed. He said to her, "Daughter, your faith has made you well; go in peace."
—Luke 8:47-48

When American women first began supporting women's missionary societies in the mid 1800s, they did not know that their sacrificial giving would change history. Missionary women launched a form of mission still important today—that of healing.

Healing remains a major focus of mission in the twenty-first century because it shows God's love for the whole person—both in bringing spiritual and physical health, and in bringing wholeness to human relationships. It is one of the chief means by which people come to follow Christ in the growing churches in Asia, Africa, and Latin America. In many cultures, the ideas of healing, salvation, and liberation are interchangeable. Because Jesus was a healer, promoting healing and wholeness remains a way to follow him in mission.

Women and Early Methodist Medical Missions in China

The ministry of healing was part of women's missionary vision from the beginning. Only a few years after sending Isabella Thoburn and Dr. Clara Swain to India, Methodist women also sent doctors and teachers to China. American women recognized that education and healing were two major paths toward reaching Asian women with the Good News. In societies that did not educate women, opening schools and clinics demonstrated the power of the Gospel to change their lives. Educating them and caring for their bodies demonstrated that women were precious in God's sight, and that God cared about women and children just as much as God cared about men. Prayer undergirded all the holistic ministries supported by women's mission groups.

Because Jesus was a healer, promoting healing and wholeness remains a way to follow him in mission.

In 1872, Methodist missionary Gertrude Howe opened a girls' boarding school in Central China. The next year, Methodist women sent Dr. Lucinda Coombs as the first woman medical doctor in all of China. In 1875, she opened the first women's hospital in the country. Howe and Coombs believed not only in the equality of women and men under God but also in equality between Chinese and Westerners. Coombs and other pioneer women missionary doctors began training Chinese women to be nurses. The first women's medical schools in India and China eventually developed from the work of Methodist women missionaries.[1] Well into the twentieth century, the vast majority of female nurses and doctors in India were Christians.

As an independent unmarried woman, Howe was often in direct conflict with male missionaries. She scandalized other missionaries by adopting four Chinese girls and teaching them English. Howe's purpose in teaching them English was to provide higher knowledge of science to her adopted children. Only by studying English, mathematics, chemistry, physics, and Latin could they qualify to enter Western medical schools in order to become physicians. Howe saved money from her small salary by living in a Chinese house and eating Chinese food. In 1892, she took five of her best pupils to her alma mater, the University of Michigan. For two years, she tutored and supported her students so that they could receive a high quality Western education. [2]

Two of Howe's students were her adopted daughter K'ang Cheng (called Ida Kahn) and Shih Mei-yu (called Mary Stone). They were remarkable in not having bound feet, the crippling condition caused by wrapping Chinese girls' feet so tightly that the bones broke and the deformed feet remained only a few inches long. Methodist women missionaries in China opposed footbinding because it damaged girls' bodies and made it difficult for them to walk or to take care of themselves. Shih Mei-yu was not an orphan, but she was put into Miss Howe's care by her parents, as they wished her to grow up to be a doctor. In 1896, K'ang Cheng and Shih Mei-yu were only the third and fourth Chinese women to earn medical degrees. They returned to China to the mission hospital at Jiujang, where Gertrude Howe lived and worked as a missionary teacher. In 1898, they treated over five thousand patients. In 1902, they treated over seven thousand.

K'ang Cheng and Shih Mei-yu had a huge impact on Chinese people. Their example of educated women with unbound feet was noticed at the highest levels of Chinese society, and they inspired many. As medical doctors, they performed operations, ran dispensaries and clinics, supervised Bible women who worked among the patients, treated crowds of people on tours of rural areas, and trained Chinese nurses. In 1903, Dr. K'ang and her adoptive mother Gertrude Howe moved to Nanchang and opened a hospital and mission center. It was the only medical facility in that region of China. Through civil wars, riots, and opposition to Christians and to educated women, Dr. K'ang ran the hospital in Nanchang until her death in 1930. [3]

Dr. Shih Mei-yu was the daughter of Methodist parents who bravely refused to bind her feet. Eventually she became one of the few official Chinese missionaries appointed by the American women's missionary society. After Dr. K'ang and Miss Howe moved to Nanchang, Shih Mei-yu partnered with another Methodist missionary, Jennie Hughes, for collaborative medical and evangelistic work. Together, they adopted children and trained Bible women, many of whom worked among the patients. To Dr. Shih, holistic healing included both physical and spiritual dimensions.

Shih Mei-yu trained numerous Chinese nurses who helped in her work. She spoke of her nurses as

> "workers filled with faith and love for the Master, who will make this self-denying work their life work, who will ask for no reward or encouragement, only the daily smile of the Lord and Master, and who will go through thick and thin, pain and suffering, only to accrue glory to the Lord." [4]

In 1915, she and her nurses treated twenty-five thousand patients. Nurses and Bible women traveled together into rural areas to meet people's physical and spiritual needs at the same time. Many of their patients became the first Christians in their villages.

In 1919, Shih Mei-yu and Jennie Hughes broke with the Methodist women's missionary society over issues of

K'ang Cheng
(called Ida Kahn).

Shih Mei-yu
(called Mary Stone).

control over their work and growing theological differences. They moved in 1920 to Shanghai, where they founded the "Bethel Bands." These groups of Chinese missionaries traveled throughout China on evangelistic tours. Some of the earliest male leaders of indigenous Chinese Christianity emerged from the Bethel Bands. Shih opened a new hospital and continued to train nurses, who both studied the Bible and became rural health workers. She pioneered the sending of Chinese women as nurse-evangelists. Dr. Shih refused demands by the Chinese government in 1928 that religious instruction for the nurses be made optional. After their Bethel Mission in Shanghai was destroyed by the Japanese in 1937, Shih and Hughes moved to the United States where they continued to train Chinese evangelists. Shih died in 1953.

Dr. Shih Mei-yu was one of the first doctors in China to send medical workers to travel through rural areas to treat people. [5] She insisted that healing involved the whole person—both physical and spiritual. Dr. Shih's lifetime of cross-cultural partnerships, modeled by her adoptive mother Gertrude Howe, and then with her own ministry partner Jennie Hughes, witnessed to the power of the Gospel to overcome ethnic and national differences. As mother of the Bethel Bands along with Jennie Hughes, she is also one of the founders of an indigenous Chinese Christianity—churches founded and run by the Chinese themselves. Chinese house churches today are inheritors of the pioneer evangelistic work of Methodist women missionaries like Dr. Shih and her partner Jennie Hughes.

Healing and Bible Women in Asia Today

Although the groundbreaking work of Dr. Shih has been largely forgotten by United Methodists, her model of holistic healing is being followed in the work of United Methodist Bible women throughout Southeast Asia. The power of the Holy Spirit for healing—spiritual, physical, and relational—continues to inspire the work of United Methodist women around the world. As Jesus said to the woman who touched the edge of his garment, "Daughter, your faith has made you well; go in peace" (Luke 8:48).

The power of the Holy Spirit for healing—spiritual, physical, and relational—continues to inspire the work of United Methodist women around the world. As Jesus said to the woman who touched the edge of his garment, "Daughter, your faith has made you well; go in peace" (Luke 8:48).

In 2001, the Women's Division of the United Methodist Church began a new training program for Bible women. For United Methodist Women, this idea goes back to the very first missionaries supported by the Woman's Foreign Missionary Society in 1869. "Bible woman" was the first professional ministry role held by indigenous, non-Western women. Along with sending Isabella Thoburn and Clara Swain to India, Methodist women collected money to support "native" Bible women. Respected local Christian women received training from missionaries, and then went into the countryside to teach women and children about the Bible. They did the hard work of rural evangelism, traveling on foot from village to village to spread the Gospel.

Without Bible women, it would have been impossible to reach Asian and African families with the liberating news of Jesus Christ. Korean, Indian, and Chinese women—often widows—received training in special schools and then went out to teach women and children. In twentieth-century South Africa, Methodist women's groups supported African Bible women who visited women in their huts. They preached and prayed and helped women who wished to be Christians but were often forbidden by their husbands. Sometimes the Bible woman partnered with a foreign missionary, and they traveled two by two into rural areas. The Bible woman would call together the local women, and together they preached and gave Bible lessons in the local language.

Without Bible women, it would have been impossible to reach Asian and African families with the liberating news of Jesus Christ.

In the mid 1900s, support for Bible woman declined. As Asian and African women became deaconesses or women's group leaders or pastors themselves, the idea of "Bible woman" seemed old-fashioned. But their heroic history remains a valuable part of women's missionary tradition. At the beginning of the twenty-first century, the Women's Division revived the idea to meet new challenges faced by women everywhere. These challenges include the dangers of HIV-AIDS and domestic violence. The "new" Bible woman movement combines the evangelistic strengths of the "old" Bible woman movement with the work of rural health and development workers.

One of the new Women's Division Bible women in the early twenty-first century was Erlincy Rodriguez. A pastor and deaconess, Rev. Rodriguez traveled through five rural communities in the Philippines. She taught women about HIV-AIDS and other health-related issues. She used special literacy techniques to teach the women, many of whom could not read. They learned about hygiene and made their own soap to earn money. Said Rodriguez, "I belong to where I am needed is my motto." [6] By 2004, United Methodist Bible women were working in rural areas of the Philippines, Malaysia, Cambodia, Indonesia, India, Fiji, Samoa, Tonga, and the Solomon Islands. In 2006, staff members of the United Methodist Women were also training Bible women in Laos, Angola, and other countries. Through the work of Bible women, many rural people have become Christians, learned to read, and adopted practices for healthier communities.

Biblical and Historical Perspectives on Healing

As the above examples from United Methodist mission history show, healing remains one of the most important and effective ways of being in mission in the way of Jesus. Studies of the early church show that Christians took care of the sick during epidemics rather than fleeing in fear and leaving their sick relatives and neighbors to die. Christian care of the sick meant not only that Christians survived epidemics at a higher rate than others but also that many who were nursed back to health became followers of Christ. Deaconesses in the early church went into non-Christian homes and served the sick and dying. Care for the sick was a major reason for the growth of the early church. Belief in the resurrection of the body set apart Christians from others, and meant that they interpreted care for people's bodies as part of their sacred calling to follow Jesus Christ.

Care for the sick was a major reason for the growth of the early church.

Catholic Sisters continued the vitally important ministry of nursing down through the centuries. In some parts of the world, nurses are still known as "Sisters." With the rise of Protestant missions during the 1800s, Christian women continued the tradition of visiting the poor in their homes and caring for the ill. As industrial cities exploded with thousands of migrant workers crowding into slums, Lutheran, Anglican, and Methodist deaconesses acted as traveling nurse social workers, caring for the sick poor in their homes. This heroic work could mean being quarantined in the homes of the poor, without electricity or running water, caring for a desperately ill mother and an entire family of children for days on end. Methodist hospitals in the United States grew from the efforts of deaconesses to take care of the sick poor.

In the 1800s, missionary societies supported the founding of clinics, hospitals, leprosaria, medical schools, and other healing ministries throughout the world. As mission workers followed Jesus in healing the sick, they modeled Christian compassion. By 1909, American Protestant women's missionary societies were supporting eighty hospitals and eighty-two dispensaries around the world.

As mission workers followed Jesus in healing the sick, they modeled Christian compassion.

Because missionary healing involved care for the whole person, women medical workers often led movements for women's rights. In 1890s India, for example, Methodist missionary Dr. Nancy Mansell led a petition drive to raise the minimum marriage age to twelve. Mansell was outraged at the high mortality rate among child brides, who were forced to have intercourse with much older men.

Dr. Katherine Bushnell infiltrated brothels run for British soldiers and lumber camps in Wisconsin where women were held as sex slaves. Her evidence led to action against the sex trafficking of women and girls. Women missionaries sought a host of social reforms to end such practices as female infanticide and foot-binding in China, female genital mutilation in North Africa, and forced prostitution in Burma. This powerful history of health activism is continued today in the work of Bible women, deaconesses, and women missionaries to educate women about the connections between HIV-AIDS and domestic violence. Many missionaries are involved in running safe spaces for women who have fled abusive relationship or who are HIV positive and have been shunned by their families.

Healing as Wholeness

As history proves, the mission of healing cannot be narrowed to the use of medical technologies. African theologian John Pobee states strongly that "healing ministry is part of the vocation of the people of God. Healing is at base a quest after wholeness of being and person, body, soul and mind." [7] This quest for wholeness does not always result in being cured physically or being completely restored to health. But healing still occurs as an expression of God's grace in our lives and affirms that God cares about our inner selves, our bodies, and our relationships with others.

Jesus' ministry as a healer demonstrates why holistic healing involves not only the body but also the mind, the spirit, and the network of human relationships. The Gospels are full of stories about Jesus healing people in the crowds that followed him. Each healing was a sign of God's kingdom present through Jesus Christ. Each healing gave people a second chance for renewed relationships with their family and friends. Exorcisms demonstrated Jesus' power over demonic evil and mental conditions that kept people from living normal lives.

Healing still occurs as an expression of God's grace in our lives and affirms that God cares about our inner selves, our bodies, and our relationships with others.

One of the most challenging instances of healing occurred in John 9, when Jesus encountered a beggar who was born blind. His disciples asked Jesus whether the man or his parents had sinned. They assumed that blindness was punishment for sin. Jesus responded that sin had not caused the blindness, but that the blindness would demonstrate the work of God. Jesus mixed mud with his saliva and spread it on the man's eyes. He ordered him to go wash the mud off in the pool of Siloam. After the beggar's sight was restored, his neighbors hardly recognized him. They sent him to the Pharisees to be examined. The Pharisees insisted that both Jesus and the man were sinners, and they threw the man out of the synagogue. The man then became a follower of Jesus, who said, "I came into this world for judgment so that those who do not see may see, and those who do see may become blind" (verse 39).

In this story, multiple types of healing are intertwined:
- *Psychological healing.* Jesus rejected the popular fatalism that some people were born in sin and thus deserved to be punished or neglected. The man's effort to help himself, after years of blindness, spoke to his spiritual condition by rejecting his "bad karma" or fate. By cooperating with Jesus and washing in the pool of Siloam, he rejected the idea that his condition was a type of punishment. As a child of God, he too deserved a life of wholeness.
- *Physical healing.* The blind man's sight was restored. With that, his ability to make a living and to have a future opened up before him. His physical healing was a sign of God's grace and gave hope for a better life.
- *Communal healing.* The blind man's healing affected his entire community. His parents and neighbors were called to rethink their relationship with him.

The Pharisees, the local religious authorities, responded to the challenges posed by his healing by rejecting him. In this particular case, we see that physical healing changed the power dynamics in the community, and in some ways things got worse for the man and his family. At the same time, the man's healing allowed him to re-engage with his community. He no longer lived the isolated life of a beggar. That he argued with the Pharisees showed his renewed confidence as a man no longer dependent on charity for his survival.

- *Spiritual healing.* After regaining his sight, the man decided to follow Jesus. His healing was not only psychological and physical but spiritual. Through being healed, the man came to see that Jesus was the son of God. His physical healing demonstrated the truth of Jesus' words—that there are other kinds of blindness than the physical. The man's final response to Jesus was "Lord, I believe."

Because of the loneliness and isolation of physical illness, the restoration of relationship is often just as important as physical healing is to those who are suffering. The healing of Peter's mother-in-law is a brief but powerful story of the connection between healing and restored relationship. It is recounted in three Gospels (see Matthew 8:14-15; Mark 1:30-31; Luke 4:38-39). One day Jesus visited Simon Peter in his home and Simon's mother-in-law was ill with a high fever. Jesus touched her, the fever left, and she rose from bed and began to serve him.

=====
The healing of Peter's mother-in-law is a brief but powerful story of the connection between healing and restored relationship.
=====

How frustrated and disappointed she must have been when the important guest visited, and she couldn't get out of bed! To feel isolated and useless can be the curses of illness and old age. But when Jesus healed her fever, Peter's mother-in-law was restored to her rightful place in serving the honored guest. The healing of Peter's mother-in-law allowed her the privilege of offering hospitality. It took her from a place of marginality in her home to the center of activity. Healing restored her usefulness and dignity and renewed her relationships with others.

> Now Simon's mother-in-law was in bed with a fever, and they told him about her at once. He came and took her by the hand and lifted her up. Then the fever left her, and she began to serve them. (Mark 1:30-31)

The story of Peter's mother-in-law points to another aspect of healing as mission. Throughout the history of Christianity, many of the best witnesses to God's love have been those who experienced healing themselves. Even though the healing may not involve the restoration of perfect health, the experience of knowing Christ's healing touch can be a powerful witness. In the 1500s, when Catholicism entered Japan, one of the most effective evangelists was a blind Japanese minstrel named Lourenço. He testified to the grace of God through song. His joy despite his blindness gave his testimony unusual power.

In the North African country Niger during the 1950s, some of the most consistent witnesses for Christ were healed lepers. Although their lives continued to be difficult because of the ravages of the disease, their joy at being healed gave them a powerful witness to share, despite their low status in Muslim society. Their roles as evangelists also gave them a purpose in life.[8] Similarly, in southern Africa today, some of the most respected healers are women who have been unable to bear children themselves, or who have overcome ill health and adversity.

Healing as Salvation

Dr. Apolos Landa Tucto is the founder of a community health project in Peru, and he coordinates a network of indigenous rural health workers. He writes that in the New Testament, the Greek words for *save* and *heal* are the same. In multiple languages, including Latin and

German, the root word for *salvation* means "healing." According to theologian Paul Tillich, "Salvation is basically and essentially healing, the re-establishment of a whole that was broken, disrupted, disintegrated."[9] Healing involves bringing God's creation back to its state of wholeness—a situation described by the Hebrew word *shalom,* in which peaceful and just relationships will prevail.

Although pain and suffering are ever-present realities in this life, our witness to Jesus Christ calls us to struggle prayerfully against them. The mission of human healing on earth provides a foretaste of the *shalom* that we anticipate in God's future kingdom. As the biblical stories of healing demonstrate, to be healed and to be saved are two sides of the same coin. Salvation and healing are the way of Jesus Christ.

United Methodists and the Mission of Healing: Nothing But Nets

(This case study was written by Rev. Douglas D. Tzan.)

Few missions can claim to have been inspired by a column in *Sports Illustrated*, but one of the most popular healing missions within The United Methodist Church today can. In a change of pace from the magazine's usual coverage, on May 1, 2006, columnist Rick Reilly illustrated the horrific toll that malaria takes on young children in Africa, alerting his readers that almost three thousand children—more than died in the September 11th attacks—die every day from the disease. More important, Reilly pointed out that this daily tragedy is easily preventable with an insecticide-treated mosquito bed net that protects children from malaria-bearing mosquitoes, and that 10 dollars covers the cost of producing, distributing, and installing these life-saving nets. Recalling the importance of nets in all kinds of sports, Reilly's column was titled, "Nothing But Nets." [10]

With those words, a campaign was born to help fight the spread of malaria, the leading killer of children in Africa. The United Methodist Church, together with *Sports Illustrated*, the United Nations Foundation, and NBA Cares (the social outreach program of the National Basketball Association), were the founding partners of the Nothing But Nets campaign, which has since grown to include many other groups, agencies, and corporations.

Part of the campaign's broad-based appeal comes from the combination of a compelling need and its ability to link to a core Methodist missional heritage. Said Bishop Tom Bickerton of the Pittsburgh Area, who has been a promoter of Nothing But Nets:

> "Today there's a three-year-old who's going to be bit by a tiny bug and, in 48 hours, she is going to die. She's the reason I do what I do. When she grows up, I pray, she will have been able to see the face of Jesus in the person who gave her that bed net. . . . To make the world a healthy place for every child has everything to do with what Mr. Wesley intended us to do." [11]

As important as the leadership of key figures has been, however, the Nothing But Nets campaign has been a grassroots effort from the beginning. In many ways, it has provided a simple and affordable way for ordinary United Methodists who lack specialized medical training to practice a holistic mission of healing. As of March 2009, United Methodists had raised more than one-fourth of the 23 million dollars the campaign had raised to date, saving the lives of over half a million children. [12] What is notable, however, is that most of the church's giving has come in small, ten-dollar increments—the cost of one life-saving bed net at a time. In addition, because the UN Foundation has covered the administrative costs of the campaign, everything that has been given has gone to provide mosquito netting.

The Nothing But Nets campaign has been a grass-roots effort from the beginning.

As is often the case, the youth and children of the church have led the wave of support for the Nothing But Nets campaign. Indeed, a spontaneous demonstration of grassroots support took place in the summer of 2007 as six thousand United Methodist Youth were gathered in Greensboro, North Carolina for the Youth 2007 gathering. On that occasion, Bishop Bickerton and soccer star Diego Gutierrez were speaking on the importance of mosquito nets for saving lives when Bickerton showed the crowd a ten dollar bill and said, "This $10 represents your lunch at McDonalds, or your snack at Domino's Pizza. Or it could represent a mosquito net that can save a life." Just then, Bickerton felt something hit his shoe. One of the youth had thrown a balled-up $10 bill onto the stage. That action opened the floodgates, and before long, over $16,000 had been thrown onto the stage. Said Bickerton, "We should be glad they didn't have any change in their pockets." [13]

One youth leader present at the event, Rick Buckingham of St. Paul's United Methodist Church in Kensington, Maryland, observed that "the Nothing But Nets campaign caught [the youths'] imagination like nothing else." [14] Will McCurry, a member of St. Paul's youth group, was one of those at Youth 2007

who put his contribution onto the stage. With the rest of his group he wanted to bring the campaign back to his home church. As a Laity Sunday speaker, McCurry took that opportunity to exhort the congregation to participate in this healing mission. Recalling Jesus' parable of the sheep and the goats and the holistic vision of mission portrayed there, McCurry said the youth of the church had been "called to Christian service through [the Nothing But Nets] campaign. Part of our Christian faith asks us to minister to the needs of our fellow human beings around the world. God has provided us with a simple and easy way to save lives and live out his word." Dramatizing his point, McCurry ended his talk by telling the congregation that in the four and a half minutes he had been speaking, nine African children had died from malaria. [15]

Children under five are particularly vulnerable to malaria, but young children have also participated in healing mission through the Nothing But Nets campaign. Indeed the simplicity of the equation, ten dollars equals a sleeping child's life, is easy for children to understand. As Katherine Commale of Downingtown, Pennsylvania said, "When the mosquitoes come, if they have a bed net the mosquitoes won't get in but if they don't have a bet net the mosquitoes will get them and they'll have a very bad disease." [16]

Katherine's family belongs to Hopewell United Methodist Church in Downingtown, Pennsylvania. After seeing a television program on malaria and its prevention and treatment, Katherine's mother Linda was haunted by what she had learned. With her daughter's encouragement, the family decided to do something about it. As a result, mother, five-year-old Katherine, and three-year-old Joseph made a diorama to illustrate that a net could cover a sleeping family. Using their diorama, the family made a presentation at their church on Labor Day weekend and quickly raised $1,500. [17] By that Christmas, the family had spearheaded an effort that had collected more than $10,000. Speaking at the 2008 General Conference in Fort Worth, Texas, Katherine reported that she had raised over $40,000. [18] By the end of

2008, now a second grader, Katherine had raised over $85,000 for Nothing But Nets.

In awarding Katherine its 2008 United Methodist of the Year Award, the *United Methodist Reporter* noted that the Nothing But Nets campaign had engaged United Methodists across the U.S., cut through bureaucratic obstacles within the church, drew praise for the church from those who have disparaged Christianity, and had placed in African homes "a small token of Methodism . . . in the form of something that's life-giving, that surrounds those who are vulnerable and keeps them safe while they sleep at night." [19]

Indeed, another part of the power of the Nothing But Nets campaign is that it enables The United Methodist Church to magnify its already existing healing missions across the global connection. United Methodists across the continent of Africa have long been engaged in malaria prevention. In the West African nation of Liberia, for example, Allen Zomonway is the project manager of the Child Survival Project at Ganta United Methodist Hospital. Zomonway first came to the hospital in the late 1980s as a nursing student. Displaced during his country's fourteen-year civil war, Zomonway returned home in 1998 to help rebuild community health care programs and to start an anti-malaria program. Even though mosquito nets were not available, he taught communities other means of mosquito control, such as cutting back brush and grass, burning the seeds of the local palm tree fruit, which acts as a mosquito repellent, moving trash sites away from homes, and emptying areas of standing water. Such community efforts have paid off, said Zomonway, "People are clearly much more knowledgeable. They can even tell you that it's the female mosquito that causes all the trouble." [20]

The largest scale example of anti-malaria outreach by United Methodists took place in November 2008. In the West African nation of Côte d'Ivoire, The United Methodist Church and Nothing But Nets partnered with that country's Health Ministry and more than half a dozen governmental and non-governmental organizations in a nationwide health campaign. The approximately six hundred thousand members of The United Methodist Church in Côte d'Ivoire played an integral part. Dorcass, a trained nurse and community health worker at an elementary school in Grand Bassam, received her nursing training at The United Methodist Church's hospital in Dabou. When she learned about the national health campaign through her United Methodist Church, she volunteered to help with net distribution and education about malaria prevention, and she convinced her daughter to join in the effort as well. Dorcass made sure that each family understood the importance of preventing mosquito bites, that children under five are most vulnerable, and how best to install the nets. [21]

Through this campaign, in the span of one week, Dorcass, and about one thousand other Ivoirian United Methodists, together with a delegation from the Texas Annual Conference, were able to distribute over eight hundred thousand mosquito nets around the country. Online video and blog entries detailing the campaign show mothers and children gathering at church parsonages and other locations. The families moved from station to station, with children getting measles vaccines, vitamin A and de-worming medicine before receiving their new bed nets. Each child had his or her left pinky finger marked with a blue marker to show they had received their nets. [22] Wrote Nothing But Nets deputy director, Adrianna Logalbo,

> "Of all the precious things I saw today (and there are many) my favorite has to be the little girl in the pink dress who was showing her blue pinky nail to all the other little children around her. Every child had blue marks on their pinkies, but that did not stop this little girl from being proud of hers. And proud she should be, for after being so patient on a hot November day. . . . It was a big day for such a little person." [23]

Jamkhed: A South-to South Health Care Model

(A case study provided by Glory Dharmaraj, PhD, Director of Spiritual Formation and Mission Theology for the Women's Division of the General Board of Global Ministries.)

In a village called Jamkhed in India, in one of the poorest parts of India, two medical doctors, Mabelle Arole and Rajanikant Arole, dedicated their lives to the most disenfranchised populations who were living in absolute poverty. They came up with an integrated approach to health care, bringing together preventive and curative services. They went beyond the model of health care given only by professionals and invented a radical model of empowering communities in the development of sustainable and comprehensive community-based primary health care initiatives. This pioneer model in the area of community-based health care, Comprehensive Rural Health Project (CRHP), started in Jamkhed, India, on September 27, 1970.

This model aims for health for everyone, including the "least of these." An integrated curative and preventive approach takes into consideration other realities on the ground—agriculture, public education, clean water, and development—and seeks to transform the community itself. The change agents are the people in the community.

The Comprehensive Rural Health Project in Jamkhed, India, pioneered the concept of community-based primary health care in the early 70s even before the Alma-Ata Conference. Raj and Mabelle Arole were able to show a remarkable drop in infant and maternal mortality rates in the villages around Jamkhed with the implementation of a primary health care program in which communities became the hub of the health system.

The change agents are the people in the community.

The Aroles carefully planned their strategy. They chose to live in Jamkhed in a backward and impoverished area of Maharashtra, India with the people they hoped to serve. They equipped a small hospital and began to train village health workers. The three principles of the program were equity, empowerment, and integration. The villagers decided on their priorities, and the Aroles helped them to fulfill them through a participatory approach.

The three principles of the program were equity, empowerment, and integration.

The General Board of Global Ministries (GBGM) in the early 1990s began to delegate health workers from Africa, Asia, and Latin America to Jamkhed for training, for periods ranging from two weeks to two months. Over the years the "Jamkhed model" has been adapted by The United Methodist Church in Bolivia, Brazil, The Philippines, Liberia, Sierra Leone, and Zimbabwe. These efforts have produced far-reaching benefits for communities in these countries. GBGM will continue to send health workers to Jamkhed to strengthen existing programs in Africa and other regions. (For more on the South-to-South Jamkhed model of transformational mission, see appendix 2.)

Conclusion: Healing as Transformational Mission

The mission of healing calls for transformation from brokenness to wholeness, from pain and suffering to peace and justice, and from sin to salvation. The mission of healing is all about caring for the whole person—spiritual, physical, psychological, and communal. Programs such as "Nothing But Nets," the work of Bible women in Asia, and the tradition of missionary medicine in India, Latin America, and elsewhere, are visible demonstrations of Christ's healing love. And in the biblical sense of *shalom,* this love brings new life to the whole world.

In the twenty-first century, Methodists everywhere are embracing healing as a metaphor for holistic mission.

For example, the mission statement of the Methodist Church of Southern Africa states that "God calls the Methodist people to proclaim the gospel of Jesus Christ for healing and transformation." The mission statement of the Methodist Church of Ireland states that it is "committed to the healing of broken persons, broken communities and an exploited environment and is active in ministries of healing, justice and reconciliation." As part of a worldwide movement of Jesus' followers, The United Methodist Church shares this witness to the transformative healing power of Jesus Christ.

In the twenty-first century, Methodists everywhere are embracing healing as a metaphor for holistic mission.

CHAPTER NOTES

1. In the nineteenth century, women's medical work was a groundbreaking activity for many reasons, including that many people believed women were incapable of studying medicine because their brains were smaller than men's brains, and that hard study would harm women's reproductive function and overload their physical and mental systems. The word *hysterical,* for example, comes from the same root word as *uterus.* By 1910, at least 10 percent of all missionaries sent by women's mission societies were medical doctors.

2. On Gertrude Howe and the context of women's missions, see Dana L. Robert, *American Women in Mission: A Social History of their Thought and Practice* (Macon, GA: Mercer University Press, 1997), 185–87.

3. On K'ang and Shih, see Kwok Pui-lan, *Chinese Women and Christianity, 1860-1927* (Atlanta: Scholars Press, 1992).

4. Shi Meiyu quoted in Connie Shemo, "Shi Meiyu" in Stacey Bieler and Carol Lee Hamrin, eds., *Salt and Light: Lives of Faith that Shaped Modern China* (Eugene, OR: Pickwick Publications, 2008), 56.

5. Shemo, 62.

6. Kelly Martini, "Bible Women Spreading Work and Word Through Asia," Global Ministries News Archives. http://gbgm-umc.org/global_news/pr.cfm?articleid=2128&CFID=12615230&CFTOKEN=98663484 (accessed January 10, 2009).

7. John S. Pobee, "Healing—an African Christian Theologian's Perspective," *International Review of Mission* 83, no. 329 (1994): 251.

8. Barbara M Cooper, *Evangelical Christians in the Muslim Sahel* (Bloomington: Indiana University Press, 2006), 178–82.

9. Paul Tillich, quoted in Apolos Landa Tucto, "Shalom and Eirene: Ministering to the Whole Person," *Lausanne World Pulse,* February 2009. http://www.lausanneworldpulse.com/themedarticles.php/1090?pg=2 (accessed April 20, 2009).

10. Rick Reilly, "Nothing but Nets," *Sports Illustrated,* May 1 2006. http://sportsillustrated.cnn.com/2006/writers/rick_reilly/04/25/reilly0501/index.html (accessed April 3, 2009).

11. Elisabeth Stagg, "Fighting Malaria," *Faith & Leadership,* March 9, 2009, http://www.faithandleadership.com/profiles/fighting-malaria (accessed April 3, 2009).

12. Jason Byassee, "United Methodists Partner to Eradicate Malaria," *Faith & Leadership,* March 9, 2009, http://www.faithandleadership.com/features/articles/united-methodists-partner-eradicate-malaria (accessed April 3, 2009).

13. Stagg, "Fighting Malaria."

14. Personal communication with Douglas D. Tzan, April 15, 2009.

15. Will McCurry, "Every 30 Seconds," *NothingButNets.net*, October 30, 2007. http://www.nothingbutnets.net/blogs/every-30-seconds.html (accessed April 15, 2009).

16. UnitedMethodistTV, "Katherine Commale (UMTV)," http://www.youtube.com/watch?v=Qk7ZnEE9MkI (accessed April 13, 2009).

17. Linda Bloom, "Raising Money for a Cause: Nothing but Nets," *United Methodist News Service*, January 5, 2007, http://archives.gcah.org/UMNews/2007/January/raising_money_for_a_cause.htm (accessed April 3, 2009).

18. MissionCast, "64. Missioncast - Nothing but Nets - Katherine Commale," http://www.youtube.com/watch?v=oHFs2VynPVc (accessed April 13, 2009).

19. Mary Jacobs, "United Methodist of the Year: Young Girl Puts Spotlight on Global Health" *United Methodist Reporter*, December 26, 2008, http://www.umportal.org/article.asp?id=4639 (accessed April 15, 2009).

20. Jody Madala and Karen A. Cheng, "Liberian Tackles Malaria Prevention with Passion," *United Methodist News Service*, April 15, 2009, http://www.umc.org/site/apps/nlnet/content3.aspx?c=lwL4KnN1LtH&b=2429867&ct=6923625&tr=y&auid=4753061 (accessed April 17, 2009).

21. Adrianna Logalbo, "Meet Dorcass," *NothingButNets.net*, November 13, 2008. http://www.nothingbutnets.net/blogs/meet-dorcass.html (accessed April 17, 2009).

22. Nothing But Nets, "Nothing but Nets in Côte D'Ivoire," http://www.nothingbutnets.net/nets-save-lives/nothing-but-nets-in-cote-divoire.html (accessed April 17, 2009).

23. Adrianna Logalbo, "Blue Pinkies," *NothingButNets.net*, November 12, 2008, http://www.nothingbutnets.net/blogs/blue-pinkies.html (accessed April 17, 2009).

Chapter Nine

Reconciliation as Mission

So if anyone is in Christ, there is a new creation: everything old has passed away; see, everything has become new! All this is from God, who reconciled us to himself through Christ, and has given us the ministry of reconciliation; that is, in Christ God was reconciling the world to himself, not counting their trespasses against them, and entrusting the message of reconciliation to us. So we are ambassadors for Christ, since God is making his appeal through us; we entreat you on behalf of Christ, be reconciled to God.

—2 Corinthians 5:17-20

On December 7, 1941, several hundred Japanese fighter planes headed for the American fleet, moored in Pearl Harbor, Hawaii. By the end of the surprise attack, fifteen American ships had been damaged or destroyed, and the U.S. air force obliterated on the ground. Over twenty-four hundred American military personnel were killed. Because of the attack on Pearl Harbor, the United States entered World War II. For the next four years, the Americans and Japanese were mortal enemies. The Japanese imprisoned Americans and their allies throughout Southeast Asia. They committed numerous atrocities, such as torturing and killing thousands of American and Filipino prisoners of war on the Bataan Death March in 1942. The United States interred Japanese Americans and deprived them of their civil rights. The war ended only after the United States dropped atomic bombs that flattened the cities of Hiroshima and Nagasaki, and the Japanese surrendered.

Patriots on both sides took heroic risks for their countries. Mitsuo Fuchida was the Japanese pilot who led the first wave against Pearl Harbor. He sent the coded message "Tora! Tora! Tora!" to indicate that complete surprise was achieved. After the successful attack, Fuchida became a national hero. He continued to lead fighter planes against the Allies until he was injured during the Battle of Midway.

http://en.wikipedia.org/wiki/Mitsuo_Fuchida

Mitsuo Fuchida.

After the bombing of Pearl Harbor, Americans clamored for revenge. One young recruit named Jake DeShazer trained as a bombardier. He was selected for a secret mission—to bomb Tokyo. A squadron of B-25 bombers departed for Japan on April 1, 1942. The "Doolittle Raiders" dropped their bombs and then crash-landed their planes because they lacked enough fuel to return to their aircraft carrier. DeShazer's crew was captured by the Japanese. While the pilot and others were eventually executed, DeShazer and a few other Doolittle Raiders spent the rest of the war in subhuman conditions in prison camps, being tortured and starved.

Although DeShazer had grown up in a Methodist church in Madras, Oregon, he was not an active Christian. But a fellow Doolittle Raider testified to him about Jesus Christ before dying of starvation. In solitary confinement, DeShazer was allowed to read the Bible for three weeks in May of 1944. As he eagerly memorized Scripture passages, he came to see the biblical promises fulfilled in the coming of Jesus Christ, and he gave his life to the Lord. He baptized himself by standing under rain that dripped from the eaves into his prison cell. Struck by Jesus' command to "love one another" (John 13:34), DeShazer began to treat his guards with dignity and respect instead of curses and hatred. He realized that following Jesus meant loving one's enemies.[1] When liberation from prison came with the Allied victory in August of 1945, DeShazer declared his intention to return to Japan as a missionary. He went to college, married, and returned to Japan with the Free Methodist Church.

Jake DeShazer.

After the war, Captain Mitsuo Fuchida became a farmer. But he was bitter and angry at the Japanese defeat, and he was determined to prove that Americans had been just as cruel to Japanese prisoners as the Japanese were to Americans. He ran into a friend from an aircraft carrier being released from imprisonment in an American POW camp. The friend told him that while in the camp, the Japanese prisoners were cared for by a young woman volunteer. When they asked her why she was helping them, she replied that her missionary parents had been beheaded by the Japanese in Southeast Asia. The forgiveness of her parents' killers

astounded Fuchida, just as it did the other Japanese prisoners. For in Japanese culture, upholding family honor would have required taking revenge and killing those who murdered one's friends and family—especially one's parents.

One day in 1948, Fuchida was handed a pamphlet entitled "I Was a Prisoner of Japan." Written by Jake DeShazer, it described how despite bombing Tokyo and becoming a prisoner of war, DeShazer had moved from hatred of the Japanese to love for them, through the grace of God in Jesus Christ. As with the missionaries' daughter, here was another case of love and forgiveness rather than hatred and revenge! Fuchida decided to purchase a Bible and read it for himself. What he read changed his life. In the example of Jesus' death on the cross and his last words, "Father forgive them, for they know not what they do" (Luke 23:34 KJV), Fuchida found a way to break the cycle of hatred and revenge. In the knowledge that Jesus died on the cross and forgave those who killed him, Fuchida realized that God had forgiven his sins as well.[2] He felt he had become a new person. He later explained,

> "Right at that moment, I seemed to meet Jesus for the first time. I understood the meaning of His death as a substitute for my wickedness, and so in prayer, I requested Him to forgive my sins and change me from a bitter, disillusioned ex-pilot into a well-balanced Christian with purpose in living."[3]

Fuchida found a way to break the cycle of hatred and revenge.

As did Jake DeShazer, Mitsuo Fuchida became a follower of Jesus Christ when reading the Bible by himself. Through their experiences of suffering and their conflicted feelings about the violence that marked service to their countries, each came to understand that Jesus' sacrifice on the cross was a powerful statement of God's love for them personally. To follow Christ was to embrace peace and forgiveness rather than hatred and violence. To follow Christ was to be reconciled to God and to humanity, including one's enemies. To follow Christ meant to testify publicly to God's love, and to share that blessing with others.

After his conversion in April of 1950, Fuchida contacted the missionaries who had given him the tract about DeShazer's experiences as a war prisoner. Within a month, DeShazer and Fuchida met and gave their testimonies together before several thousand people in Osaka, Japan. They each decided to be an "ambassador of Christ," preaching the Gospel of peace and reconciliation to Japanese and Americans alike. Despite much discouragement and opposition, they spent the rest of their lives testifying to God's love and forgiveness. Part of their witness was their reconciliation with each other—the pilot who led the attack on Pearl Harbor, and the Doolittle Raider who bombed Tokyo.

To follow Christ was to embrace peace and forgiveness rather than hatred and violence. To follow Christ was to be reconciled to God and to humanity, including one's enemies. To follow Christ meant to testify publicly to God's love, and to share that blessing with others.

The message of God's love, and the forgiveness each experienced through Christ, was especially meaningful to people of the other race. When DeShazer preached in Japan, he met Japanese whose family members had been killed by American bombers. Many who hated Americans found peace and healing through hearing DeShazer speak. One young woman whose fiancée had been killed in the Doolittle Raid went to a service ready to assassinate him. But said DeShazer, the "power of Jesus" changed her life "from hatred to love. . . What a pleasure it is to strive for peace in this Christian way rather than to come with airplanes, bombs, and guns." [4] During his thirty years as a missionary in Japan, DeShazer helped to found over twenty churches.

Similarly, when Fuchida preached in the United States, many who had lost their loved ones at Pearl Harbor went to hear him speak. Some gave him money for his evangelistic work. One woman who had lost her husband at Pearl Harbor, and who hated the Japanese, met Fuchida and exclaimed "Praise God, for the attacker of Pearl Harbor has come to our country in the name of Christ! Now I can forgive all things in His name." [5] In another incident, Fuchida met the widow of an officer who had died on the battleship *Arizona* at the same moment their son was born in the naval hospital. She wanted her son to shake Fuchida's hand "in token of Christian brotherhood." [6]

When Christians seek to mend relationships that have been separated or shattered, they are witnessing to the Good News of Jesus Christ.

Through their mission work until their deaths,[7] DeShazer and Fuchida tried to live out the message of the Good News, that

> in Christ God was reconciling the world to himself, not counting their trespasses against them, and entrusting the message of reconciliation to us. So we are ambassadors for Christ, since God is making his appeal through us; we entreat you on behalf of Christ, be reconciled to God. (2 Corinthians 5:19-20)

Few stories of reconciliation are as dramatic as that of Jake DeShazer and Mitsuo Fuchida. But the healing and reconciling work of Christ is needed now as much as it was after the Second World War. Reconciliation means restoring wholeness to what is broken. Because there is so much brokenness in the world today, reconciliation remains a central goal of the church's mission. When Christians seek to mend relationships that have been separated or shattered, they are witnessing to the Good News of Jesus Christ.

Biblical and Historical Roots of Reconciliation as Mission

As with hospitality and healing, reconciliation is a deeply biblical theme that underlies the mission of the church in the twenty-first century. In the mission of hospitality, God's love through Christ is revealed as we welcome others to join us in community. In the mission of healing, we visibly demonstrate God's love for the whole person—body, mind, and spirit. And in the mission of reconciliation, we seek to mend what is broken—peoples' relationships with God, with each other, and with all of God's creation. As ambassadors for Christ, in the healing power of the Holy Spirit, we share God's love with the whole world. Hospitality, healing, and reconciliation are different approaches to the mission of restoring the wholeness that is God's purpose for our lives.

Reconciliation with God

We experience joy in following Jesus Christ, not just because he healed and taught people, but because through his death and resurrection he provided the path for mending a broken world. The work of Jesus Christ in restoring the relationship between God and humanity is the first meaning of reconciliation as described by the apostle Paul. Paul wrote to the Roman believers,

> For if while we were enemies, we were reconciled to God through the death of his Son, much more surely, having been reconciled, will we be saved by his life. But more than that, we even boast in God through our Lord Jesus Christ, through whom we have now received reconciliation. (Romans 5:10-11)

For his followers, the death and resurrection of Jesus Christ is the ultimate sign that God loves the world. In becoming human, God identified with our sufferings, failures, and weaknesses. In dying on the cross, he chose to take on the pain of human vulnerability rather than to commit violence by fighting or by seizing earthly power. In the resurrection, he promised us life over death. Just as God became one with us through becoming human in Jesus Christ, so is humanity unified with God. The resurrection of Jesus carries in it the assurance of humanity's permanent reconciliation with its Creator. We become whole with God through Jesus' victory over sin and death.

Hospitality, healing, and reconciliation are different approaches to the mission of restoring the wholeness that is God's purpose for our lives.

This idea of reconciliation was so important to Paul that a recent document by the World Council of Churches indicates that it is the "key [to] Christian identity:"

> Paul uses the term reconciliation in exploring the nature of God, to illumine the content of the gospel as good news, and to explain the ministry and mission of the apostle and the church in the world. The term 'reconciliation' thus becomes an almost all-embracing term to articulate what is at the heart of the Christian faith. [8]

In traditional theological terms, the idea of being united with God through the crucifixion and resurrection of Jesus is often called the "atonement." While theologians disagree over the exact definition of the atonement, it is easy to remember it as "at-one-ment." In other words, the idea behind the atonement is being restored to oneness with God—reconciliation between God and the people God loves. The idea of atonement was very important to John Wesley, the founder of Methodism. In 1778, he wrote to Mary Bishop, "Nothing in the Christian system is of greater consequence than the doctrine of Atonement. . . . What saith the Scripture? It says, 'God was in Christ, reconciling the world unto himself.'" [9]

The resurrection of Jesus carries in it the assurance of humanity's permanent reconciliation with its Creator. We become whole with God through Jesus' victory over sin and death.

As "ambassadors for Christ," as Paul stated in 22 Corinthians 5:20, we are witnesses to wholeness and the restoration of human nature to its divine capabilities through Christ. This joyous message defines the mission of reconciliation. As stated by the World Council of Churches:

> Mission as ministry of reconciliation involves the obligation to share the gospel of Jesus Christ in all its fullness, the good news of him who through his incarnation, death and resurrection has once for all provided the basis for reconciliation with God, forgiveness of sins and new life in the power of the Holy Spirit. This ministry invites people to accept God's offer of reconciliation in Christ, and to become his disciples in the communion of his church. It promises the hope of fullness of life in God, both in this age and in God's future, eternal kingdom. [10]

Reconciliation among People

The second area of reconciliation discussed by the apostle Paul is reconciliation among people. Human reconciliation flows from God's reconciliation with us through Jesus Christ. The cross and the resurrection form the foundation for reconciliation between human beings because they make it clear that reconciliation begins with God. Restoring wholeness seems nearly impossible without divine help. By reaching down to us through Jesus Christ, God gives human beings the courage to reach out to one another. In the moving accounts of Jake DeShazer and Mitsuo Fuchida, both men gained the strength to forgive themselves and to forgive their enemies by grounding their lives in the story of Jesus' death on the cross and his joyous resurrection. Unconditional love and acceptance by God empowers people to cross boundaries in acceptance and forgiveness of their enemies. God's action to reconcile breaks the vicious cycle of violence, revenge, and more violence that characterizes the world of sinful humanity.

God's love, given freely, liberates us to love others.

Because reconciliation begins with God, we need not wallow in our powerlessness over sin, feeling inadequate and sorry for ourselves. God's love, given freely, liberates us to love others. In the book of Ephesians, Paul talks about the enmity between Jews and Greeks in the early church. How could they be reconciled to each other, and find unity across racial and ethnic divisions? The answer to human hatred and disunity is Christ's spirit of peace, and his creation of a united "new humanity" through his death on the cross. Paul states of Christ in Ephesians 2:15-18:

> He has abolished the law with its commandments and ordinances, that he might create in himself one new humanity in place of the two, thus making peace, and might reconcile both groups to God in one body through the cross, thus putting to death that hostility through it. So he came and proclaimed peace to you who were far off and peace to those who were near; for through him both of us have access in one Spirit to the Father.

The Christian idea of reconciliation thus leads directly toward peacemaking and acceptance of fellow human beings despite our differences. Fuchida and DeShazer clearly understood these connections. Being accepted and forgiven by Christ, they accepted and forgave each other for the horrific acts of bombing and killing their fellow countrymen. They renounced violence and turned toward peace-making and unity between Japanese and Americans. As "ambassadors of reconciliation," they worked as hard to make peace as they had in making war. Throughout the history of Christianity, the mission of reconciliation has involved forgiveness, peacemaking, interracial unity, conflict transformation, and bringing forth the justice necessary for continued healthy relationships among human beings.

One of the most significant examples of reconciliation as mission occurred in the evangelization of Fiji during the 1800s. The Fiji Islands were broken into seven warring kingdoms. Warfare included cannibalism, and the use of over twenty-five different kinds of war clubs. During the 1800s, Christianity spread through the South Pacific through islanders, who traveled to enemy territory in their long canoes and landed unarmed to spread a message of peace. Many indigenous missionaries were killed and eaten.

Throughout the history of Christianity, the mission of reconciliation has involved forgiveness, peacemaking, interracial unity, conflict transformation, and bringing forth the justice necessary for continued healthy relationships among human beings.

A year after his conversion, the Tongan Methodist Joeli Bulu (d. 1877) went to Fiji as a missionary. Over the next forty years, Bulu spread the message of peace and reconciliation among the Fijians. While serving on the northern island of Vanua Levu, Bulu was persecuted. The non-Christian Fijians stole his pigs, killed his chickens, and spoiled his bread pits. Cannibals destroyed twenty or thirty Christian villages on that one island. One morning, the cannibals surrounded Bulu's village to kill all the Christians. Bulu had the villagers sit down in the grass and wait peacefully for their deaths. The war cry sounded, and the cannibals burst in. As they stood with their clubs and spears above the heads of the peaceful Christians, they felt a power take them over, and they could not strike. One man presented a whale's tooth, a Fijian sign of atonement, to Bulu and said, "Joeli, you are a true man. We have spoiled your bread: we have killed your chickens: we have taken your pigs: we have treated you badly. But you are a true man, and your God is a true God. Take this atonement and feel free to tell us the story of your God." [11]

Inspired by Jesus as the prince of peace, who died on the cross rather than resorting to violence, the Fijians renounced warfare and became Christians. They united in peace with their traditional enemies, including with Tongans and Samoans. Many became Methodists, and the Fijians themselves became missionaries to other ethnic groups in New Guinea. Visitors today can see the baptismal font, made from the pot in which cannibals cooked their victims. The stone slab on which victims' brains were bashed out has become the altar. In the light of reconciliation through Jesus Christ, the symbols of war became symbols of peace and inter-ethnic unity. The Communion feast, itself a celebration of the sacrificial blood and body of Jesus Christ, carried deep meaning for those who had renounced cannibal warfare and become unarmed peace-bearers.

In the light of reconciliation through Jesus Christ, the symbols of war became symbols of peace and inter-ethnic unity.

Another historical example of reconciliation and peacebuilding as mission was the work of Darrell Randall, an American Methodist missionary to South Africa in the 1940s. Arriving there at the beginning of apartheid, he cofounded the Wilgespruit Fellowship Centre in 1947. This center in Johannesburg became a key ecumenical and interracial meeting place for leaders who opposed apartheid. As racial separatism enforced by the apartheid regime reduced the possibilities of peaceful interaction, Randall and his wife Mildred challenged the system by meeting with black African leaders such as Walter Sisulu, Nelson Mandela, and Desmond Tutu. Randall bore the message of pacifism and peaceful reconciliation among races. During his career as missionary and then as professor at Methodist-related American University in Washington, D.C., Randall sponsored and affiliated with a number of Christian groups for nonviolence, as well as the International Fellowship of Reconciliation.

The Wilgespruit Fellowship Centre remains involved in peaceful reconciliation movements today. Under Randall's successors, the center continues to sponsor multiracial leadership training, self-help projects, and community-based conflict transformation and mediation.

During the early 1990s, the center's commitment to peaceful conflict resolution was an effective witness when violence broke out between black ethnic groups that supported different political parties in the Meadowlands section of Soweto. Through its "Negotiation and Community Conflict Programme," Wilgespruit intervened to rebuild trust and relationships between the warring parties. They guided a community-based monitoring process that lasted several years, and the zone of killing became a "zone of peace." The cessation of ethnic violence has lasted to the present in Meadowlands, in contrast to other areas with similar problems. [12]

During the twentieth century, some of the greatest names in Methodist missions, such as E. Stanley Jones (India), Bishop Ralph Dodge (Rhodesia/Zimbabwe), and Richard Deats (Philippines), spent their lives working for peace, justice, and reconciliation across ethnic and racial divisions. There were many connections between the Methodist missionary community of the mid-twentieth century and the nonviolent resistance of the American civil rights movement.

One notable leader was Mia Adjali, the daughter of Norwegian Methodist missionaries in Algeria. During the 1960s, Adjali ran the Church Center for the United Nations, supported by the Women's Division. In that position she provided hospitality and support for African liberation movements to end apartheid and colonialism. Through seminars on decolonization and social justice, Adjali educated many United Methodists on world issues and provided a Christian witness at the United Nations. [13]

Reconciliation with the Cosmos

The third kind of reconciliation about which Paul writes is the reconciliation of the cosmos—of God's creation. Speaking of Christ as the "firstborn of all creation," Paul writes that

> in him all things hold together. . . . For
> in him all the fullness of God was

pleased to dwell, and through him to reconcile to himself all things, whether on earth or in heaven, making peace by the blood of his cross. (Colossians 1:15-20)

While the basic idea of cosmic reconciliation through Christ lies in early Christian philosophy, it has become more popular in recent decades as a rallying cry for Christian environmentalism. If Christ was with God from the beginning of time, then he cares about all of creation, not only about human salvation. Since Jesus died for the whole world, then the realm of peace and justice must include all of God's creation, not just human beings.

Paul's idea of cosmic reconciliation gives a biblical foundation to efforts to restore the earth and to mend creation. Grassroots movements and scholars are drawing upon the biblical idea of reconciliation to support activities like tree-planting, simple lifestyles, stewardship of the environment, and helping rural peoples to remain on the land. In the first chapter of Genesis, we read that God created the cosmos and pronounced it good. Since the goal of mission is to spread the Good News of salvation through Jesus Christ, then mission as reconciliation includes witnessing to the Good News that Jesus died to restore the wholeness of creation.

Since Jesus died for the whole world, then the realm of peace and justice must include all of God's creation, not just human beings.

Over the past thirty years, all major branches of Christianity have thought about what it means to extend the saving work of Christ beyond individual human redemption. Pope John Paul II declared the great missionary St. Francis of Assisi the patron saint of ecology in 1979. John Paul II called for laity to draw upon the power of the resurrection "to restore to creation all its original value." [14] In 1989, mainline Protestants and Orthodox, through the World Council of Churches, embraced the ideas of "justice, peace, and the integrity of creation" as intrinsic to the nature of mission. In 2004, evangelical leaders met at Sandy Cove and pledged to advance God's reign by making "creation care a permanent dimension of our Christian discipleship."[15] Recent opinion polls of evangelical Protestants show that earth care is one of their top five priorities. Across many traditions, Christians in the twenty-first century believe that the wholeness and reconciliation desired by God include creation. Human beings have a special obligation to take care of what God has created.

Mission as reconciliation includes witnessing to the Good News that Jesus died to restore the wholeness of creation.

Mission work has always been concerned with the earth. The "father of Protestant missions," William Carey, helped found a botanical garden in India along with translating the Bible into Bengali and other languages. Many generations of agricultural missionaries have focused on sustainable agriculture for the support of the people. Medieval missionaries in Holland built dikes to reclaim land from the sea. In the 1900s, Protestant missionaries collected plant specimens and studied deforestation and conservation of water resources. Mission schools often held annual "arbor days" during which students went out to plant trees. Missionaries have defended local land rights and sustainable land policies, even at the cost of their lives. [16]

One environmental mission that received some support from Lutherans, Dutch Reformed, and United Methodists in the 1990s was that of the ZIRRCON, a grassroots movement of African-founded churches in Zimbabwe. Along with traditional religionists, rural churches in Masvingo Province planted up to a million trees a year over a fifteen-year period. Through tree-planting in areas that had been denuded of trees and wildlife, they worked to "clothe" the earth, which they often referred to as Christ's "body." They drew upon the power of Christ's death and resurrection by holding tree-planting Communion services. Participants confessed their sins against the environment, took Communion, and then planted seedlings. As co-workers with Jesus Christ in his work of cosmic reconciliation, the motto of the churches affiliated with ZIRRCON was Colossians 1:17, "In Christ all things hang together." Because these rural churches participated actively in healing ministries, they interpreted their environmental mission as a natural extension of Christ's ministry as a healer. [17]

The mission of reconciliation begins with God's saving work in Jesus Christ. Secure in the knowledge that God is the source of wholeness and unity, followers of Jesus around the world witness to renewed relationships between God and humanity, among human beings, and between humanity and God's creation. The mission of reconciliation involves hard work and learning many skills, including those of peace-building, conflict transformation, justice-seeking, and earth care. But as Robert Schreiter points out, reconciliation is more a "spirituality" than a "strategy." [18] To be an "ambassador of Christ" requires first and foremost being a person united with God in prayer.

To be an "ambassador of Christ" requires first and foremost being a person united with God in prayer.

United Methodists and the Mission of Reconciliation Today

In situations of violence and injustice, reconciliation remains an essential part of United Methodist witness to the Good News. The following contemporary story of reconciliation was shared in an interview given by United Methodist Bishop Ntambo Nkulu Ntanda to Professor Pamela Couture, Academic Dean of Saint Paul School of Theology, as part of a research project, "'Where's the Peace to Keep?' Peacemaking of Luba Congolese in Kamina in the Democratic Republic of Congo." [19] Bishop Ntambo testifies to the power of prayer for reconciliation between enemies. His testimony also points to the importance of spiritual leadership and hospitality shared by the church in situations of violence.

During the regime of Congo dictator Mobuto Sese Seko (1965–1997), soldiers representing the Mobuto government roamed the countryside, pillaging civilian villages. The Mayi-Mayi movement arose as a loosely organized network of militia groups that defended the civilian population against the government soldiers. After the overthrow of Mobutu in 1997, Africa's first "World War" began in the Democratic Republic of Congo, involving nine African nations—and up to twenty nations from other continents—and now counting 5.4 million persons dead. During this war the Mayi-Mayi reemerged as militias under the control of local commanders. As the Mayi-Mayi never represented an organized political party, they were not included in the political peace processes that ended the war.

Many Congolese say that the Mayi-Mayi "was a good movement that went wrong." Rather than protecting the local population, various influences turned the Mayi-Mayi against the local villagers whom they terrorized. The Mayi-Mayi often included child soldiers, some of them recruited from Methodist congregations. In 2004 the Congolese government turned to Bishop Ntambo Nkulu Ntanda, the Bishop of North Katanga Annual Conference, to bring the Mayi-Mayi into the peace process. Bishop Ntambo was asked to convene a peace conference in Kamina at which the Mayi-Mayi commanders would negotiate with local government and religious leaders. Bishop Ntambo talks about his role, and that of United Methodists, in the peace conference.

A UMNS photo by Billy Reeder.

Bishop Ntambo Nkulu Ntanda greets students during a covenant service to support a Wesley Foundation in the Congo.

Bishop Ntambo: "It was one day I was home, someone called me on the phone. Said bishop, 'You will have big news.' After a few hours I got the phone call. The governor said, 'Well, bishop, we are thinking to have conference, peace, how we can bring peace to our area. We need to host peacemaking conference and we choose you to host that for all the people, including myself.'

"I said, 'Which people, whose area?'

"'People from Kalemie, from Kabalo, from Lubumbashi, the whole Katanga, all of them will come to Kamina.'

"I said, 'That was my dream and my hope, because people have been suffering. Who will be coming?'

"He said, 'The Mayi-Mayi key leaders, all the soldiers, key leader generals, all the police, all the chiefs of the villages, the king, all the administration, all the church leaders, bishops and so on, and so on.'

"'But how many people?'

"They said, 'At least 120.'

"'How to feed them?'

"'We ask you to feed them.'

"'How to lodging?'

"'We ask you to give them lodging.'

"'How transportation?'

"'We ask you to do transportation.' So I can say, 100 percent"!"

Pamela Couture: "And then they want you to keep peace, too!" (Laughter).

Ntambo: "It was a curse."

Pamela: "But I suppose if you're feeding them, housing them, transporting them, that helps them also."

Ntambo: Exactly. And I said, 'How are we to be in touch with them? How to do invitations?'

"He said, 'Well, on the side of government, we will do. But on the side of Mayi-Mayi, we ask you to do it.'"

Pamela: "So you had to invite the Mayi-Mayi."

Ntambo: "This is how Rev. Kabongo is so important. When you are in Kamina, he can share with you."

(Rev. Kabongo, United Methodist District Superintendent in Kamina and a relative of a key Mayi-Mayi leader, Chinja-Chinja, was sent by motorbike to their native village four hundred miles away, to convince Chinja-Chinja to attend the peace conference. Rev. Kabongo was able to persuade Chinja-Chinja to attend.)

Ntambo: "[The Mayi-Mayi] are people who are very very mean, who were accused as cannibals. I got to convince all of them to come to Kamina. Ma'am, it wasn't easy. Now the men, when all of them came, I hosted them. I said to myself, 'OK, this time, you are scared.' Before, I enjoyed it. I said, 'They are coming; we are doing reconciliation.' But now, they start arriving. The whole town was under terrors because the Mayi-Mayi came with all their guns. The soldiers, the side of government, also came very well armed. And all of them were threatening to fight in Kamina. And the man who they were waiting for [Chinja-Chinja] was on his way. And when he arrived at ten kilometers from Kamina, he sent a message. The governor said, 'I'm not going to host him; you take him to Bishop Ntambo.'"

Pamela: "So he was taken to your house."

Ntambo: "He was taken to my house, wearing what witches wear to protect them against bullets and so on. When he arrived, just before he entered to my house, he said, 'Grandpa, I want you to pray for me.' He kneeled, I prayed for him. He said, 'we are not going to get peace unless you people of God are involved.'

"I said, 'Amen.'

"He said, 'I believe in God. I'm not fighting for human beings; I'm fighting for justice, for dignity. I'm defending [President] Kabila. Kabila has brought peace to us. The people are destroying the good will the man has given us. I am on the side of the president. I am a soldier of God. I am going to defend Kabila, to protect our own people.'

(Organizing logistics for the assembly required more than group facilities. Rather, each leader had to be provided food and lodging that communicated respect as the dignitary he claimed to be.)

Ntambo: "And instead of being 130 people, we had 300 people."

Pamela: "How did you feed them?"

Ntambo: "That is a good question. It was help from UMCOR. They sent us $10,000 so we were able to buy food."

Pamela: "And what did you feed them?"

Ntambo: "First of all, we bought cows and fish, because they pretended to be dignitaries."

Pamela: "Because you needed to gain credibility, and some of the credibility comes in using the symbols of power. Food and the particular kind of food are part of the symbols of power."

Ntambo: "Exactly. High hospitality. Besides cows and fish, I had to buy goats and chicken to welcome all the key leaders. A chicken or goat is a sign of welcome.'

Pamela: "I wondered about that; you can't feed them beans and rice!"

Ntambo: "Oh, no."

Pamela: "What about termites?"

Ntambo: "No way! They will leave! *(laughter).* They have their own rules. The chiefs don't want to eat together with everybody. You have to find food for them, personally, and a place to eat separately. And the Mayi-Mayi, they were the key people in that conference. You need to treat them as kings; you have to be like slaves to them. I used all the skills of . . . diplomacy. All the means of diplomacy."

(While the diplomatic logistics were being cared for, the bishop became the mediator between enemies.)

Pamela: "What did you do to get them talking to each other? And talking in a way that would be productive?"

Ntambo: "You know, there were steps to come before that successful meeting. One was good relationships. I have very good relationship with governor and all his staff, very good relationship with military . . . ah, trusted by the sides of enemies of opposition. So by good relationships I was open to everybody. I have open contacts with everybody. I was loyal to everybody. And I didn't play games. It was truth from the beginning until the end."

Pamela: "Did people try to play games with you?"

Ntambo: "All the time. Even some tried to corrupt. I was honest with them, and I showed love and concern and understanding when they were reporting to me. I became an advisor to all sides. You call, say, the chief—you stay with them, you talk, discuss, give direction; you call the Mayi-Mayi people—stay with them, talk, discuss; I go to the governor—I talk, discuss—and you can hear why this one is angry, this one why they are angry. You don't report everything to them. You need to choose what to report to them that can bring the reconciliation."

Pamela: "So you almost served as a priest in different places with different groups."

Ntambo: "And another strategy was to share with them how much we lost in the fight. What gain did we get by destroying our own country? I was telling them how blessed we are as a country. Congo has all kind of minerals; we have ten months of rainy season. I told them how fortunate we are. We can raise all kind of livestock. We have good soil; we can plant all kind of plants. But look where we are compared to other countries.

Zambia has only three months of rainy season, but they eat full time. There is no war; they love one another. I mean, I shared with them the blessings from God. So all those were the kinds of things we were sharing. And they felt guilty—all of the same—what are we doing? . . . And by feeling guilty and confessing, so they committed to start new style of life. And that made things successful."

(Prayer proved important to a successful peace conference.)

Pamela: "So did you pray with them?"

Ntambo: "Ya. That was my role. You may have strategies, you may have skill and wisdom, but Pam, you need someone to refer to as example. Whatever I share with you, it is the love to my people. For me that love reached the high rank when I looked at Jesus. And not fanaticism, not to please people or to gain confidence or money. When I look at the cross and see. Why did he die? Just he wanted to save human beings, he didn't account suffering, he didn't account the loss of his own dignity; the goal was clear to him to serve human beings as a savior."

Pamela: "It's passion."

Ntambo: "A great passion. When people look at you and find such kind of passion and love for them, accomplishment for them; they will accept, they will follow you, they will commit to do whatever you need. And this is what happened in Kamina. I don't think when I go back now I'll be seen the same way *(laughter)*, but during that time . . ."

Pamela: "Right."

Ntambo: "I may say, I confess, that type of model of life convicted men to accept whatever we were approaching them with—criticism or giving them as advice—they absorbed everything within them. Not respect to me, but to see the future of the country, the benefit of the future generation and what great impact can be done once they follow the type of advice and wisdom we were sharing to them. So that was really great, and it was also good time to share with them the message of Christ."

Pamela: "I'm hearing imitation of Christ."

Ntambo: "Yes. Let me say, just to confirm the importance of prayer; when we finished, we stood as a big gathering, hand in hand. But first, before I got there, when I sent the young man for Chinja-Chinja, I felt I was going to fail my purpose. I cried. I said, 'Why did I accept this?' because all the pieces, all the fight was coming. I said, 'We will end up with people killed.' It was in my yard—where we had farewell gathering when you were in Kamina—I knelt, in a very bright moon. I cried. I said, 'God, why me?' That was all threatening, all my personal feeling."

Pamela: "Gethsemane."

Ntambo: "Yeah. Second, when the rebel came, the head of rebels and asked me to pray for them, he didn't see me a rich man in Kamina with goats and cows; no, a man of God.

"Third, the governor, when he received this rebel, it was the key. The governor and the rebel said, 'Bishop, we want you to pray for us.' He knelt and I prayed for them, which helped.

"The fourth was at the end of the gathering, because more than 500 people showed up, but we said 300—it was a big gathering. And I asked the bishop of Catholic to give prayer, and the Muslim, and all, we ended with that prayer.

"But when you look at the cross, you can see the compassion. You can see the love of one another, love your neighbors, you can see the patriotism, you will learn, you will see the dignity of humanity. What I want to share is, Pam, you feel the presence, you need God and you feel his presence once it's accomplished. Let me try to explain that.

"What I mean is, you feel like God is far from you when this one is angry with you, this one wants to do bad things, and you have to bring all together to make them reconcile, to unify, to reconcile. But as a man, you feel like I failed in my mission. And now you want badly the intervention of God. It's like the time your wife is giving birth. And the doctor comes and tells you, if you don't pray she's dying. You feel that only the presence, only with God's presence here, that my mission can be accomplished. So, without God you can't do anything. That's what I mean. It's time you see how great that is. And it's time, once the mission is accomplished, Pam, you say, thanks, God. He's a living one. That was the time I felt that presence."

Conclusion: Reconciliation as Transformational Mission

The ultimate inspiration for the mission of reconciliation lies in the vision of the new heaven and earth, described in the book of Revelation. That which is broken, sinful, or wasted will be replaced by the fullness and wholeness of God's new creation. God will dwell with God's people and wipe away their tears.

"Death will be no more;
mourning and crying and pain
will be no more,
for the first things have passed away."

And the one who was seated on the throne said, "See, I am making all things new." (Revelation 21:1-5)

This hope for abundant life is what gives Christians courage to engage in the difficult mission of reconciliation. As the stories of Jake DeShazer, Mitsuo Fuchida, Bishop Ntambo, and others show us, Jesus Christ frees his followers to cross cultural and political boundaries with his message of forgiveness and healed relationships. We seek peace, justice, and unity with others because we recognize that reconciliation has already taken place through Jesus' work on the cross. Christ liberates us from our fears. As ambassadors of Christ, we walk in the power of the resurrection.

Hope for abundant life is what gives Christians courage to engage in the difficult mission of reconciliation.

CHAPTER NOTES

1. C. Hoyt Watson, *DeShazer* (Spring Arbor, MI: Saltbox Press, 1991), 48–53.
2. Gordon W. Prange, *God's Samurai: Lead Pilot at Pearl Harbor* (Washington, DC: Brassey's, 1990), 209.
3. Fuchida, quoted in Charles R. Hembree, *From Pearl Harbor to the Pulpit* (Akron, OH: Rex Humbard World Wide Ministry, 1975), 55.
4. DeShazer, quoted in Watson, 83; Hembree, 50.
5. Quoted in Prange, 243.
6. Prange, 248.
7. DeShazer died in 2008, and Fuchida in 1976.
8. Commission on World Mission and Evangelism, Athens Assembly Preparatory Paper #10, "Mission as Ministry of Reconciliation," World Council of Churches. http://www.oikoumene.org/en/resources/documents/wcc-commissions/mission-andevangelism/cwme-world-conference-athens-2005/preparatory-paper-n-10-mission-as-ministry-of-reconciliation.html (accessed May 2, 2009), para. 12.
9. http://www.wesley-fellowship.org.uk/WesBulletin23_2.html
10. World Council of Churches, para. 33.
11. Quoted in Alan R. Tippett, *The Deep-Sea Canoe: The Story of Third World Missionaries in the South Pacific* (Pasadena, CA: William Carey Library, 1977), 39.
12. See Davin Bremner, "South African Experiences with Identity and Community Conflicts," *Journal of Peace Research* 38, no. 3 (2001): 393–405.
13. Mimi Edmunds, "The 1960s: Making Connections," in William Minter, Gail Hovey, and Charles Cobb, Jr., eds., *No Easy Victories: African Liberation and American Activists over a Half Century, 1950-2000* (Trenton, NJ: Africa World Press, 2008), 94–97.
14. Quoted in Allan Effa, "The Greening of Mission," *International Bulletin of Missionary Research* 32, no. 4 (2008): 171.
15. Quoted in Ibid., 173.
16. See Dana L. Robert, *Christian Mission: How Christianity Became a World Religion* (Chichester, UK: Wiley-Blackwell, 2009), 110–113; Willis Jenkins, "Missiology in Environmental Context: Tasks for an Ecology of Mission," *International Bulletin of Missionary Research* 32, no. 4 (2008): 176–84.
17. Zimbabwean Institute of Religious Research and Ecological Conservation. For the history and work of ZIRRCON, see Marthinus L. Daneel, *African Earthkeepers: Wholistic Interfaith Mission* (Maryknoll, NY: Orbis, 2001).
18. See Robert Schreiter's writings on reconciliation, including Schreiter, *Reconciliation: Mission and Ministry in a Changing Social Order* (Maryknoll, NY: Orbis, 1992), and *The Ministry of Reconciliation: Spirituality and Strategies* (Maryknoll, NY: Orbis, 1998).
19. Interview of Bishop Ntambo Nkulu Ntanda by Pamela D. Couture, May 9, 2008, TGIF Restaurant, Indianapolis Airport, Indianapolis, Indiana. Used by permission.

Conclusion

Joy to the World! Mission in the Age of Global Christianity

When United Methodists sing "Joy to the World! The Lord is Come!" we declare ourselves a people in mission. We witness to the promises of forgiveness and wholeness that came into the world through the life, death, and resurrection of Jesus Christ. Although life is full of pain and brokenness, the Good News tells us that these are not the final answers to human destiny. As followers of Jesus, we live in the joy of God's presence in our lives and in confident hope of life eternal.

We witness to the promises of forgiveness and wholeness that came into the world through the life, death, and resurrection of Jesus Christ.

Mission and evangelism take place in human history between the first coming of Jesus and the fulfillment of the final Revelation vision:

> After this I looked, and there was a great multitude that no one could count, from every nation, from all tribes and peoples and languages, standing before the throne and before the Lamb, robed in white, with palm branches in their hands. They cried out in a loud voice, saying, ""Salvation belongs to our God who is seated on the throne, and to the Lamb!" (Revelation 7:9-10)

Today, more than at any time in human history, people from different cultures and nations are followers of Jesus Christ. Christians live in Africa, Asia, Europe, and the Americas. The existence of this worldwide church does not mean that the age of cross-cultural mission is finished. Rather, it means that United Methodists share the privileges of mission and evangelism with a multi-cultural community of fellow witnesses!

The Bible shows that there are many ways of participating in mission. The earliest followers of Jesus Christ proclaimed the Gospel to the world, witnessed through lives of love and holiness, and welcomed those who were different than themselves. These biblical practices continue into the present. United Methodists inherit the Wesleyan tradition of "free grace," the idea that God's loving presence is available to all who seek it. This message of grace means that mission is not a matter of spreading guilt and fear but of responding joyfully to God's love. The message of free grace leads us to preach salvation for individuals, to cross boundaries for the sake of forming new Christian communities, and to work for peace and justice as part of Jesus' vision of the kingdom of God. As followers of Jesus, we try to live out our mission in the way he did, and we invite people everywhere to join us in following him.

The message of free grace leads us to preach salvation for individuals, to cross boundaries for the sake of forming new Christian communities, and to work for peace and justice as part of Jesus' vision of the kingdom of God.

In the twenty-first century, United Methodists prayerfully practice mission in the fellowship of a worldwide church. Some of the most important ways of being in mission, practiced by Christians throughout the world today, are hospitality, healing, and reconciliation. All three of these mission practices emphasize wholeness—reuniting people with the God who created them, people with each other, and humanity with God's creation. United Methodists are involved in all these forms of mission—both in the United States and around the world.

The transformation that we seek today is that of taking what is broken and restoring it to fullness in the light of the Good News of Jesus Christ. In unity with "heaven and nature," let us sing, "Joy to the World! The Lord is Come!"

Suggestions for Further Reading

Abraham, William J., and James E. Kirby, eds. *Oxford Handbook of Methodist Studies*, Oxford Handbooks in Religion and Theology. Oxford: Oxford University Press, 2009.

Adeney, Miriam. *Kingdom Without Borders: The Untold Story Of Global Christianity* Downers Grove, IL: InterVarsity Press, 2009.

Anderson, Gerald H., ed. *Biographical Dictionary of Christian Missions*. New York: Macmillan Reference USA, 1998.

Arias, Mortimer. *Announcing the Reign of God: Evangelization and the Subversive Memory of Jesus*. Philadelphia: Fortress Press, 1984.

Chilcote, Paul Wesley, and Laceye C. Warner, eds. *The Study of Evangelism: Exploring a Missional Practice of the Church*. Grand Rapids: William B. Eerdmans, 2008.

Coleman, Robert E. *The Master Plan of Evangelism*. Grand Rapids: Revell, 2006.

Cracknell, Kenneth, and Susan J. White. *An Introduction to World Methodism*. New York: Cambridge University Press, 2005.

Dharmaraj, Glory E. *Mutuality in Mission: A Theological Principle for the 21st Century*. New York: The United Methodist Church, 2001.

Gallagher, Robert L., and Paul Hertig. *Landmark Essays in Mission and World Christianity*. Maryknoll, NY: Orbis Books, 2009.

Gittins, Anthony J. *Ministry at the Margins: Strategy and Spirituality for Mission*. Maryknoll, NY: Orbis Books, 2002.

Gunther, W. Stephen, and Elaine Robinson, eds. *Considering the Great Commission: Evangelism and Mission in the Wesleyan Spirit*. Nashville: Abingdon Press, 2005.

Harman, Robert J. *From Mission to Mission: The History of Mission of the United Methodist Church, 1968-2000*. Vol. 5 The United Methodist Church History of Mission Series. New York, NY: General Board of Global Ministries, The United Methodist Church, 2005.

Hunter, George G. *To Spread the Power: Church Growth in the Wesleyan Spirit*. Nashville: Abingdon Press, 1987.

Johnson, Todd M. and Ross, Kenneth R., eds. *Atlas of Global Christianity*. Edinburgh: Edinburgh University Press, 2009.

Kim, Sebastien, and Kim, Kirsteen. *Christianity as a World Religion*. London: Continuum, 2008.

Kimbrough, S. T. *We Offer Them Christ: Stories of New Missions with Witnesses in Their Own Words*. New York: General Board of Global Ministries/United Methodist Church, 2004.

Kirk, J. Andrew. *What Is Mission?: Theological Explorations*. Minneapolis: Fortress Press, 2000.

Messer, Donald E. *Breaking the Conspiracy of Silence: Christian Churches and the Global Aids Crisis*. Minneapolis: Fortress Press, 2004.

Nuessle, John Edward. *Faithful Witnesses: United Methodist Theology of Mission*. New York: General Board of Global Ministries, The United Methodist Church, 2008.

Pohl, Christine D. *Making Room: Recovering Hospitality as a Christian Tradition*. Grand Rapids: William B. Eerdmans, 1999.

Priest, Robert J. *Effective Engagement in Short-Term Missions: Doing it Right!* Pasadena: William Carey Library, 2008.

Robert, Dana L. *Christian Mission: How Christianity Became a World Religion*. Chichester, UK: Wiley-Blackwell, 2009.

———. *American Women in Mission: A Social History of Their Thought and Practice*. Macon, GA: Mercer University Press, 1997.

Thomas, Norman E., ed. *Classic Texts in Mission and World Christianity*. Maryknoll, NY: Orbis Books, 1995.

The United Methodist Church. *Grace Upon Grace: The Mission Statement of the United Methodist Church*. Nashville: Graded Press, 1990.

Walls, Andrew F. *The Missionary Movement in Christian History: Studies in Transmission of Faith*. Maryknoll, NY: Orbis Books, 1996.

Whiteman, Darrell, and Anderson, Gerald H., eds. *World Mission in the Wesleyan Spirit*. Franklin, TN: Providence House Publishers, 2009.

Study Guide

By Toby Gould

Note: Many of the ideas in this introduction were borrowed from the study: *God's Mission, God's Song* by Joyce D. Sohl (Women's Division, GBGM, 2006). Thanks to Joyce for her generous spirit! Some ideas came from Brenda Connelly, my colleague in mission study leading for many years. Thanks, Brenda!

Introduction

Mission studies have a long and rich history. The first mission study book of this kind was published in 1901 by a committee of women from different denominations (see Harriett Jane Olson, "Responsively Yours: Schools of Mission a Legacy of Women," [*Response,* April 2009, page 4], reprinted in Appendix 1). These studies can have profound and surprising effects on the participants. Some people have found themselves pursuing a mission calling based on what they first learned in one of these classes. While not all of us will prepare to become a missionary following this course, a goal of every study is to send all of us back to our homes and our churches to advocate for and participate in some mission effort. This study invites us to step back and reflect on the meaning of two key terms in theology and discipleship, *mission* and *evangelism*. The last session of this study will invite our participation in both of these aspects of our Christian lives.

While most studies focus on an area of mission concern—Native American study, globalization, particular countries like Sudan, India and Pakistan—we are now invited to look at *why* we are involved in mission and *how* we proclaim the Good News in Christ Jesus. What

are the biblical mandates for mission? Does Christ call each of us to be an evangelist?

One hundred years ago, the first World Missionary Conference was held in Edinburgh, Scotland. At the same time, church women were celebrating a fifty-year jubilee of the founding of the first women's missionary society. In 2010, there will be a follow-up to the Edinburgh conference and celebrations of one hundred fifty years since that founding of the women's missionary society. This study gives us the opportunity to "catch up" with the changes in direction, goals and methods of mission work in those one hundred years.

Prepare for the Study

The words *mission* and *evangelism* bring images to our minds. For some of us, these are profound terms with historical and contemporary importance. For others, images of both mission and evangelism come from personal experience. For most of us, these terms have meaning at the heart of our faith.

The purpose of this study is to look at the meaning of both mission and evangelism within the context of the last one hundred years. But this is not just a historical trip into the past. By the end of this study, each of us should have gained perspective on our definitions of these two terms and their interdependence.

The text for this study, *Joy to the World: Mission in the Age of Global Christianity* by Dana L. Robert, is an essential part of learning. This study guide is based on the text, and readings from the text must be completed before each session. As the leader of your study group, you must be familiar with the text. There is too much information, too many important people and concepts, to leave reading to the last minute. As each of the nine chapters presents a complete concept or covers a particular period of history, try to read through an entire chapter at a sitting. The Bible readings in the text are the foundation of the study, so as you read each chapter, read through the appropriate Bible verses as well.

Goals of the study

- Learn about the 1910 mission conferences and reflect on their significance for mission today.
- Gain an understanding of United Methodist and predecessor churches' history in mission.
- Forge definitions of and the relationship between *mission* and *evangelism*.
- Increase our understanding of God's mission in the world.
- Affirm our role in God's mission and increase our mission actions.
- Explore the challenges for mission today, especially in the U.S.
- Learn biblical perspectives on mission and apply them to our lives.

Your Preparation as Leader

1. Be prepared spiritually. Pray about this study. Open your heart to God's guidance. Remember that the participants will bring their own experiences and faith journeys to this study. Be open to different ways of viewing concepts and directions for mission and evangelism.
2. Read and study books in the bibliography and on the reading list. Both mission and evangelism are vocations and fields of study. Missionaries, evangelists, and scholars have written insightful books in both fields. Your understanding of this study will be broadened as you read widely.
3. Make this study a worshipful experience. Bring articles for a worship center to be created in your classroom. If you have access to a class list in advance, participants can be asked to bring for the worship center items that represent an important event or description of mission or evangelism for that person.
4. Make the space an environment of learning. Posters, photographs, and quotations can be mounted on construction paper or display boards and placed around the room. Articles and pictures from *New World Outlook* and *Response* are particularly useful to this study. A table of books and other resources related to the study can be prepared. If the Internet is available, go to the GBGM website http://new.gbgm-umc.org/ for mission updates that can be collected between classes and posted. Again, If you have access to a class list in advance, participants can be asked to bring resources for display. Often a circle of chairs leads to more open discussion than a leader/class setup. Plan space for a variety of small group interaction.
5. Gather your supplies in advance: hymnals (*The United Methodist Hymnal*, or *UMH*, and *God's Mission, God's Song*, music or CD), paper, nametags, pens, pencils, chalk and chalkboard, markers, newsprint, easels, and masking tape.. If you use presentation software (e.g., PowerPoint) or outline your session electronically, make sure that the room can be darkened sufficiently and that there is a surface for projection. If you do not bring your own projection devise, check on availability and try out the equipment well in advance.
6. Pay attention to comfort. People learn best when they feel comfortable. Learn how to regulate temperature so the room is neither too or too cold. Sitting in folding chairs for two hours without a break hurts almost everyone. Take rest breaks and move around; stand-up breaks for one minute can ease back pain! Variety in the activities offered will also keep participants focused on the themes.
7. Enter into a covenant with the class that includes confidentiality in the class setting, that welcomes discussion and even disagreement; and that agrees on politeness and acceptance of others at all times.
8. Encourage preparation by the participants. Each person should have the text and a Bible for use in the classroom.

Note: be sure the invitation to the study includes the information that participants should read chapters 1–2 of the text prior to the first session of the study.

9. Most will want to take notes and jot down assignments. Encourage participation in discussions and group activities. Have volunteers lead worship and present group reports.

10. Prepare a detailed agenda for yourself and an outline agenda for the participants. The session's theme, worship responses, questions for discussion, and assignments for future sessions can go in the participant's agenda. Your detailed agenda will divide your session into time segments and should include preparatory material and items to bring to class.

11. Journaling. For many participants in any adult education experience, time and effort can be enriched by keeping a journal through the course. This journal can start with preparation for the class and continue through mission projects that follow. In your introductory note to the participants or at the first session, if no class list is available ahead of time, suggest journaling to the class. Keep a journal yourself!

12. This study should not end at the last session! Activities are provided that lead participants and leaders to plan future efforts in mission and evangelism.

Remember:
Successful mission studies lead to action!

Session One

Purposes
- To introduce the themes of mission and evangelism.

Preparation
- Assemble the worship center for the classroom.
- Make sure you have nametags, pens, pencils, makers, newsprint, tape, extra Bibles, and enough copies of the *United Methodist Hymnal* (*UMH*) for all participants.
- Make sure you have a copy of the text and a Bible with appropriate passages marked in each.
- Set up and test any electronic equipment you will use during the class.
- Create a banner for the front of room: "Mission and Evangelism" or "Joy to the World!"
- Create a resource display of books, magazines, articles, audio/visual resources.

Opening Worship (20 minutes)
Bring the class together. Ask that all be in an attitude of worship, Have the call to worship, hymn and journal question available for the class use.

Call to Worship
Come to Christ, that living stone, rejected by the world, but in God's sight chosen and precious.

We have responded to Christ's call, and seek to be built into a spiritual house, a living reminder of God's presence on earth.

Once we were no people, but now we are God's people, called out of darkness into God's marvelous light. Therefore we sing with the church in all ages:

Blessed be your name, O God, our Redeemer. By your mercy we have been born anew to a living hope through the resurrection of Jesus Christ from the dead.

(Ruth Duck in *The United Methodist Book of Worship* (Nashville, The United Methodist Publishing House, 1992), #457. Used by permission.)

Song: "Jesus Shall Reign" (UMH #157)

Meditation
Read the biblical text (Revelation 7:9-10 NRSV):

> "After this I looked, and there was a great multitude that no one could count, from every nation, from all tribes and peoples and languages, standing before the throne and before the Lamb, robed in white, with palm branches in their hands. They cried out in a loud voice, saying,
>
> 'Salvation belongs to our God who is seated on the throne, and to the Lamb!'"

And the author's words (see p.11):

> John of Patmos wrote these words at the end of the first century A.D., when the tiny community of Jesus' followers struggled under persecution by Roman authorities. John's vision of the gathered followers of Jesus, who were called out from every nation, tribe, people, and linguistic group, has inspired Christians ever since. Today, in the twenty-first century, John's hopeful dream seems more like a prophecy. For during the lifetimes of the people reading this book, Christianity has undergone one of the biggest changes in its two-thousand-year history. It is now a multi-cultural faith, with believers drawn from every continent, and from multiple nations, tribes, and people groups.

Ask the questions:

- What are "the biggest changes" that have gone on in your life of faith and in your faith community during your lifetime? How have these changes affected your church and your directions of mission?
- Have participants journal their answers to these questions. Inform them that their responses will not be read to the class. Explain that the external work of mission requires an inner life of prayer and reflection. Invite everyone to continue to journal their thoughts and concerns throughout all of the class sessions.

Getting Acquainted (30 minutes)

- Have nametags available if participants do not already have them.
- Ask participants to introduce themselves and tell briefly why they are in the class. In a School of Christian Mission, ask also for hometown and home church. As class leader, you can begin this process.
- Invite the class to divide into groups of three or four, and let them know that these will be the discussion groups for the duration of the course. (I have found that participants choose more dynamic groups themselves than any of my devising).
- Post the following questions where all participants can see them easily (on newsprint, whiteboard, electronic presentation slides, etc.):

   What has the mission of Jesus Christ in the world meant to you personally?

   What is the most important incident of evangelism that has happened to you?

- Ask the small groups to spend ten minutes on each question. This exercise is designed to help small group participants get to know one another and to facilitate open communication throughout the course. There is no need to bring responses back to the whole class.

Overview of Study (30 minutes)

This book is divided into three sections of three chapters each. Read aloud from the author's introduction:

Part I sets the biblical and historical context for the reality that Christianity is now the largest world religion, comprising roughly one-third of the population. The idea that the Good News is intended for all has helped it spread across many boundaries and barriers. The church today includes persons from all cultures, in all the inhabited regions of the world. Mission and evangelism in the twenty-first century take place within these new global realities. This section discusses changes in the Christian population, mission structures, and women's mission work over the past century.

Part II discusses the theological foundations for Christian mission. It draws primarily upon the New Testament and on Methodist history as sources for United Methodist understandings of mission and evangelism. It discusses the meaning of Jesus Christ as the foundation for Christian mission, and the meaning of the church as a community sent by God into the world as witnesses. Chapter 6 identifies the Wesleyan tradition of free grace as the particular contribution of Methodism to world mission.

Part III examines several contemporary practices of world mission. These models of mission are rooted in both the Scriptures and in history, and are emphasized today by Christians around the world. In the mission of hospitality (see chapter 7), God's love through Christ is revealed as we welcome others to join us in community. In the mission of healing (see chapter 8), we visibly demonstrate God's love for the whole person—body, mind, and spirit. And in the mission of reconciliation (see chapter 9), we seek to mend what is broken—peoples' relationships with God, with one another, and with all of God's creation. As ambassadors for Christ, in the healing power of the Holy Spirit, we share God's love with the whole world. Hospitality, healing, and reconciliation are all ways of celebrating God's intention to bring hope and wholeness to the world through Jesus Christ.

Small Group Discussion (20 minutes)

- What were the issues dividing Jewish and non-Jewish Christians in the first century? What were the outcomes of these divisions? What are the issues dividing churches today? Have "new folks" come into your church and raised issues that were uncomfortable for "old-timers"? Remember, old-timers do not need to be old in years; they may just have been in place for a time and have a stake in the future direction of the church. Which one are you? What does this say about mission?

- Read the stories of United Methodist missionaries to Africa in the nineteenth and twentieth centuries, and the emergence of missionaries within Africa today (see United Methodists and the Changing Face of World Missions, pp. 18–22). What issues are raised by these churches for Western churches?

- The work of Mbwizu Ndjungu in Senegal is characterized as "holistic" because it includes healing, feeding, and visiting those in prison. Take a few minutes and write down (on newsprint) all the ministries of your church(es). After your group list is as complete as you can make it, have someone in the group read Matthew 25:35-36. Now consider together how holistic your mission work is? Where could you get more involved in local and/or global mission?

Bible Study (30 minutes)

Read (or ask a volunteer to read) Acts 10:9-16; 44-48. Peter's dream opens up faith in Jesus to those thought unclean and outside the Jewish faith in Peter's time.

Peter says, "Can anyone withhold the water for baptizing these people who have received the Holy Spirit just as we have?" (verse 47). The twentieth century was a time of amazing growth in Christianity among those who had never heard the Gospel before. How open are we today to offering the water of baptism to all who have received the Holy Spirit but are very different from us in belief and practice? *(10 minutes)*

Read from the author's text (p. 26):

> In 2010, Christian groups around the world are celebrating the centennial of Edinburgh 1910 with conferences, study programs, and seminars. Exactly one hundred years after the original conference, representative delegates from all the major church traditions—including this time Catholics, Orthodox, Protestants, and new non-Western denominations—are meeting in the same church hall in Edinburgh, Scotland. But why remember Edinburgh 1910 at all? What was so important about a conference of missionaries and church leaders a century ago? What exactly is being celebrated?

Chapter 2 helps to answers these questions. In your small groups, discuss these questions as you look back one hundred years to Edinburgh 1910 (see pp. 25–29).

- Why remember Edinburgh 1910?
- What was so important about a conference of missionaries and church leaders a century ago?
- What exactly is being celebrated?

Assignments for Session Two

Read chapters 3–4

Recruit a worship team to lead worship for session 2, and provide a hard copy of the devotions.

- Recruit a presentation team to help set the stage for a History of Mission presentation. Tell the team to use written and Internet resources to describe the six locations and times visited by the "space traveler" in chapter 4 of the text (pp. 61–64).

Closing Prayer (in unison)

Risen Christ,
as you journeyed with the two who traveled the
     Emmaus Road
travel with us on our journey of faith.
In our encounters on the way
give us compassion to listen to the other's story,
patience to explain what may seem obvious
     to ourselves,
and courage to make ourselves vulnerable,
so that others may encounter you through us
and we may rediscover you through them. Amen.

("Week of Prayer for Christian Unity 2010,"
preparatory materials)

Session Two

Purposes

- Explore the significance of the 1910 women's missionary conference and the pivotal role of women in mission.
- Gain an overview of the history of mission.

Preparation

- Make sure you have a copy of the text and a Bible with appropriate passages marked in each.
- Set up and test any electronic equipment you will use during the class.
- Check with the worship and presentation teams to make sure they are prepared.
- Review recent issues of Response magazine and search the Women's Division website (http://new.gbgm-umc.org/umw/) and prepare a list for the segment on Women in Mission. Make copies of the list for the class.
- Have a roll of paper at least twelve inches wide and six feet long for the timeline. Mark six equal sections on the roll, and label each one with a time and place as listed in the "Mission from Outer Space" segment.

Opening Worship (20 minutes)

Call to Worship

One voice:	We are called from every place.
Many voices:	**We are called by Jesus.**
One voice:	We are called to be peacemakers.
Many voices:	**We are called by Jesus.**
One voice:	We are called to see injustice and make it right.
Many voices:	**We are called by Jesus. May justice roll down like waters.**

Song: "Justice Comes as River Waters Flow"
(*God's Mission, God's Song.* The sheet music for this song is available for download from www.umwmission.org/joytotheworld)

Prayer

Invite the group to join in prayer, naming those places in God's world in need to peace and justice. After each intercession, the group will respond, **Jesus, hear our cry.**

Meditation

- Read Acts 9:36-42 aloud where Luke tells the amazing story of Peter's encounter with the only woman in the New Testament who is called a "disciple."
- In chapter 3 (p. 42), the author asks, "Why was the only person Peter raised from the dead a widow? And why was a leader of widows called a disciple?" What is the significance of Tabitha to the early church and the church today?" Ask for responses to these questions.

Women in Mission (40 minutes)

Read aloud the 1910 summary of the ideals of the women's missionary movement:

> To seek first to bring Christ's Kingdom on the earth, to respond to the need that is sorest, to go out into the desert for that loved and bewildered sheep that the shepherd has missed from the fold, to share all of privilege with the unprivileged and happiness with the unhappy, to lay down life, if need be, in the way of the Christ, to see the possibility of one redeemed earth, undivided, unvexed, unperplexed, resting in the light of the glorious Gospel of the blessed God, this is the mission of the women's missionary movement.

(Helen Barrett Montgomery, *Western Women in Eastern Lands* (New York: The Macmillan Company, 1910), 278; quoted in Dana L. Robert, *American Women in Mission: A Social History of Their Thought and Practice* (Macon: Mercer University Press, 1996), 268.)

After reading chapter 3, you are familiar with a summary of the history of women's missions. It is a rich history, rich in scholarship and lay study, rich in fund raising for ambitious mission projects, rich in dedication of woman missionaries who gave their lives to Christ in mission.

- List on newsprint what you know about women in mission today. Look back through chapter 3 for specific stories of women in mission *(hand out copies of the list you prepared ahead of time from* Response *and the GBGM website)*. When you have finished your list, reread the 1910 statement written by Helen Barrett Montgomery. Put yourself in Montgomery's position for today's mission work by women.
- Working in small groups, write a statement of the ideals of United Methodist Women today. To help you formulate your statement:

  Refer to the purpose of United Methodist Women, stated here and found online at *UMW 101* (http://new.gbgm-umc.org/ UMW/about/umw-101/).

  The Purpose of United Methodist Women. The organized unit of United Methodist Women shall be a community of women whose purpose is to know God and to experience freedom as whole persons through Jesus Christ; to develop a creative supportive fellowship; and to expand concepts of mission through participation in the global ministries of the church.

  Review chapter 3 and note ideals that take a more prominent position than others. Give those ideals more prominence in your statement.

  The language of faith has changed considerably since Ms. Montgomery wrote her statement. Use words comfortable to you.

Don't worry about polishing the language in the short time available. It is more important to get your ideals written down in some fashion.

- Take ten minutes for each group to present its statement. Close this segment with prayer, keeping on your hearts, those women in your community and around the world engaged in the mission of Jesus Christ.

Note: Men participating in the study should not feel excluded from this exercise. The themes and goals of a local unit should be instructive to all.

Break (10 minutes)

Mission from Outer Space (30 minutes)

In chapter 4, the author describes the journey of a visitor from space, who lands on earth to look at Christians in mission over the centuries. Report to the class your journey to Christian mission over the centuries.

Invite the presentation team to share what they learned about the six locations and times described in the space traveler's journey.

Divide into your usual groups, letting each group choose one of the following dates and places.
- Jerusalem in A.D. 37
- Nicea in 325
- Coast of Ireland in 600
- London in 1840
- Lagos, Nigeria in 1960
- Your home church now

Each group should create a report of two to three minutes for a news broadcast. Remember the theme of this reporting is *mission*. How are Christians in these places and times involved in mission?

After hearing all the reports, post the following questions for small group discussion:

- How would you describe the mission of your church to that interplanetary visitor?
- What do you have in common with the other representative groups? How are you unique?

Tape up the timeline sheet you prepared, and have each group write in their descriptions and responses to the questions.

"Who Do You Say That I Am?" (20 minutes)

In chapter 4, the author describes the mission of Jesus in various ways: Jesus as Lord (pp. 66–67), Jesus as Messenger and Message (pp. 67–68), Word, Sign, and Deed (pp. 68–69). These descriptions take us in many directions. How do you respond to these descriptions in terms of the ways you carry out Christ's mission?

- Write out your response to the following questions, and then share your responses with your small group.
- Do you follow Jesus as your Lord?
- Is Jesus the unique messenger of God's word to you to be in mission?
- What is the content of Jesus' message to you?
- How do you carry out that mission in word, sign, and deed?
- Each group should post three headings on newsprint—"Jesus as Lord," "Jesus as Messenger and Message," "Word, Sign, and Deed"—and collect the words and phrases that help describe or define these phrases for the group. The sheets should then be posted on the wall.

Lead the class in creating a theology of mission. This might begin with the words, "We believe in Jesus as Lord, our leader, redeemer . . ." or "We believe in Jesus as Messenger and Message that the kingdom of God is at hand . . ." or "We believe in Jesus as Word, Sign, and Deed, the word of Good News to the Poor . . ."

Closing Worship (10 minutes)

Use "The Summons" from John Bell of the Iona Community (p. 74 in the text). After reading each stanza aloud as a group, pause one minute for personal reflection.

Song: Tenemos Esperanza
(*God's Mission, God's Song*. The sheet music for this song is available for download from www.umwmission.org/joytotheworld)

Closing Prayer
Ask for prayers to strengthen Christ's mission in the world.

Assignments for Session Three
- Read chapters 5–6
- Ask for volunteers to present short (two- to three-minute) sketches of the following individuals: Olaudah Equiano, William Apess, Thomas Coke, John Stewart, Melville Cox, Ann Wilkins, Ellen Johnson-Sirleaf, Phoebe Palmer, and E. Stanley Jones. Each sketch should include a description of the person's missionary efforts.

Session Three

Purposes
- To increase our understanding of evangelism
- To find links between evangelism and mission
- To learn about United Methodist history in mission and evangelism

Preparation
- Make sure you have a copy of the text and a Bible with appropriate passages marked in each.
- Set up and test any electronic equipment you will use during the class.
- Download and play the video clip "I am the church" by Josh Longbrake http://vids.myspace.com/index.cfm?fuseaction =vids.individual&VideoID=14099118.
- Have hymnals available for each participant.
- Have newsprint or poster paper and markers available for the exercises in this session.
- Make sure everyone has read chapters 5 and 6 of the text.

Opening Worship (20 minutes)
Play the video "I am the church" by Josh Longbrake.

One of the hurdles to evangelism in this new century is explaining the church to those outside the walls. Many people do not come from "churched" backgrounds. Many people are seeking faith in their lives. Christian faith can be as mysterious to them as other world religions often are to us. For instance, we understand the differences and similarities between our church and other churches in town (Do we?), but those outside our hallowed walls don't have a clue. Who is the church? It's one thing to sing this song in Sunday school with elementary-age children; it's another to sing it with those who claim our same Lord and Savior Jesus Christ, but with whom we disagree about almost everything else. This is a major challenge in practicing evangelism in our time.

In the video clip are many different faces, including some faces few of us see in our churches. Now that we have seen this collage of faces, it is time to look in the mirror. Are we as welcoming as the words on the sign on the church's front lawn? Carroll Wise, one of the early leaders in pastoral counseling defined that discipline as "meeting a person at the point of his or her need." Dr. Wise meant that we should not bring our preconceptions with us when we interact with people. Rather, we should listen to the story of the person in front of us and respond to the concern on that person's heart.

What face do we truly show the world when we open our hearts, our minds, and our doors to inquiring people? List the positive and negative aspects of your church's face—to those entering the doors for the first time and to those who encounter you *as* the church in day-to-day life. How might you improve that image?

Song: "We Are the Church" (UMH #558)

Prayer: "Litany for Christian Unity" (UMH #556)

How Do We Practice Evangelism? (20 minutes)

The Book of Discipline of The United Methodist Church 2008 says, "The mission of the Church is to make disciples of Jesus Christ for the transformation of the world. Local churches provide the most significant arena through which disciple-making occurs" (The United Methodist Church, 2009), ¶120.

Kathleen Norris writes in *Amazing Grace* (New York: Riverhead Books, 1998), "Evangelism is a scary word even to many Christians, I have often heard people who are dedicated members of a church say, "I hate evangelism" or "I don't believe in it," or, usually from the shy, more introverted members of a congregation, "I'll do anything else for this church, but don't ask me to serve on the evangelism committee" (p. 300). Norris says that the best evangelism is the "show, don't tell kind." This means "living in such a way that others may be attracted to you and your values, but not taking this as a license to preach" (p. 302).

In a church I (Toby Gould) served as pastor, one couple took it upon themselves to meet all newcomers to that congregation. Each Sunday at coffee hour, Dorothy and Jack would listen to the newcomer's stories and tell them about our church. That same afternoon, this couple would take a homemade pie and deliver it to the newcomers along with a church newsletter. Jack and Dorothy did this faithfully, without regard to the perceived status of the newcomers or without asking about their faith or church membership. It was an act of "doing" evangelism.

Break into small groups and share ways that you have "done, not preached" evangelism.

Alternate small group questions: If we take the definition of mission as "sending" seriously (see the text p. 79), how do we break out of the mold of church as community center and become the church sent into the world? Or can the church as community center be seen as "sending?" Do we "receive" mission efforts from other churches, especially those of other cultures and places? An important mission concept is *mutuality in mission.* No one church sends mission. No one church receives mission from others. Rather, mission is give and take among Christians.

An Inventory of Mission (30 minutes)
In chapter 5, the author describes three major categories of mission:
- Proclaiming the Gospel to the world.
- Witnessing through love and holiness.
- Inclusion through healing and receiving.

In small groups, create an inventory chart of your church's (or churches') mission efforts in each of the three categories. For the purpose of this exercise, you

will need to rely on your own knowledge, but for a fuller inventory, search through your church's annual report, newsletter, website, written sermons, or whatever else you have to put flesh on these theological (missional) bones. You might use the following classifications:
1. Mission work by individuals.
2. Mission work by groups (such as United Methodist Women, your youth program, United Methodist Men, Volunteer in Missions teams) or the congregation as a whole.
3. Mission done through financial gifts, apportionments, special mission giving.

In this way you can inventory your church's evangelistic and missional efforts. What percentage of your church's budget goes to mission?

Post the charts together before the whole class. As a class, find at least five new "avenues of mission" from the inventories the groups have created.

Question for discussion: Many congregations participate in short-term mission trips in the U.S. and elsewhere. It is important to connect these trips with both the theological reasons for missions and a strategy to bring long-term results. Consider a mission you have been on or that you know about. What was the theological significance of the trip? What effects has the trip had on the participants, your congregation, and the persons served?

United Methodist Who Have Gone Out Before Us (30 minutes)
An old phrase in the mission field speaks of missionaries "going out" to do mission. The text is rich in examples of those whose lives have been spent "doing" evangelism and mission, though the term "going out" looks far different today than it did one hundred years ago. On pages 94–102 of the text, the author tells us of women and men who gave their lives to missionary endeavors.

Have class members present their prepared sketches of Olaudah Equiano, William Apess, Thomas Coke, John Stewart, Melville Cox, Ann Wilkins, Ellen Johnson-Sirleaf, Phoebe Palmer, and E. Stanley Jones.

When the sketches are finished, have small groups discuss the following question: What commonality in motive, conviction, or source of faith do you find in these individuals?

Alternate exercise: "Social holiness" is a term unique to Methodists and other Wesleyans. How would you define social holiness? More important, how do you live out social holiness?

Alternate exercise: The author proclaims, "Because God loves us, we are free to make disciples and transform the world" (p. 104). How do you see this happening in our time, in our church, in our community?

Alternate exercise: The author writes, "For United Methodists, evangelism is the heart of mission" (p. 102). Draw the outline of the human body on newsprint or poster board. Draw an outline of a human heart within the body, proportionate and properly placed. Then draw lines for blood vessels to head, hands, and feet. Label the heart "Evangelism" and the body "Mission." Write in words describing the functions of the heart, vessels, and body (e.g., heart=speaking a Gospel word; body=feeding those who are hungry, vessels=carrying the strength of prayer to mission).

Closing Worship (10 minutes)
Song: God of Our Foremothers
(God's Mission, God's Song)

Prayer
One: Gracious God, you have called us from many places and from our individual lives to be part of your mission to your world. Having heard the stories of those who have gone before us in your mission, we feel the weight of your call to us. Grant us strength for the journey, vision for the way, a heart to love those we find difficult to love. *(Intercessions from the class may be invited.)*

All: **Surround us with your grace. Guide us with your Spirit. Give us hope in the name of your Son, Jesus Christ. Amen.**

Assignments for Session Four
*   Read chapters 7–9.
*   Recruit a group to prepare the Commitment Service and provide copies of the service.
*   Recruit a group to prepare the Action Plan for Hospitality.
*   Hand out copies of the Discussion Topics, and invite the small groups to choose three possible topics to prepare for 20-minute discussion.

Session Four

Purposes
- To dedicate ourselves to practice mission and evangelism in our lives.
- To practice hospitality in our communities to those in need, to Christians who practice their faith in ways differing from ours, and to those of other faiths.

Preparation
- Make sure you have a copy of the text and a Bible with appropriate passages marked in each.
- Set up and test any electronic equipment you will use during the class.
- Obtain enough envelopes for the Commitment Service.
- Make sure groups are ready to present.

Opening Worship (20 minutes)
Songs
- "Rescue the Perishing"
  (*God's Mission, God's Song* #70; also on CD)
- "*Momento Novo*"
  (*God's Mission, God's Song* #29; also on CD)
- "In Mission Together"
  (*God's Mission, God's Song* #76; also on CD)

Scripture: Luke 14:15-24
The story of the banquet is instructive in many ways. The directive of the host to invite those who live on the street to the banquet was even more outrageous to the original hearers of the story than it is today. It's difficult to come up with a parallel situation that we would feel at a personal level, but consider this: Invite only homeless people to your daughter's wedding and reception. (If you can come up with something more uncomfortable, please substitute.) If the example seems either silly or far-fetched, remember that first-century Palestine lived in a caste system under the rule of Roman tyranny. Observant Jews (notably Pharisees) survived by keeping the religious rules of their time. Jesus' words would not only have been offensive and theologically unacceptable, but would have shaken the social structure at its foundations. Read pp. 112–113:

> The book of Matthew also emphasizes the importance of hospitality from the perspective of both host and guest. Shortly after Jesus' birth, his family became refugees in Egypt to escape King Herod's attempts to murder him. This meant that the child Jesus experienced what it was like to be a refugee in a foreign country, in need of charity and hospitality from Egyptians. Today the Coptic Christians of Egypt still use icons or paintings of the holy family as refugees to symbolize their spirituality and their important place in Christian history. Egyptians showed hospitality to a Jewish refugee family. In sheltering the baby Jesus, they welcomed God into their midst.

Matthew records the most profound words of Jesus about hospitality in chapter 25. As in the book of Luke, outreach to the stranger is lifted up as a sign of God's kingdom of justice and mercy. Jesus talks of the end times and God's final judgment.

> "Then the king will say to those at his right hand, 'Come, you that are blessed by my Father, inherit the kingdom prepared for you from the foundation of the world; for I was hungry and you gave me food, I was thirsty and you gave me something to drink, I was a stranger and you welcomed me, I was naked and you gave me clothing, I was sick and you took care

of me, I was in prison and you visited me.' Then the righteous will answer him, 'Lord, when was it that we saw you hungry and gave you food, or thirsty and gave you something to drink? And when was it that we saw you a stranger and welcomed you, or naked and gave you clothing? And when was it that we saw you sick or in prison and visited you?' And the king will answer them, 'Truly, I tell you, just as you did it to one of the least of these who are members of my family, you did it to me.'" (Matthew 25:34-40 NRSV)

Christine Pohl, in her important book on the practice of Christian hospitality, writes, "God's invitation into the Kingdom is tied to Christian hospitality in this life" (*Making Room: Recovering Hospitality as a Christian* Tradition (Grand Rapids: William B. Eerdmans, 1995), 22).

In this famous passage from Matthew, it becomes clear that in caring for the unknown and needy "other," the followers of Jesus are caring for God. In God's kingdom, every person is valued and loved and carries the image of God inside himself or herself. Thus hospitality to strangers is a way to proclaim the Good News of God's love for all persons. Hospitality as a form of mission enacts what the great missionary Saint Francis meant when he allegedly said, "Preach the Gospel always, and when necessary use words."

The idea that Jesus Christ can be found in the stranger has energized ministries of hospitality throughout the history of Christianity. Monasteries sheltered and fed strangers in early Christian Europe. The root word of *hospitality* is the same as that for *hospital* and *hostel* and *hospice*. The founding of hospitals to care for the sick poor was an important pioneer ministry of churches over the centuries. Hostels sheltered pilgrims and strangers. The hospice movement is a modern-day effort to provide dignified care for the dying. John Wesley, the founder of Methodism, insisted that his followers obey Jesus' words in Matthew 25 to feed the poor, clothe the naked, welcome strangers, and visit prisoners. Early Methodists founded societies to support the urban poor, who were needy strangers in the cruel cities of the industrial revolution.

After all this, the question is "How revolutionary is Christian hospitality?" Break into small group discussion.

An Action Plan for Hospitality (20 minutes)

Chapter 7 ends, "Hospitality is a form of mission in the way of Jesus. It transforms both the host and the guest. The practice of hospitality witnesses to the life, death, and resurrection of Jesus Christ. It changes people, and it can change the world." Be prepared to be transformed. Devise an Action Plan for Hospitality for practicing Christian hospitality where you live.

Invite the group to share the Action Plan for Hospitality they prepared for the session. Discuss the plan together.

Topics for Discussion (60 minutes)

Each topic is designed as a 20-minute discussion for small groups or the entire class. These discussions should take the balance of the session, leaving enough time for the Commitment Service. At the end of session 3, have small groups choose three of the topics to present as a 20-minute discussion.

1. The story of the actions of churches in Jena, Louisiana is a moving one (see pp. 109–110). In order to gain the most from this story, look at the courageous acts

of hospitality of people of faith in Jena. List the actions that you think made a difference.

2. Chapter 8 is a treasury of exciting and important mission stories. The work of women missionaries in China is instructive on many levels. Gertrude Howe's pioneering efforts were "often in direct conflict with male missionaries." Clearly, concern for the needs of women was a strong component of the philosophy and praxis of many foreign women missionaries. Such activities as the advocacy of the end of foot binding and the efforts to educate Chinese women were not universally appreciated by male missionaries or by mission-sending organizations. What contemporary issues facing missionaries are strongly related to women's concern's?

3. One unfortunate thread of mission work is the fracture that can take place between indigenous mission efforts, often begun by mission-sending agencies, and those who take up these mission efforts locally. The author mentions the fundamentalist-modernist divide that occurred between Shih Mei-yu and Jennie Hughes with the Methodist women's missionary society (see pp. 122–123). This break is repeated in many places throughout the world and continues today. How can we work together in mission when our theologies differ greatly? Can we support mission efforts of those doing good work in the name of Jesus Christ, even while disagreeing on basic theological principles?

4. One of the most dynamic mission efforts in The United Methodist Church today is the revival of Bible Women in Asia and Africa. This nineteenth-century concept has found new life in the twenty-first century. Reread the section on Healing and Bible Women in Asia Today (see pp. 123–124). Discuss the dynamics of the Bible Women movement. The example of Rev. Erlincy Rodriguez is particularly illustrative. Discuss the implications of this revival.

5. I doubt that there are many United Methodists or basketball fans in this country who have not heard of the "Nothing but Nets" campaign to combat malaria. It is a wonderful mix of secular and sacred, not-for-profit organizations and publicity campaigns, basketball players and UM kids. One of the great by-products of this effort has been the involvement of United Methodist children and youth. When second graders raise $85,000 for Nothing but Nets, something important is happening. Have the children in your church been involved in this effort? If so, what have been the results for the children as well as the success of the campaign? If not, what can your class do to introduce this program to your church's children? In what other ways can children and youth be involved in mission?

6. At Jamkhed, India, doctors developed a "radical model of empowering communities in the development of sustainable and comprehensive community-based primary health care initiative" (see p. 130; also see appendix 2). The General Board of Global Ministries has sponsored dozens of community health volunteers from Africa, Asia, and Latin America to train in Jamkhed in community-based health care. Health practices created at a local level in India have been passed on and adapted to southern hemisphere communities. This community-based model fosters sharing between workers in communities, rather than a top-down approach of imposing medical "expertise" from North America or Europe. If you were starting a mission program in your community to meet a local need, how would you involve the recipients of that program, in planning, organization, and completion of the project?

7. Reconciliation can be a powerful tool in the world (see chapter 9). The Truth and Reconciliation Commission in South Africa is one example of people working on personal and national levels to affect reconciliation among people who have been separated for generations. What global issues today would benefit from a truth and reconciliation commission? (Suggestion: perform a Google search to find places where truth and reconciliation commissions

have been active, and read about their issues and process.) If several issues emerge, divide the class and work on individual issues as groups. Define the problem and create steps for implementing a reconciliation process for this particular issue. A reconciliation process should include but is not limited to defining the issue(s) that divide(s), understanding the history that created the division or injustice, allowing for a thorough airing of grievances, choosing steps to right the injustice and heal the divisions. Note: This is not a short or simple process, but a discussion can open an issue that has been ignored by a community or a nation.

8. "When Christians seek to mend relationships that have separated or shattered, they are witnessing to the Good News of Jesus Christ" (see p. 135). The story of Mitsuo Fuchida and Jake DeShazer is dramatic. Most of us have not seen combat in anyone's air force, let alone been involved in the two most famous raids of the Pacific theater in World War II, but we all have relationships that need mending. Spend some time reflecting on the broken relationships in your life. What can you do to mend that relationship? In what ways do you need to ask for God's help?

9. Review the various models of mission highlighted in the case studies of chapters 7–9. In what ways are they similar? How do they differ? Which models demonstrate transformative mission; which models include charity? Discuss the benefits and drawbacks of the various approaches to mission.

Service of Commitment (20 minutes)

Song: "The Church of God Is Not a Temple"
(God's Mission God's Song)

Scripture: 2 Corinthians 5:17-20

This passage in 2 Corinthians defines and prescribes reconciliation to those who follow Jesus Christ. Rather than studying or discussing the text, meditate on its definitions and its prescriptions. One approach is to reflect on each phrase as defined by punctuation. For instance, consider the first phrase, "So if anyone is in Christ." Does this refer to you? Are there any exceptions allowed in this phrase? Are you prepared as someone who is "in Christ" to take on the prescriptions that follow? Paul's writing is logical and formulaic. As you meditate on each phrase, the depth and gravity and liberation in Paul's theology become clear. Completing this exercise individually, noting significant learning or insights for each phrase.

If anyone is in Christ,
there is a new creation:
everything old has passed away;
see, everything has been made new!
All this is from God,
who reconciled us to God through Christ,
and has given us the ministry of reconciliation;
that is, in Christ God was reconciling the world to God,
not counting their trespasses against them,
and entrusting the message of reconciliation to us.
So we are ambassadors for Christ,
since God is making God's appeal through us;
we entreat you on behalf of Christ,
be reconciled to God.
(2 Corinthians 5:17-20 NRSV, adapted)

Following this meditation, instruct participants to work in silence, and write down their promises to work in mission and to be an evangelical witness to Jesus Christ.

Post the following questions where everyone can see them:

- What difference will this study make in your leadership?
- What will you do in your local unit and local church to help others become involved in mission and evangelism?
- If you are involved at the conference level, how will you help focus and renew the call to mission and evangelism?

These promises can be placed in self-addressed envelopes with the participant's name and address, sealed, and placed in the worship center during the singing of the final song. Three months after class, the leader will mail the envelopes to the participants.

Song(s):
- "Lord, Your Church on Earth"
  (*God's Mission God's Song*)
- "Go, Make of All Disciples"
  (*UMH #571*, optional)

Benediction (in unison)
Let us go into God's world, discerning God's purposes, strengthened by those who have gone before us, secure in the knowledge that Christ calls us into mission. May our steps be sure. May our hands and hearts be open. May we proclaim God's glory in all that we do. Amen.

Appendix 1

Responsively Yours: Schools of Mission a Legacy of Women

Harriett Jane Olson
Women's Division, Deputy General Secretary

Why is it that United Methodist Women sponsors the Schools of Christian Mission in each Annual Conference in the United Methodist Church, working either alone or cooperatively with others in the conference? Why do we study a country, an issue and a spiritual growth topic each year?

Have you ever stopped to wonder?

Did you notice when the United Methodist General Board of Global Ministries and the Women's Division started producing the mission studies previously prepared by the National Council of Churches' Friendship Press? Do you know that Women's Division now has taken the lead on development of these studies with input from our colleagues at Global Ministries?

It's a long story! As amazing as it was, the 1869 gathering of the women of the Methodist Episcopal Church on Tremont Street in Boston, Mass., was not an isolated incident. What happened there, in response to the dire picture of women's lives in India painted by Clementine Butler—wife of missionary William Butler who was home on furlough—was echoed in other denominations.

From the beginning of our mission story in the 1800s, the mission work of women to women has had ecumenical connections. From the missionary wives sent by church boards to the single women sent by women's missionary societies, our foremothers were concerned both that the Gospel should be preached and that women and children around the world should be touched through education and health care. The physical and spiritual condition of women and children was beyond the reach of the male-dominated denominational boards, so the women's mission movement had much in common across denominational lines. They took up responsibilities that those in need could not have done for themselves — speaking in public, traveling unaccompanied, teaching that was nearly preaching, and of course, caring for the sick and for women in childbirth.

Women participating in the London Missionary Conference of 1888 organized the World's Missionary Committee. At their meeting in 1900 they formed a committee for united study to provide "reliable information about mission." The series provided a history of mission and a contextual study about mission with women and girls. This focus on how Christian mission was being experienced "on the ground" was quite different than studies of mission that were available at the time. The study guides were designed to prompt reflection among the participants about how they could take action to improve the situation of women and girls around the world. Eventually, the Federal Council of Churches and the National Council of Churches provided a structure within which this work took place. In 1998 all of Global Ministries and Women's Division shared this work, with Women's Division assuming a larger share of the responsibility in 2006.

Ecumenical Schools of Christian Mission in which teachers were to be prepared for the material that they would teach in the coming year began in 1904. The approach to mission of the women's societies didn't always match the approach of the denomination's mission boards. Similarly, the information that we receive in Schools of Christian Mission sometimes doesn't match what we learned in our own secondary or undergraduate study. Our view is not always the version of history told by the victors. Our interest is not quite so much in what leader emerged victorious from what battle, whether this is a battle of bullets or of words. We have much more interest in what was and is experienced by the real people for whom Jesus both lived and died.

No wonder that our Schools of Christian Mission authors sometimes surprise us with the positions they take! No wonder that the teachers and leaders of our schools still receive special training and additional information to help them!

In this year's geographic study, we look at Sudan. We look not only at Darfur, but we look at a whole nation. A nation that is both blessed with assets and at war with itself. This learning will inform us as citizens of the world and as sisters of the women of Sudan. It will also inform our planning and our giving—so we will take action as a result of our study.

Appendix 2

Jamkhed: A South-to-South Health Care Model of Transformational Mission

Glory Dharmaraj, PhD
Women's Division, Director of Spiritual Formation and Mission Theology

In a village called Jamkhed in India, in one of the poorest parts of India, two medical doctors, Mabelle Arole and Rajanikant Arole, dedicated their lives to the most disenfranchised populations who were living in absolute poverty. They came up with an integrated approach to health care, bringing together preventive and curative services. They went beyond the model of health care given only by professionals and invented a radical model of empowering communities in the development of sustainable and comprehensive community-based primary health care initiatives. This pioneer model in the area of community-based health care, Comprehensive Rural Health Project (CRHP), started in Jamkhed, India, on September 27, 1970.

This model aims for health for everyone, including the "least of these." An integrated curative and preventive approach takes into consideration other realities on the ground—agriculture, public education, clean water, and development—and seeks to transform the community itself. The change agents are the people in the community.

"Primary Health Care—Now More than Ever"
(Cherian Thomas MD, Executive, Health & Welfare, UMCOR)

On October 14, 2008 the World Health Organization (WHO) launched its *World Health Report 2008* with the title: "Primary Health Care—Now More Than Ever." Dr. Margaret Chan, the director-general of WHO, noted in her speech that the report was being launched in Almaty, Kazakhstan at the thirtieth anniversary of the Alma-Ata Conference on Primary Health Care held in 1978. WHO, in a press release, stated:

> In a wide-ranging review, the new report found striking inequities in health outcomes, in access to care, and in what people have to pay for care. Differences in life expectancy between the richest and poorest countries now exceed 40 years. Of the estimated 136 million women who will give birth this year, around 58 million will receive no medical assistance whatsoever during childbirth and the postpartum period, endangering their lives and that of their infants. [1]

The news release goes on to note that "vast differences in health occur within countries and sometimes within individual cities. In Nairobi, for example, the under-five mortality rate is below 15 per 1000 in the high-income area. In a slum in the same city, the rare is 254 per 1000."

The Comprehensive Rural Health Project in Jamkhed, India, pioneered the concept of community-based primary health care in the early 70s even before the Alma-Ata Conference. Raj and Mabelle Arole were able to show a remarkable drop in infant and maternal mortality rates in the villages around Jamkhed with the implementation of a primary health care program in which communities became the hub of the health system.

The Aroles carefully planned their strategy. They chose to live in Jamkhed in a backward and impoverished area of Maharashtra, India with the people they hoped to serve. They equipped a small hospital and began to train village health workers. The three principles of the program were equity, empowerment, and integration. The villagers decided on their priorities, and the Aroles helped them to fulfill them through a participatory approach.

The General Board of Global Ministries (GBGM) in the early 1990s began to -delegate health workers from Africa, Asia, and Latin America to Jamkhed for training, for periods ranging from two weeks to two months. Over the years, GBGM has sent over 300 persons to Jamkhed to learn the principles of community-based primary health care and on their return home, many of them were able to put into practice what they learned in Jamkhed.

In September 2008, eight persons (four from Sierra Leone and four from Liberia) attended a two month training program. One of those who attended was Angeline Willicor from the Ganta United Methodist Hospital in Liberia. In March 2009, Karen Cheng and Jody Madala wrote a story about Angeline's work with the community in HIV/AIDS prevention and care, which can be accessed at: http://new.gbgm-umc.org/umcor/newsroom/releases/archives09/beggingthemtolive.

Over the years the "Jamkhed model" has been adapted by The United Methodist Church in Bolivia, Brazil, The Philippines, Liberia, Sierra Leone, and Zimbabwe. These efforts have produced far-reaching benefits for communities in these countries. GBGM will continue to send health workers to Jamkhed to strengthen existing programs in Africa and other regions. Claudia Maia, GBGM missionary working in Mozambique and Florence Mefor, also a GBGM missionary, working in Zimbabwe attended the September 2009 training.

Jamkhed has championed the use of the Jaipur Foot for those who have lost their lower limbs. The low-cost prosthesis made out of rubber and aluminum has proved to be very durable and effective. Dr. Arole helped to estab-lish the Jaipur Foot prosthesis in Angola and Sierra Leone. The Angola workshop was destroyed during the war, but Amara Lappia and his two colleagues continue to produce and fit the Jaipur Foot at the workshop in Bo, Sierra Leone. They returned to Jamkhed in October 2008 for a two-week refresher course.

Community Health: Latin America[2]

Dalva Maria de Oliveira Ribeiro lives in the community of Eldorado, just outside Porto Velho, a city in the Amazon rainforest of northwestern Brazil. Dalva Maria is blind and one of her gifts is playing the accordion.

Eldorado has been settled by people who migrated from southern Brazil seeking, but not finding, better economic conditions. Because of the poverty of the migrants in Eldorado, many children are malnourished and there is a high rate of infant mortality. Members of the community have been uprooted from their culture and family support systems.

Dalva Maria decided to offer her musical gift to the community and began playing for the children. They would gather at a local home to sing with her and enjoy the accordion music. Before long she had 150 children coming daily.

Holistic Outreach for Children

Dalva Maria decided she had to do more for the children than play and sing with them. She began to teach them to read and write and raised money to feed them. The community recognized the need for a center for the children and a gathering place for the neighborhood women. Together they built a Methodist Church with a community room for children's and women's programs. The singing sessions grew into a day care and a community center for women and children of all ages. In Brazil, children attend school for only three or four hours a day. The rest of their learning is done through assignments and schoolwork to be done at home.

The center provides children with meals and help with their homework. The children participate in team sports where they learn leadership skills and teamwork. They also paint, do other arts and crafts, have access to a library, and learn about God and God's role in their lives. Local women and mothers were trained to work with the children. They also learned a variety of handicraft skills to generate income for themselves and their families.

How CCPHC Helps

Dalva Maria and the others who work with the children are concerned with the physical, emotional, mental and spiritual well-being of the children. They have gained valuable tools for addressing the children's health needs through Comprehensive Community-Based Primary Health Care (CCPHC) training-a rapidly growing ministry of the United Methodist Committee on Relief.

People from all over Latin America attended the most recent CCPHC training session, held in Dalva Maria's community of Porto Velho. Through Comprehensive Community-Based Health Care training, local community workers learn that health care is not just about treating disease, health means wellness, staying well, leading a healthy lifestyle. Participants at the Porto Velho training included nurses, community development practitioners, church leaders, pastors, activists, teachers, doctors and dentists. Training sessions are held periodically in different locations in Latin America and they include discussions of health for the elderly, children, infants, adolescents, pregnant women and nursing mothers.

Access to Health through Training

Most people in rural and poor urban communities have little access to hospitals, clinics, and doctors. So they learn about how they can promote health through alternative methods. People learn that except in cases of serious illness or accident they have the resources within their own communities to prevent and treat illness and maintain a good standard of health.

Community health workers learn about nutrition, herbal medicine, treatments for common illnesses like diarrhea and malaria, mental health and well-being, women's health problems, prenatal and postnatal care, care of chronic diseases like tuberculosis and leprosy, family planning, dental care and the importance of a balanced lifestyle and lifelong education. They also address larger quality of living issues that affect the overall health of a community-safe drinking water, improvement of land and the production of nutritious food, animal care, and income-generation for women and other vulnerable groups. The underlying assumption of CCPHC is that most communities, no matter how poor they are, have sufficient knowledge, human and material resources to live a healthy life.

Participants take the skills and knowledge they gain from training sessions back to their communities and local projects. At the center in Porto Velho, Dalva Maria and the other workers are able to address the nutritional needs of the children, monitor their growth, and educate the children in good hygiene, dental care, and other practices that will help them lead healthy lives.

A Growing Ministry

Other participants in the training session have taken the skills and knowledge they gained back to their own projects and ministries. For example, many pastors in Latin America run children's programs with up to 400 children at a time. With CCPHC training, they are able to provide the skills and mentoring to keep children mentally and physically healthy. In Rio de Janeiro, participants take their newly gained skills and knowledge back to three centers where they work with destitute and homeless children from infancy to age 21. In addition to recreation and schooling, the centers provide a home for a number of homeless children, nutritious meals, comprehensive health screening, and dental care.

The Comprehensive Community-Based Health Care movement is growing every year, not only in Latin America, but in Africa, Asia, and Europe. In Latin America, UMCOR supports projects in Argentina, Bolivia, Guatemala, Venezuela, Nicaragua, Colombia, Brazil, and Ecuador.

Testimonies

The words of the following health coordinators and health promoters speak loudly about the success of CCPHC in different regions.

Eluzinete Garcia (Brazil): "My time in Jamkhed helped me to discover my own potential and motivated me to work with poor communities. The church has a responsibility not just to run clinics but to raise people's consciousness about their health and their rights."

Elisa Quiroga (Bolivia): "Before CCPHC training, we were not very clear about what we were doing. Now our commitment has been challenged and deepened. We have found alternative ways to work in communities. We have learned to be creative and to start from basic things in our work with people."

Beth Ferrell (Mozambique) reports: "In 1994, the Community Development and Preventive Health Course Project was initiated for pastors' wives and churchwomen from all over Mozambique. It was to address the needs of underserved areas and to promote preventive rather than curative care as a more fiscally responsible approach in places such as Mozambique where there are limited resources. For example, in 1995 and 1996, Mozambique was listed as the poorest country in the world by the World Bank and the United Nations. In 1997, Mozambique 'graduated' to become the world's next-to-poorest country.

"This ongoing community health program to empower women in Mozambique has been well received and continues to be necessary if women are to attain the abundant life Jesus talks about in John 10:10.

"The course is a very basic one. It focuses on sanitation, hygiene, clean drinking water, adequate nutrition, family planning, maternal and child health care, and disease prevention, recognition, and treatment. It is a vehicle to achieve positive results in all these areas through community development and use of existing resources. Continued cooperative efforts among course participants in the same locale and faithful prayer support for all members of the group are encouraged.

"The participants return to their homes, communities, and church groups to share what they have learned. This enriches the lives of others at the basic level of need. Ideas regarding how to generate income are also discussed. These ideas depend to a great extent on land, roads, rainfall, material available for crafts, and tourists."

NOTES

1. http://www.who.int/mediacentre/news/releases/2008/pr38/en/index.html (accessed September 4, 2009).
2. http://new.gbgm-umc.org/umcor/work/health/community-health/latin-america/?search=Dalva Maria deOliveira Ribeiro (accessed September 4, 2009).

About the Authors

Dr. Dana L. Robert

Truman Collins Professor of World Christianity and History of Mission
Boston University School of Theology

A leading historian of Christian mission, Dana Robert has been teaching at Boston University since 1984. Her books include *American Women in Mission: A Social History of their Thought and Practice* (1997), *Christianity: A Social and Cultural History* (co-author 1997), and *Christian Mission: How Christianity Became a World Religion* (Wiley-Blackwell, 2009). Robert has directed nearly sixty doctoral dissertations in mission studies and the history of world Christianity. Former students hold teaching and ministry positions around the world. Robert directs the Center for Global Christianity and Mission at the Boston University School of Theology, the oldest United Methodist seminary in the United States (see website, http://www.bu.edu/cgcm/).

Robert is a lifelong United Methodist from Baton Rouge, Louisiana. She serves on the Committee on Faith and Order for the denomination. With her husband M.L. Daneel, an expert on African Indigenous Churches, she regularly participates in mission outreach in Masvingo, Zimbabwe. She has two sons, Samuel and John, and lives in Somerville, Massachusetts.

Reverend Dr. Toby Gould

Toby Gould, a United Methodist minister, retired in 2007 as Project Manager for Mission Studies for the Women's Division of the General Board of Global Ministries. He oversaw the writing, editing, and publishing of the resources for the studies. Reverend Gould has taught numerous schools of Christian mission across the United States.

Reverend Gould served as the pastor of churches in New York and Connecticut, most recently at Memorial United Methodist Church in White Plains. New York. He was Executive Secretary for Ministries with Persons with Handicapping Conditions for the General Board of Global Ministries, 1980–1985, and wrote several books and articles in that field.

Toby wrote the study guides for spiritual growth studies, *The Bible: the Book that Bridges the Millennia, Volumes 1 and 2*. He has contributed articles to many publications, including *Upper Room Disciplines*, 2002 and 2003.

Toby and Merri Gould live in a 140-year-old farmhouse in Charlemont, Massachusetts with their Australian Shepherd, Justin.